Library Networking

Library Networking

M. Ram

RANDOM

RANDOM PUBLICATIONS

NEW DELHI (INDIA)

Library Networking

ISBN 978-93-5111-246-4

Published in 2014 in India by
RANDOM PUBLICATIONS
4376-A/4B, Gali Murari Lal, Ansari Road
New Delhi-110 002
Phone : +91-11-43580356, +91-11-23289044
e-mail: randomexports@gmail.com, sales@randompublications.com, info@randompublications.com

Type Setting by : Keystoneprintads, Delhi-110051
Printed at : Thomson Press (India) Ltd.

Preface

The world has been witnessing a knowledge and information explosion during the past few decades. Over 10 million journal articles are published every year besides news items, editorials and articles that are appearing in popular print media. Information professionals who would be the leaders in the twenty-first century depend on information for their work. Access to information holds the key to development. Libraries which are store houses of knowledge and information, and information centers which disseminate knowledge and information, form two important components of present day society.

While there is a deluge of information on one hand, the cost of collecting, processing, storing and disseminating information has been spiraling up on the other hand. This calls for heavy budgets for libraries even to maintain a reasonable level of acquisition of journals, books and reports. Estimates show that a three to fourfold rise in library budgets will be needed by AD 2000 to maintain the same acquisition level as in 1990. Information buying power of libraries has been declining year after year. Because of this, resource sharing and cooperative functioning through networking have become inescapable for libraries and information centres worldwide. India is no exception; for that matter, it is even more necessary to network libraries in newly developing countries like India than in the developed nations. Efficient resource sharing can be achieved by using the recent advances in information technology for realising a network of libraries. Information technology signifies the coming together of the disciplines of electronics, computer hardware and software, communications (in particular telecommunications), artificial intelligence and human/ machine interface.

During the last six to seven years, library and information activities in the country have entered a new era. Individual libraries are coming out of the proverbial "Berlin Wall"around them. They are trying to form a larger community in an effort to tackle the ever increasing demands for better services, quantitatively and qualitatively, in an environment already over strained by financial pressures. Forced, motivated, or logic driven, the librarians are coming out of their shell in large numbers.

I thank all members of my team who have helped in the preparation of the book. My special thanks go to "Random Publications" who have published the book.

– M. Ram

Contents

1

Networking

A network is a social structure made of nodes which are generally individuals or organizations. It indicates the ways in which they are connected through various social familiarities ranging from casual acquaintance to close familial bonds. Networking is basically an inter institutional arrangement intended to break information isolation. The term was first coined by Barnes. Networking involves a set of skills and activities relying heavily on effective interpersonal communication for gathering, processing, and moving information in organisation. Networking is a set of behaviors that take place within the context of organisations. However, networking has become a popular term in the day to day conversation and is often considered to be related to job seeking and personal advancement with an emphasis on self-promotion and trying to use others for ones' own ends. None of us can survive in business or other profession without a strong network of information and referral sources. Every person has a network of old schoolmates, relatives, colleagues from former jobs or leisure activities, and friends.

The critical factor is your mindset towards networking– recognising networking as important, not a waste of time. Networking is valuable not simply because of the information you gather, but because of the sense of cooperation or goodwill that you create. Networking is often considered as the hidden side of organizational leadership. The human network is the social structure composed of individuals, friends, collaborators or other organizations connected through technology using a variety of devices - personal computers, mobile phones, gaming consoles and PDAs. In many instances the term is described synonymously with the architecture of participation. It is the intersection of communications networks and social networks - a telecommunications network where people are the endpoints.

DEFINITION AND CONCEPT OF NETWORKING

Networking is the building and maintaining of relationships with a wide range of individuals, groups, or institutions who share common interests, goals, or expertise. Networking implies that the relationships between people are the determining factor in programs. Women face different challenges than men in the workplace. To meet these challenges successfully women need to network. Networking is about sharing information, ideas, resources, opportunities.

Members of a network look to each other for advice, tips on jobs, careers and employment and create a support system for each other. These informal strategic alliances can benefit you greatly. Networking is emerging as an important concept in the study of professional effectiveness and advancement, leadership, and organisations. It has been linked to studies of leadership power and influence skills, careerdevelopment and promotion tactics, organisational structure and communication processes. Networking has become popularised and is often considered to be related to job seeking and personal advancement, with an emphasis on self-promotion and trying to use others for one's own ends.

NEED FOR NETWORKING

In any organisation there are structured groups like different departments, or work groups and unstructured or informal groups. Individuals' involvement in unstructured groups is important, because networking is becoming the best way to accomplish things in organization. Albrecht and Ropp have found that workers discussed new and innovative ideas in an unstructured group more freely than in a structured group or in a hierarchical role relationship.

VARIOUS FEATURES OF NETWORKING

Networking is characterized by the following features:

- Ongoing, purposeful interaction
- Cooperation
- Relationships
- People centeredness
- Complex and diverse interconnections
- Open ended and flexible progression

NETWORKING COMPONENTS

It is essential to approach networking systematically. In order to develop a good network you should be able to answer the following types of questions:

- In which organisations/ events do you need to be visible?
- What kinds of referral sources do you need, and where/ how can you meet them?
- Who can influence potential people to choose you, and how can you meet them?
- Who are already your advocates and can introduce you to others?

Different people have different attitudes to networking. All persons are not natural net workers. Some can develop strong networking skills with a little help, and others are really not comfortable meeting strangers especially in new cultures. You would find different attitudes towards networking among different types of net worker as you can make out below.

- The Passive Net worker: They have little interest in meeting new people. Instead, they will gravitate to people they already know, wasting the chance to expand their contacts.
- The Inquisitive Net worker: This type of people takes initiative but behaves like a detective interrogating suspects. They draw out other people and may learn a lot, but sooner of later the fact that they do not share any information will make others stop trusting them.
- Social Net worker: This type takes appropriate initiative in meeting new people but keeps the conversation on a social level. They may be very popular and receive many social invitations – and so can be very valuable in your networking strategy. However, they need to understand how to engage in commercial information exchanges as well.
- Dedicated Net worker: They initiate appropriately and are constantly looking for ways to be helpful to others. In return, the latter often share with them valuable market information and intelligence. These staff members are the heart of your networking team and should receive your active support and are rewarded for their efforts.

Even some of those who have strongly supported the view that effectiveness of networking centres around, the objective to further ones' own interest have started seeing the limited scope of this self serving framework. They say that knowing how to network is practivally knowing how to be helpful to the people with whom we work and ask for help in return. In reality, interdependence not independence is the key to getting somewhere in the work world. Such attitude expresses what is best about networking ability to create an effective support system for yourself that also works to the advantage of others. Networking is now becoming as emerging style of functioning within the organization. People are increasingly learning from one another horizontally; everyone is becoming a resource for everyone else; and each person is receiving professional support and assistance from many directions. In this scenario, one can identify the following as strategies for successful networking

- Finding the right track to multiple sources of information related to a project;
- Bridging the information flow between functions such as finance and marketing;
- Communicating by both formal and informal means to accomplish projects;
- Doing things and/or gathering information without overpowering others;

- Managing the give and take of information flow within an organization or between organizations, often outside formal organization lines and;
- Facilitating the interchange among individuals who serve as resources to obtain a specific goal.

It has been found that networking can be a decisive factor in the woking of a successful organisation. Research has proved that workers are more likely to talk about new ideas with those colleagues with whom they also discussed work and personal matters.

Tacit knowledge is shared relatively easily between individuals within the community, often without ever being made explicit. And those who are well integrated into networks of social relationship at work are more likely to participate in decision making.

They can see clearly how they contribute to group performance and share in the rewards of group performance. It has also been found that highest number of innovation has taken place in those organisations where collaboration, free flow of information and coalitions built of supporters are the dominant characteristics.

NETWORKING THROUGH INFORMATION AND COMMUNICATION TECHNOLOGY

Nowadays, organisations are investing in ICT that create intra-organisational electronic network. The purpose is to have "bridging ties" between geographically dispersed organisational members. The main objective is to provide a platform to communication through which individuals working on similar problems may quickly ask each other for help on task related problem. Educators and policy makers need to stay alert to the need for programs that maintain the principle of providing a positive, useful, and quality service.

- *Professional Development:* New Technologies, while helpful in certain key ways, also create new problems, the foremost of which is training individuals (learners and teachers) how to implement them in a cost-effective manner. Sometimes the training process becomes very expensive, and nearly counterproductive (when in the midst of repaid platform and software changes). The Internet promises, in some respects to be relatively easy to train on and with.
- *Technological Lifelong Learning:* Using Online networking technology and the Internet not only provides adult learners with new opportunities for literacy and basic skills instruction but the use of these technologies themselves provide new technological literacy skills that adult learners can utilize in the work place, for personal reasons, and in the future for additional lifelong learning at higher levels.

In sum, Internet-based network technology is one of the most promising areas for literacy work in the world. The benefits of this technology seem well matched with the following problems in the literacy field:

- The dispersed and diverse population of adult learners,
- The limited and thinly distributed expertise in learning diagnosis, and
- The need to connect learners and instructions interactively in an asynchronous manner that takes advantages of learners needs for independence along with their unavailability for formal classroom instruction.

The uses of technology for adult literacy and adult education have been growing exponentially in recent years, from computer-assisted instruction to the information highway and to the simple improvements engendered by the use of personal computers in management and information systems.

TECHNOLOGY, THE INTERNET AND ADULT LITERACY

One can argue that in theory, electronicbased technologies are a source of exponential growth in the field of adult literacy. All things being equal, that is, inexpensive access to broadband width of internet facility, uninterrupted supply of power and clear link between literacy and poverty alleviation, it is possible to effectively work on the interface between technology, the Internet and adult literacy.

Electronic Technologies

Computers, wireless communications, videotapes, and the like – are now being incorporated into elementary, secondary, business, and college level education. Adult literacy programs, in contrast, still lag far behind in using these newer technologies for instruction. Studies show that many adult literacy programs have a foothold in technology, but this is mainly in the use of microcomputers for administrative purposes, not instructional ones. Economic considerations clearly are a major impediment to technology implementation in adult literacy programs.

Need of Network in Adult Literacy

These technologies hold enormous promise for the future because they can:

- Reduce the isolation that many adult literacy providers and students experience,
- Facilitate communication among staff and students within and between programs
- Increase access to high quality materials and emerging research,
- Streamline administrative and reporting processes, and
- Help to provide the delivery vehicle for innovative instructional and staff development approaches.

However, we need to keep in mind that across these new technologies, there is also inadequate staff training and lack of information on effective implementation and specialised uses.

ADVANTAGES OF NETWORKING AND INTERNET TECHNOLOGY

There are some clear advantages of networking and Internet technology both for adult learners and for adult literacy programs. For learners, this would include

- Reaching learners outside of the classroom,
- Using learning time more efficiently,
- Sustaining motivation
- Individualizing instruction and
- Providing access to information tools.

For adult literacy programs, this would include:

- Improved recruiting and training of learners,
- Improving curriculum
- Meeting staff development needs
- Enhancing assessment and curriculum, and
- Streamlining coordination, management and administration.

INTERNET SERVICES

The Internet allows each of us to share information and resources such as government documents, electronic publications, online books, media publishing, human anatomical images, computer software, bibliographic and full-text databases, speeches, live concerts, animal sounds, and motion videos. The Internet's dynamic nature is delivered from world citizens contributing their time, resources and energies to each other. Users consult electronic resources at libraries; download computer shareware and software upgrades. A few usages of the Internet can be listed.

- To trade with people or other organizations
- To access information on Internet, you need a browser-software. Examples of the browser can be Netscape, Internet Explorer etc.

The World Wide Web (WWW) can be defined as a hypertext, multimedia, distributed information system that provides links to hypertext documents, as well as too many other Internet tools and databases. There are several features that are unique to the Web that make it the most advanced information system to appear on the Internet to date.

Network-based Information Services:

- Resource Sharing, Virtual Libraries, Computer Mediated Communication, Web Publishing, Other Services
- Infrastructure Requirements Hardware, Software, Human ware, Technologies for Networking, Network architecture etc
- Organization of Information Resources Digital resources, Nonprint

media, Content creation, Metadata tools, Research networks, Institution networks etc

- Network Policy and Governance Participation in INFLIBNET, Legal and Copyright issues, Economics of centralised database services Institutional policies etc.

ELECTRONIC NETWORKS OF PRACTICE (ENOPS)

In an effort to replicate traditional social networks electronically, organisations are now investing in computer-mediated communication technologies to facilitate knowledge sharing regardless of time and space constraints. These emergent virtual communities are referred as electronic networks of practice (EnoPs). Needles to say, communication within this network of practice occurs primarily through computer-based communication technologies suh as bulletin board, listservs etc. One of the main characteristics of ENoPs is that the participants in the network interact with one another to help each other solve problems. By posting a message, individuals seeking help can reach out others who can provide valuable knowledge and insight in response.

The posting of messaes and responses is recorded like a conversation beteen participants. This shows active mutual engagement in problem solving; and the characteristic of mutual engagement distinguishes it from more static form of electronic knowledge exchange, such as document repositories and other types of database. Another characteristic of an ENoP is the fact that the technology supports any number of participants. As a result knowledge seekers are not limited to asking only experts whom they personally know or able to identify, thus increasing the possibility of connecting with someone willing and able to help.

In addition, knowledge in an ENoP is typically archived and available to all participants in the network. This ultimately creates and online repository of questions and answers that can be referred to later by any individual regardless of the fact whether he or she had participated in the original discussion. The value of an ENoP increases dramatically as the number of participants rises. Moreover, in an ENoP, participation is open to anyone with a desire to interact.

The electronic links created by the Internet and related technologies that enable individuals to communicate are practically ubiquitous, thus membership is open to anyone with a desire whether they want to participate as well as how often they participate. They have the choice to determine what they want to contribute, choosing what knowledge they are willing to disclose as well as the length of the message they contribute influencing the quality and helpfulness of the knowlede exchanged. The characteristic of discretionary choices regarding participation and knowledge sharing differntiates an ENoP from other form of virtual work, such as virtual teams in which the members of participants are expected to coordinate effects to deliver a specific outcome. In addition to these, participants in an ENoP are strangers.

Knowledge exchange is an ENoP occurs between people regardless of personal acquaintance, familiarity or location. Since participation is voluntary, knowledge seekers have no control over who responds to their questions. On the contrary, in a traditional social network, people typically know one another and interact overtime creating expectations of obligations and reciprocity that are enforced through social sanctions.

WHY OF NETWORKING

Electronic Networks of Practice is an excellent means of improving one's own level of technical competence. Additionally it helps to keep current with technical developments as well as to know who was actively working in different areas. Technically or otherwise people gain competitiveness. There seem to be a variety of reasons why people help each other. As the saying goes, nothing comes free, in order to receive help from the network, individuals feel obligated to help others in return, a strong sense of reciprocity. In some organisations, like knowledge management companies, helping others is a part of their job.

Through their participation they are able to improve level of technical competence of network as a whole and ultimately enhance organisation's competitiveness in the market. The participants of EnoP gain exposure to critical new ideas. They get help and advice not available locally. Studies indicate that individuals participate in EnoPs outperform their colleagues who primarily rely on their colleagues for knowledge and advice. A database of all the postings/ questions can be made. This shall help individuals to find previously discussed topics as well as a means to educate people on how to use email or list serve technology give here examples of Adult education/ community participation questions.

PROBLEMS ASSOCIATED WITH NETWORKING

In case of List serve mailing lists, even though mail is received in the mail box, yet there is much unsolicited mail. The receiver has to go through that. It wastes his much time which otherwise could be utilised in some productive work. In a discussion form, the participants are required to enter forum actively otherwise he/she gets no postings of the network. An online CoP may be ephemeral and the knowledge created may be lost, unless proper infrastructure is in place that can sustain what may be learned.

ENOP AND PARTICIPATION AND HELPING OTHERS

Higher levels of participation and tenure in the EnoP are associated with both acquisition of knowledge from participation in the network and contributing knowledge to others. In addition, both knowledge acquisition from and knowledge contribution to the network are positively related to individual performance. Level of participation in the network is more important for supporting positive knowledge outcomes than the length of time an individual has participated. This implies that newcomers to the network can reap the same benefits of participation as long as standing participants. EnoPs are a type of collective in which the knowledge exchanged and created is the collective's public good. Mutual engagement in an EnoP is open and voluntary. Participation typically results in the creation of a knowledge repository of archived messages that is available to all individuals regardless of their original participation.

KNOWLEDGE SHARING AND ELECTRONIC NETWORKS

Tacit knowledge is shared relatively easily between individuals within the community, often without ever being made explicit. Furthermore, these tightly knit social structures facilitate the creation of a shared identify through the development of a common language and social capital (such as norms of behaviour, trust, and obligation), resulting in strong social ties between individuals.

These characteristics have been argued as essential for the continuous incremental improvements in the community's practice and the reason why CoPs are centres for learning and innovation within organisations.

In contrast, as mentioned above, interactions in an EnoP are limited text based, asynchronous, computermediated communication. As a result, the ability of members to develop a shared identity and common language through narration, collaboration and social construction is hampered. However, EnoPs have a greater reach than CoPs and support the creation of weak electronic "bridging ties" between unlimited numbers of like minded others from across the globe.

Due to the extensive reach of these networks, individuals benefit from EnoPs since they gain access to new information, expertise, and ideas that are often not available locally.

COMPUTER NETWORKS

NETWORKING THROUGH COMPUTERS

A computer is emerging and no one could keep himself/herself away from it any longer. But, what are the types of a network within the arena of computers? Those are LAN, MAN and WAN. Not only this, there are certain topologies associated with it and there are certain components which carry out these functions. We need to acquaint ourselves with these technical words and their usages when we move to the area of networking through computers and extend its use in reaching out to adult learners. Let's discuss in detail about seemingly strange terms and their everyday applications.

Types of Network

Based on geographical dispersion of computers there are mainly three types of network.

- Local Area Network: In this type of network computers and other communication devices are in a small area and are connected together (networked). The area can be single building, cluster of buildings in the same campus. Examples can be Local Area Network of Lab in which you may be working or a library which you may be using.
- Metropolitan Area Network: A Metropolitan Area Network is basically a bigger version of LAN and normally uses similar technology. It might cover a group of nearby corporate offices or it can be in a city. It can be private or public.
- Wide Area Network: Computers can be farther apart like covering cities, countries or even continents. The computers are connected by telephone lines or radio waves or optical fibres.

Network Topologies

Topology refers to the shape of a network or network's layout. How different nodes in a network are connected to each other and how they communicate is determined by the network's topology. There are four most common network topologies, namely,

- Star Topology: All devices are connected to a central hub. Nodes communicate across the network by passing data through the hub.
- Bus Topology: All devices are connected to a central cable, called the bus or backbone.
- Ring Topology: All devices are connected to one another in the shape of a closed loop, so that each device is connected directly to two other devices, one on either side of it.
- Mesh Topology or Point to Point Network: Devices are connected with many redundant interconnections between network nodes. In a true mesh topology every node has a connection to every other node in the network.

Network Components

The following are essential components for computer networking.

- Network hardware
- Transmission media
- Network software

Network Hardware

The basic component of computer network hardware is a computer. Computers on a network can be divided into two categories,

- Server and
- Clients or nodes.

Server is the computer of higher power, and speed. It costs more. To this computer resources are attached. And the clients, also known as nodes access, are the resources which are attached to server. In peer to peer computer networks there are no servers.

Transmission Media

Communication of data propagation and processing of signals is called transmission. Signals travel from transmitter to receiver via a path. This path is called medium. Medium can be guided or unguided.

Guided Media

In guided media, data is sent along a physical path i.e. cables. There are several types of cables used in network. The type of cable chosen for a network is related to the network's topology, protocol and size. Different types of cables:

- Coaxial cable looks like cable that brings the cable TV signal to television.
- Twisted pair copper wire cable looks like phone cable. Twisted pair cables come in two varieties, a. shielded and b. unshielded.
- Optical fibre cable

Unguided Media

Here no wire is installed. The data communication is predominantly sent by radio waves and microwaves.

Network Card

We will discuss about networking software. But hardware has also to be connected. Most important part of connection is the network card. This is the middle part of connection. These cards are 8 bit cards, 16 bit cards and 32 bit cards. Each card has its own method of sending information (network protocol) through the cable. The most commonly used is Ethernet Protocol. A network card is called Interface card, network adapter, a NIC etc. It is a circuit board or chip which allows the computer to communicate to other computers on a network.

Modem (MODulator/ DEModulator)

A modem converts digital signals (computer signals) from the computer into analogue signals for transmission and vice versa for reception over a telephone line. There are four basic types of modems for a PC:

- External,
- USB,
- Internal and
- Built-in.

External and USB are set on your desk outside the PC, while as Internal and Built-in are inside the PC. Present day modems have 56 kilobites per second speed. ISDN (Integrated Services Digital Network) circuits are digital. In this conversion from digital to analogue is not required.

Switch

Switches are basically bridges, but usually have multiple ports. Switches connect network segments, using a table of addresses to determine the segment on which a packet needs to be transmitted.

Hubs

A hub is used to connect multiple computers and devices via a dedicated cable. It is cheap and connections are easy. It generally has 4, 8, 12, 24 ports.

Router

These are used to connect networks and to determine the optimal path along which the network traffic should be forwarded. They are occasionally called gateways. There are other network devices like repeaters, bridges, ports, etc.

Network Operating Software

Network operating software (NOS) is a collection of software and associated protocols that allow a set of autonomous computers, which are interconnected by a computer network, to be used together in a convenient and costeffective manner. It is similar to any other operating system like windows, DOS, etc. except it operates over more than one computer. It controls operation of the network system, including who uses it, when they can use it, what they have access to, and which network resources are available. At a basic level, the NOS allows network users to share files and peripherals such as disks and printers. They provide data integrity and security. The examples can be categories of NOS: The NetWare, LAN Manager, Solaris and Windows 2000 etc. The main categories of network software are:

- Peer to peer software and
- Client/ Server-based

Peer to Peer Software

In peer to peer networking operating software users can share resources and files located on their computers and can access shared resources on other computers. There is no central server. All computers in the network are equal. They have similar capabilities and resources. Examples of Peer to peer network software are Windows XP, Windows 98. When you are working in Microsoft Office Word under Windows environment, you can share the shared documents. It is possible because Windows XP is peer to peer networking software.

Client Server Based (Two Tier)

This software is in two parts. One part which includes functions and services resides in one or more exclusive (dedicated) computers. This part is called server. It provides security and access to resources. Another part called 'client' resides on other computers (nodes/ client). They access resources on the server. The network operating system allows multiple users to simultaneously share the same resources irrespective of physical location. Examples of Server based networking software are: Novel Netware, Windows NT, UNIX, Window 2000 etc.

Client Server Based (Three Tier)

Here a client-software is split into two parts.

- Browser (user-interface) (thin client)
- Logic.

Thus two tier client-server becomes three tier architecture. The logic which describes how to access and process data is moved to a new server. This new server is server for thin client. Nothing changes in the server side.

LAN

Standards for LAN are Ethernet, LocalTalk (for Macs), Token Ring, the most popular in Ethernet Protocol. It allows for linear bus, star or tree topologies. Data can be transmitted over twisted pair, coaxial or fibre optic cable at a speed of 10mbps.

INTERNET

The Internet is a network of networks. It connects millions of computers and thousands of computer networks throughout the world. The Internet has revolutionised our society, our economy and our technological systems. The Internet represents one of the most successful examples of the benefits of sustained investment and commitment to research and development of the information infrastructure.

The Internet Society (ISOC) defines the Internet as a "global network of networks" which enables computers of all kinds to directly and transparently communicate and share services throughout the world. It provides for both communications capabilities and information services. It also constitutes a shared global resource of information, knowledge and means of collaboration and cooperation among countless diverse communities. For communication on Internet it uses standard protocol which is called transmission control protocol, Internet Protocol or TCP/IP. Standardized communication protocols allow similar, dissimilar, near and distant computers to communicate with one another. The Internet protocols and standards are being defined from time to time by various international organization and committees after rigorous testing and reviewing.

Trends

You may like to know about Internet 2 nd Internet 3, which reflect future rends in computer networks.

Internet 2

It is a consortium being led by 200 universities working in partnership with industry and government to develop and deploy advanced network applications and technologies, accelerating the creation of tomorrow's Internet.

Internet 3

It includes the US Government's initiative to provide high andwidth network service.

Adult Education

There are discussion groups and e-mail lists relating to adult learning. You may try to access some of the following resources.

Discussion groups

- alt.education.distance is a group that focuses on learning over the Internet, a form of distance education.
- bit.listserv.edtech is an adult education discussion group.
- misc.eeducation.adult is an adult education discussion group.

Email Lists

- ADNET is the adult education network
- URL: listserv@alpha.acast.nova.edu
- DEOS-L is the international forum for distance learning.
- URL: listserv@psuvm.psu.edu
- DISTED is an online chronicle of Distance Education and Communication
- URL: listserv@alpha.acast.nova.edu

IMPORTANCE OF INTERNET

The Internet is an "enabling technology". When its introduction is sensitive to local values and committed to local capacitybuilding, it offers important opportunities to

- Open dialogue: Low cost networking facilitates knowledge sharing, awareness of alternative perspectives, more open exchange
- Improve governance: Raising efficiency, transparency, participatory systems
- Improve social and human rights conditions: Expands access to better quality education, healthcare, disaster relief capacity and other services

- Reduce poverty: Opens new opportunities for bypassed groups (women, the poor, rural populations, children)
- Introduce economic opportunities: E-commerce, ICT-sector development etc.
- Improve environmental management, GIS: Food security early warning systems.
- Support indigenous knowledge: Communities document their knowledge.

Disadvantages of Internet

Advances in communication media (VoIP, Instant messaging, email), based on Internet technology have made computer mediated communication more rich and cheap. Yet, today, this potential for knowledge sharing is not fully realized. Indeed, the internet is by nature an anonymous medium in which people find it hard to place their trust. As a result, people who have had few or no face-to-face meetings are not likely to share knowledge.

Benefits of Internet

It supports and encourages the new learning environment, which is based on principles of active learning-reflecting the change in the culture of education from teacher-centred to learnercentred. The Internet can be used for a variety of purposes from a library. Some of the purposes are

- To exchange e-mail instantly with institutions in India or abroad
- To participate in teleconferences with people on topics of internet or research problems like adult education
- To find out educational information from universities libraries and book stores all over the world
- To search on-line library catalogues for bibliographic data and other databases for textual data
- To have access to electronic journals, newsletters and in-house information of many organisations and institutions.

CASE STUDIES – I

Here we will discuss about the network that focuses on teachers and another network that focuses on learners. Then we will talk about a network that links literacy efforts and also about futures trends.

ALTIN: Focus on Teachers

The gradually increasing use of instructional technology and online communications in the field of adult literacy is creating both new opportunities and reviving old challenges.

ALTIN

The purpose of the Adult Literacy Technology Innovation Network

(ALTIN) technology training program, begun in the mid-1990 was to provide basic instructional technology staff development for adult literacy teachers, including the basics of instructional technology and electronic online communications in a useful and userfriendly way, while at the same time building a network of practitioners who can, after the six months of training, assist other literacy programs and practitioners by means of a mentoring process. ALTIN has shown that an electronic training network works best when participants have established a human network among themselves when they are able to identify commonalities of interest and need, have established a level of trust and commitment among themselves, and can identify areas of collaboration and communication that will result in mutual benefit. Face-toface meetings appear to make such a people-to-people connection easier, helping to increase the level of trust, facilitating the identification of areas of mutual interest and concern among participants, and increasing the accountability and commitment that participants have to each other online.

SHELCOM: Focus on Learners

The shelter communications Literacy Network was an experimental Internetbased computer writing project for adults living in homeless shelters in Philadelphia, USA. The project began in 1993 and completed in 1995. These poorly educated adults also suffered from a variety of problems associated with drug and alcohol use. SHELCOM showed that such disadvantaged populations can be reached effectively through the Internet, in spite of the initial low literacy abilities of many participants.

Literacy Link

Distance education for learners and teachers: Literacy Link, funded by the U.S. Department of Education is designed to serve the large numbers of Americans who require additional basic skills instruction. As an Internet-based lifelong learning system, Literacy Link has two major goals:

- To increase the access of adults to learning opportunities that will enable them to obtain their high school diplomas, and
- To improve the quality of instruction available to individuals and adult literacy providers nationwide through enhanced resources and expanded staff development.

Literacy Link is one of the first and most comprehensive initiatives to harness the power of the Internet to provide instruction and demand to adult learners, as well as communities, libraries, schools and homes.

Conclusions and Future Directions

The above case studies illustrate a few of the opportunities that have become available through Internet. Some of them are staff development, reaching out to the disadvantaged, and taking advantage of the convenience of learning in the home or community. In the ALTIN case study, it was found that human networks are an essential component to the electronic networks that are now easily and cheaply available on the Internet. The SHELCOM project demonstrated that new technologies can be implemented with even the most difficult to reach and difficult-to-retain populations, using fairly simple networking and word-processing techniques. Literacy Link deals with how distance education can provide a cost-effective and comprehensive selflearning system for adult education in the home and community.

CASE STUDIES – II

Production of information and its dissemination through network can be most effective if it comprises local content. We will discuss here importance of local content and creation of local content in India. Then we will look at creation of information that is demanddriven. There will be short pieces of information on creation of rural knowledge repositories and local websites, databases, bulletin boards and e-mail lists.

Information Production and Dissemination through Network

Importance of Local Content

An education centre can provide people in the community with access to computers to send and receive information. Centre should translate the need to provide people with access to content that they can use in their daily lives. Persons may need such practical content as adult literacy programs, information on public benefits, information on health, consumer and credit information, and information related to employment and training. If a woman in the village has access to the Internet, she will not necessarily be able to use the information to improve her child's health because trying to get information from the Internet is like drinking from a fire hose – you don't know the source of the water.

Local content is a big challenge for an adult education centre. A multi-nation study by the International Institute for Communication and Development or IICD suggests that "easier access to globalized knowledge is fast turning us into 'consumers' of distant and potentially irrelevant information". Local content, the report says faces intense competition because big content initiatives by other groups tend to push their external content onto local communities. In the same vein, another IICD report suggests developing countries are being invaded by foreign ideas and values that may undermine or overwhelm local cultures.

Generation of Local Content in India

Here is a case study of a village knowledge centre. It shows how staff dealt with the issues of local, relevance and language. The centres, established in Pondicherry on the southeast coast of India by the M.S. Swaminathan Research Foundation (MSSRF), demonstrated ingenuity, creativity and sensitivity in developing their information products. In one case, coastal villages were highly dependent on weather and tides information. Many fishermen were not literate.

Village Knowledge Centre downloaded whether reports from digital network information and converted that to audio. The audio versions were then played on loudspeakers in the open air. In addition, project volunteers in the villages built their own information resources in the center to complement the external databases thereby providing local and localized information on agricultural, health and government programs for low-income people, for example, a directory of general and crop insurance schemes; a list of about 130 schemes available as entitlements to rural families; a directory of hospitals and medical practitioners in Pondicherry – grouped according to their specialisations; bus and train schedules covering Pondicherry and two nearby towns; and pest management information for the sugarcane crop.

The content in the above cases is based on Dagron and Harris. Information must be locally relevant and respond to the information needs of the potential users. In such ways these services shall contribute to social and economic community development and to sustainability of the adult education setup.

Demand Driven Information Production in the Warna Wired Village Project

The project area is a cluster of 70 villages in the Sangli district of Maharashtra, India. The project has been jointly implemented by the Government of India through the National Informatics Centre, the Government of Maharashtra and the Warna Cooperative Society.

This project was initiated to serve the information needs of the farmers for different crop cultivation practices of major crops, sugarcane cultivation practices, pest and disease control, marketing information, dairy and sugarcane processing information, and other agriculture-related services. Apart from information retrieval, there are two client based applications to serve the farmers' needs through the computer booths installed in each village:

- The Dairy Information Centre; and
- The Sugarcane Information System.

In the Dairy Information System, information on all farmers who are part of the dairy system is maintained. Other details available to members of the dairy co-operatives include the quantity of milk supplied by each farmer, fat content, billing information and credit details. This information is maintained and updated at the central database on a daily basis. In the Sugarcane Information System, information on shareholders is maintained. There are about 200-350 shareholders in each village for the sugarcane crop. This system maintains details of the cultivation schedule, the quantity harvested and supplied to the society, deductions effected by the society towards, credit, and the net income due to the farmers. This data is available with respect to each shareholder. Booth operators of Paragoam, Bhairwadi, Kuralap and Panhala report that an average of 20-25 farmers visit the computer booths every day for information on crop cultivation practices and disease control, marketing, dairy and sugarcane billing details, etc.

Creating Rural Knowledge Repositories

Tele-centers in Kannivadi and Samiarpatty developed a database on indigenous knowledge on issues such as livestock management, integrated pest management, the practices of the farmers in cultivating 42 crops focusing on pest and disease management. A database on the local expertise has been developed in the form of a rural yellow page. The information consists of consisting of names, addresses and information of various village professions such as blacksmiths, carpenters, plumbers, masons, nurses, traditional healers, etc.

Similarly, a local consultant has been employed to gather information about all the development programmes in the region. This database would provide the information regarding the objectives of the programs, eligibility for participation, etc. Details of experts in agriculture and health are also kept in the tele-centers. Camps are organized where experts and villagers meet and discuss various issues in specific subjects. These discussions are captured in audiocassettes and video photography. In a form of question-answer, the discussions are kept in a database. Camps such as livestock management, credit management, and women's health are being organized. The activities of the region are captured in Thagaval Thinnai (information courtyard) where information on agriculture and horticulture prices in the regular local markets, weekly markets and informal markets, social and cultural events, training programmes, visits of experts, local entertainment, weather reports, local employment opportunities, and news from regional newspapers are regularly given and supplied through local area network.

Moreover prints-out of some of the location-specific and very vital information are being pasted at the public places every day. Thus, Tagaval Thinnai is available both in 'online' form as well as in print form. The animators collect the information through formal channels such as web sites and informal channels such as contacting the traders. Some of the main sources of the information are agricultural extension agencies, the block development office, commission agents of the flower market at Nilakotai (a market town), Gandhigram, a deemed university etc. The information is collected and provided on a daily basis.

Local Websites

A local website with the help of users of adult education centre can guide to relevant information. The website can, on the one hand, be a medium for introducing information on the community with information provided by the community. On the other hand, the website will provide links to useful information sources and present information that has been interpreted into the local languages. The website can further link to online distance learning material and/or local databases.

Databases

The tele-center manager in collaboration with project volunteers can build their own databases. These shall be locally generated and, hence, locally and personally relevant information sources that can include details of government programs for low-income rural families (dependent on the context of the particular community); local market prices for grain; local farming families; a directory of insurance plans for both crops and input prices; pest management plans for local products; a directory of local hospitals, medical practitioners and their specialities; a regional timetable for buses and trains; and a directory of local veterinarians, cattle, and animal husbandry programs, etc. Databases could further include a collection of application software and reference material, such as CD ROMs relevant for responding to local needs. Most software producers donate license for their software to NGOs or community groups upon request, so if a NGO is in need of software, it can contact the producer.

Bulletin Boards

Bulletin boards present an easy-to-realize method of presenting gathered information to a wide number of community members. Bulleting boards could be placed outside the adult education centre building and/or different focal points within the community and be updated regularly.

Email Lists

Email lists allow the posting of questions, receiving of news updates, and sharing of experiences via email within a group that you define. An email list is identified by a single name, such as mail- list@server.com. A message is sent to the mailing list name and it is automatically forwarded or broadcast to all the addresses in the list. These mailing lists can be extremely helpful in connecting users of adult literacy programmes to share experiences. For example, Chasquinet, an Ecuador-based NGO, hosts a telecenter in Latin America and the Caribbean.

PARTICIPATION IN APPLICATION NETWORK

The participation in collaborative networks enables information to flow from and to rural communities, facilitates dialogue between communities, intermediaries and development organizations, fosters coordination of national and local development efforts and overcomes physical barriers to knowledge and information sharing. Networks provide information and help regarding particular topics, as well as access to the Internet, mail connections, radio connections, and e-mail. Generally, these applications use inexpensive storeand- forward systems to provide information on agriculture, public health, medicine, and the environment.

Example for an Application Network: FarmNet

Farmer Information Network (FarmNet) is a network of rural people and supporting intermediary organizations, such as extension services, using ICTs and conventional communication media to facilitate the generation, gathering and exchange of knowledge and information. Operated by farmers and their organisations, FarmNet links farmers to each other and to the resources and services, they need to improve their livelihoods. Design of a FarmNet with the Uganda National Farmers' Association found that the best approach was to enhance existing communication efforts (face-to-face, local radio, publications) with the use of simple e-mail based communication system for information on markets, improved agricultural technologies and weather conditions.

2

Participatory Networks: The Library as Conversation

AN OVERVIEW

Knowledge is created through conversation. Conversations can take place between friends and colleagues in the 'here and now.' But, they can also take place over centuries, with the participants changing but the theme remaining the same, and the conversation being recorded in thousands of artifacts, like books, pictures, and digital files. In many conversations users need sophisticated processes to facilitate the conversation. Facilitation not only enriches conversations with diverse and deep information, it also serves as a memory keeper, documenting agreements and outcomes to facilitate future conversations.

The library serves this vital role for many communities. The implication of this rather abstract concept is that libraries are in the conversation business. This theoretical argument can be seen in traditional brick-and-mortar libraries as library speaker series, book groups, and even the collection development processes. Yet online, the library has fallen far short of this ideal of conversation facilitator. Key library systems, such as the catalogue for example, are at best one-way conversations.

Libraries have a great opportunity to provide invaluable conversational, participatory infrastructure to their communities online. By adopting concepts and technologies from Web 2.0 and tightly integrating them into their services, libraries can advance not just their communities but also their positions within them. The opportunities inherent in participatory networks have not emerged because of current Internet developments such as Web 2.0, but, rather, these technologies make it easier to meet an identified and long-standing role of libraries. Wikis, blogs, and recommender systems replace dial-up bulletin boards and local databases as a means to empower our communities.

What's more, these technologies can bring the ideal of the participatory model to our most fundamental library systems. Libraries should adopt participatory network concepts and software not because they are new or sexy, but because they match our most fundamental mission: knowledge creation and dissemination. This document describes the participatory model of libraries and provides an overview of current Web 2.0 technologies and a brief discussion of how current Library 2.0 efforts point the way to an even greater change in library as a facilitator of conversations. Specific challenges and opportunities of participatory networking are reviewed. Finally, the authors recommend the creation of a shared participatory test bed for libraries.

This network would not only experiment with new collaborative Web technologies, but also work with library organisations and vendors to speed innovation in traditional library systems. Finally, the network test bed would create a shared infrastructure to provide participatory technologies – such as Wikis, blogs, and RSS feeds—to libraries for inclusion in their day-to-day services.

THE GOAL

Knowledge is created through conversation. Libraries are in the knowledge business. Therefore, libraries are in the conversation business. Some of those conversations span millennia, while others only span a few seconds. Some of these conversations happen in real time. In some conversations, there is a broadcast of ideas from one author to multiple audiences. Some conversations are sparked by a book or a video or a Web page. Some of these conversations are as trivial as directing someone to the bathroom. Other conversations centre on the foundations of ourselves and our humanity. It may be odd to start a technology brief with such seemingly abstract comments. Yet, without this firm, if theoretical, footing the advent of Web 2.0, social networking, Library 2.0, and participatory networks seems like a clutter of new terminology, tools, and acronyms.

In fact, as will be discussed, without this conceptual footing, many library functions can seem disconnected, and the field that serves lawyers, doctors, single mothers, and 8 year olds fragmented. The scale of this technology brief is limited; it is to present library decision makers with the opportunities and challenges of participatory networks. It is only a single piece of a much larger puzzle that seeks to present a cohesive framework for libraries. This framework will not only fit tools such as blogs and Wikis into their offerings, but also will show how a more participatory, conversational approach to libraries in general can help libraries better integrate current and future functions.

Think of this document as an overview or introduction to participatory librarianship. Readers will find plenty of examples and definitions of Web 2.0 and social networking later in this chapter. However, to jump right into the technology without a larger framework invites the rightful skepticism of a library organisation that feels constantly buffeted by new technological advances. In any environment with no larger conceptual founding to measure the importance of an advance in technology or practice selection of any one technology or practice is nearly arbitrary. Without a framework the field becomes open to the influence of personalities and trendy technology.

Therefore, it is vital to ground any technological, social, or policy conversation into a larger, rooted concept. As Susser said, "...to practice without theory is to sail an uncharted sea; theory without practice is not to set sail at all." For this chapter, the chart will be conversation theory.

The core of this brief is in four sections that follow:

- A conceptual framework for understanding and evaluating participatory networks;
- A discussion of key concepts and technologies in participatory networks drawn primarily from Web 2.0 and Library 2.0;
- A merging of the conceptual framework with the technological discussion to present a sort of roadmap for library systems development; and
- A set of recommendations to foster greater discussion and action on the topic of participatory networks and, more broadly, participatory librarianship.

LIBRARY AS A FACILITATOR OF CONVERSATION

So let us return to the concept that knowledge is created through conversation. This notion stretches back to Socrates and the Socratic Method. However, the specific foundation for this statement comes from 'Conversation Theory,' a means of explaining cognition and how people learn. It is not the purpose of this chapter to provide a detailed description of Conversation Theory, a task already admirably accomplished by Pask. Rather, let us use the theory as a structure upon which to hang an exploration of participatory networking and, more broadly, participatory librarianship.

The core of conversation theory is simple: people learn through conversation. Different communities have different standards for conversations, from the scientific community's rigourous formalisms to the religious community's embedded meaning in scripture to the sometimes impenetrable dialect of teens. The point remains, however, that different actors establish meaning through determining common definitions and building upon shared concepts. The library has been a place where we facilitate conversations, though often implicitly.

The concept of learning through conversations is evidenced in libraries in large initiatives like information litreacy and teaching critical thinking skills and in the smaller events of book groups, reference interviews, and speaker series. Library activities such as building collections of artifacts inform scholars' research through a formal conversation process where ideas are supported with evidence and methods. Similarly, preservation efforts, perhaps of wax cylinders with spoken word content or of ancient maps that embody an ongoing dialogue about the shape and nature of the physical world, seek to save, or at least document, important conversations. Common use of the word 'conversation' is completely in accordance with the use of the term in Conversation Theory.

The term is, however, more specifically defined as an act of communication and agreement between a set of agents. So, a conversation can be between two people, two organisations, two countries, or even within an individual. How can a conversation take place within an individual? Educators and school librarians may be familiar with the term 'metacognition,' or the act of reflecting on one's learning. Yet, even the most casual reader will be familiar with the concept of debating oneself. The point is that a conversation is with at least two agents trying to come to an understanding. Also note that those two agents can change over time. So, while Socrates and Plato are dead the conversation they started about the nature of knowledge and the world is carried forward by new generations of thinkers...same conversation, different agents. People converse, organisations converse, states converse, societies converse.

The requirements, in the terms of Conversation Theory, are two cognitive systems seeking agreement. The results of these conversations, what Pask would call 'cognitive entanglements,' are books, videos, and artifacts that either document, expand, or result from conversations. So, while one cannot converse with a book that book certainly can be a starting point for many conversations within the reader and within a larger community.

If the theory is that conversation creates knowledge, the library community has added a corollary: the best knowledge comes from an 'optimal information environment,' one in which the most diverse and complete information is available to the conversant. Library ethics show an implicit understanding of this corollary in the advocacy of intellectual freedom and unfettered access. Libraries seek to create rich environments for knowledge and have taken the stance that they are not in the job of arbitrating the conversations that occur or the 'appropriateness' of the information used to inform those conversations. As will be discussed later, this belief in openness of conversations will have some far-reaching implications for the library collection and is an ideal that can never truly be met.

For now, the reader may take away that conversation theory is very much in line with current and past library practice, and it also shows a clear trajectory for the future. The value to this viewpoint is not just theoretical; it has real consequences and uses. For example, much of library evaluation has been based in numeric counts of tangible outputs: books circulated, collection size, reference transactions, and so on. Yet this quantitative approach has been frustrating to many who feel they are counting outcomes but not getting at true impact of library service. Librarians may ask themselves, "Which numbers are important...and why?" If libraries focused on conversations there might be some clarity and cohesion between statistics and other outcomes. Suddenly, the number of reference questions can be linked to items cataloged or to circulation numbers...they are all markers of the scope and scale of conversations within the library context.

This approach might enable the library community to better identify 'important' conversations and demonstrate direct contributions to these conversations across functions. For example, a school district identifies early litreacy as important. There is a discussion about public policy options, new programmes, and school goals to achieve greater litreacy in the K-5 grades. The library should be able to track two streams in this conversation.

The first is the one libraries are used to counting; that is, the library's contribution to K-5 litreacy. But the library can also document and demonstrate how it furthered the conversation about children's litreacy in general. It could show the resources provided to community officials. It could show the litreacy pathfinders that were created. The point of this example is that the library is both participant in the conversation and facilitator of conversation. The theoretical discussion leads us to a discussion about the second topic of this technology brief: pragmatic aspects of the knowledge as conversation approach, or a participatory approach as it will be called.

As new technologies are developed and deployed in the current environment of limited resources, there must be some means of evaluating their utility. The utility of a technology is appropriately measured against a given library's mission, which is in turn developed to respond to the needs of the community that library serves. First, however, let us identify some of the new technologies and describe them briefly.

PARTICIPATORY NETWORKING, SOCIAL NETWORKS, AND WEB 2.0

Let us now move from the theoretical to the operational. The impetus behind this chapter is the relatively recent emergence of a new group of Internet services and capabilities. Suddenly, terms like Wiki, blog, mashup, Web 2.0, and biblioblogosphere have become commonplace. As with any new wave of technological creation, these terms can seem ambiguous and they also come wrapped in varying amounts of hype. They may all, however, be grouped under the phenomenon of participatory networking. While we now have a conceptual framework to evaluate these technologies that support participatory networking, we still need to know the basics of the terminology and technologies.

This section outlines key concepts in the pragmatics of participatory networking. The section after this one will join the theoretical and operational to outline key challenges and opportunities for the library world. We begin with Web 2.0

WEB 2.0

Much of what we call participatory networking, at least the technological foundation of it, stems from developments in 'Web 2.0.' As with many buzzwords, the exact definition of Web 2.0 is not clear. It is more an aggregation of concepts that range from software development to abstractions. What pervades the Web 2.0 approach is the notion that Internet services are increasingly facilitators of conversations.

Web 2.0 Characteristic: Social Networks

A core concept of Web 2.0 is that people are the content of sites; that is, a site is not populated with information for users to consume. Instead, services are provided to individual users for them to build networks of friends and other groups. The content of a site, then, comprises user-provided information that attracts new members of an ever-expanding network.

Examples:

- *Flickr*: Flickr provides users with free Web space to upload images and create photo albums. Users can then share these photos with friends or with the public at large. Flickr facilitates the creation of shared photo galleries around themes and places.
- *The Cheshire Public Library*: The Teen Book Blog at the Cheshire Public Library offers book reviews created only by the students who use the library.
- *Memorial Hall Library*: The Memorial Hall Library in Andover Massachusetts offers podcasts of poetry contests in which the content is created by students.
- *Libraries in MySpace*: MySpace searches show that there are MySpace sites for hundreds of individual libraries and scores of library groups. Alexandrian Public Library. This practice is growing among public libraries and is an attempt to reach out to users in their preferred online environments. In this venue, the more friends a library MySpace site has the more successful it may be considered. The Alexandrian Public Library has 75 friends and 15 comments. The Brooklyn College Library has 2195 friends and 270 comments.

Web 2.0 Characteristic: Wisdom of Crowds

There has been some research into the quality of mass decision-making. That research shows how remarkably accurate groups are in their judgements. Web 2.0 pools large groups of users to comment on decisions. This aggregation of input is facilitated by the ready availability of social networking sites. Certainly, this approach of community organisation and verification of knowledge also has its detractors.

Many, for example, question the wisdom seen in some entries of Wikipedia. Yet, recent articles have compared this mass editing process favourably to traditional sources of information such as the Encyclopaedia Britannica.

Web 2.0 Characteristic: Loosely Coupled APIs

API is short hand for 'Application Programming Interface.' It provides a set of instructions that a programmer can use to communicate between applications. APIs allow programmers to incorporate one piece of software they may not be able to directly manipulate into another. For example, Google Maps has made a public API that allows Web page designers to include satellite images into their Web pages with little more than a latitude and longitude. APIs vary in their ease of integration. Loosely coupled APIs allow for very easy integration using high-level scripting languages.

Web 2.0 Characteristic: Mashups

Mashups are combinations of APIs and data that result in new information resources and services. This ease of incorporation has led to an assumption of a 'right to remix.' In the world of open source software and the creative commons, the right to remix refers to a growing expectation among Internet users that they are not limited by the interfaces and uses presented to them by a single organisation.

Web 2.0 Characteristic: Permanent Betas

The concept of a permanent beta is, in part, a realisation that no software is ever truly complete so long as the user community is still commenting upon it. For example, Google does not release services from beta until it has achieved a sufficient user base no matter how fixed the underlying source code is. Permanent beta is also a design strategy. Large applications are broken into smaller constituent parts that can be manipulated separately. This allows large applications to be continually developed by a more diverse and distributed community.

Web 2.0 Characteristic: Software Gets Better the More People Use It

An increasing number of Web 2.0 sites emphasise social networks, where these services gain value only as they gain users. Malcolm Gladwell recounts this principle and the work of Kevin Kelly with an earlier telecommunications network, the network of fax machines connected to the phone system: "The first fax machine ever made...cost about $2,000 at retail. But it was worth nothing because there was no other fax machine for it to communicate with.

The second fax machine made the first fax machine more valuable, and the third fax made the first two more valuable, and so on...When you buy a fax machine, then, what you are really buying is access to the entire fax network—which is infinitely more valuable than the machine itself." With social networking sites, and all sites that seek to capitalise on user input, the true value of each site is defined by the number of people it can bring together.

Examples

Amazon

A classic example of this characteristic is Amazon.com. Amazon sells books and other merchandise, but, in reality, Amazon is very much about the marketing of information. Amazon gains tremendous value by allowing its users to review and rate items. The more people use Amazon and the more they comment, the more visibility these active users gain and the more credibility markers they take on.

Web 2.0 Characteristic: Folksonomies

A folksonomy is a classification system created in a bottom-up fashion and with no central coordination. This differs from the deductive approach of classifications systems like the Dewey Decimal System, where the world of ideas is broken into ten nominal classes. It also differs from other means of developing classifications where some central authority determines if a term should be included. In a folksonomy, the members of a group simply attach terms to items and the aggregate of these terms is seen as the classification. What emerges is a classification scheme that prioritises common usage over semantic clarity.

CORE NEW TECHNOLOGIES: AJAX AND WEB SERVICES

As we have jut discussed, Web 2.0 is little more than set of related concepts, albeit with a lot of value being currently attached to these concepts. These concepts are supported by two underlying technologies that have facilitated Web 2.0 development and brought a substantially new user experience to the Web. The first is AJAX, which allows a more desktop-like experience for users. The second is the advent of Web services. These technologies are not necessary for Web 2.0 concepts, but they have made Web 2.0 sites much more compelling.

AJAX

AJAX stands for Asynchronous JavaScript and XML. It is a set of existing Web technologies brought together. At the most basic, AJAX allows a browser and a server to send data back and forth without needing to refresh the entire Web page being worked on. Think about the Web sites you work with. You click on a link, the browser freezes and waits for the data, then draws it on the screen. Early versions of sites like MapQuest would show a map. If you wanted to zoom into the map, you would press a zoom icon and wait while the new map, and the rest of the Web page was redrawn. Compare this to Google Maps, where you click in the middle of a map and drag left or right and the map moves dynamically.

This kind of interaction we are used to in desktop applications. Click and drag has become second nature on the desktop and AJAX is making it second nature on the Web, too. Another advantage of AJAX is that it is open and requires only light programming skills. Javascript on the client and almost any server side scripting language are easily accessible languages. This fact allows for both fast development and easier integration with existing systems. As an example, it should now be easier to bring more interactive Web interfaces to existing online catalogues.

Web Services

Web services allow for software-to-software interactions on the Web. Using Web protocols and XML, applications exchange queries and information in order to facilitate the larger functioning of a system. One example would be a system that uses an ISBN number to query multiple online catalogues and commercial vendors for availability of a book. This simple process might be part of a much larger library catalogue that shows users a book and its availability. The point is that unlike federated search systems such as Z39.50, Web services are small. They also tend to be lightweight, and are aggregated for greater functionality.

LIBRARY 2.0

Library 2.0 is a somewhat diffuse concept. Walt Crawford, in his extended essay Library 2.0 and 'Library 2.0' found 62 different views and seven distinct definitions of Library 2.0. It is no wonder that people are confused. However, it is natural for emerging ideas and groups to function in an environment of high ambiguity. For use in this technology brief the authors see Library 2.0 as an attempt to apply Web 2.0 concepts to the purpose of the library. In the words of Ormsby, "The purpose of a library is not to ... showcase new gadgetry ...; rather, it is to make possible that instant of insight when all the facts come together in the shape of new knowledge."

How the applications are used will determine whether they support Ormsby's "instant of insight." Many libraries and librarians are already pursuing this goal. Some, for instance, are using blogs to reach other librarians, their own users, and potential users.

They are using Wikis to deliver reports, teach information litreacy, and serve as repositories. One has developed an API that allows WordPress posts to be directly integrated into a library catalogue. Clearly, the Internet and newer tools that empower users seem to be aligned with the library mission. After all, librarians blogging and allowing the catalogue to be 'mashed up' can be seen as an extension of current information services. But this abundance of new applications poses a challenge.

Given the speed with which new tools are invented, librarians may find it difficult to create strategies that include all the desired services that they make possible. For every new application that becomes available, library administrators must decide whether it can serve the library, how to use it, and how to find additional resources to manage it. This problem stems from focussing excessively on the technology. Librarians should, instead, focus on the phenomena made possible by the technology. Most important of these phenomena, the library invites participation.

As Chad and Miller state:

- Library 2.0 facilitates and encourages a culture of participation, drawing upon the perspectives and contributions of library staff, technology partners and the wider community. Library 2.0 means harnessing this type of participation so that libraries can benefit from increasingly rich collaborative cataloguing efforts, such as including contributions from partner libraries as well as adding rich enhancements, such as book jackets or movie files, to records from publishers and others.
- Library 2.0 is about encouraging and enabling a library's community of users to participate, contributing their own views on resources they have used and new ones to which they might wish access.
- With Library 2.0, a library will continue to develop and deploy the rich descriptive standards of the domain, whilst embracing more participative approaches that encourage interaction with and the formation of communities of interest.

The carte blanche statement that users participating in the library is 'good,' however, is insufficient. Library administers must ask, 'What is the ultimate goal?' In summary, current initiatives in the library world to bring the tools of Web 2.0 to the service of Library 2.0 are exciting and innovative, and more to the point, they are supportive of the library's purpose. They may, however, incur costs, such as monitoring blogs and Wikis and creating content and corresponding with users that stretch already inadequate resources even further. Ultimately, the value of Library 2.0 concepts requires us to answer some important questions: will they be used to further knowledge, or will they simply create more work for librarians? What does the 'next version' of Library 2.0 look like? Is its mission the same and just the tools different? What makes the library different from MySpace... simply a legacy? Should we incorporate new services into the current library offerings? How do we, as facilitators of conversations, point the way to the next generation of library? It is hoped that some of the concepts in participatory librarianship may answer these questions and help further the innovations of the Library 2.0 community.

PARTICIPATORY NETWORKS

The authors use the phrase participatory networking to encompass the concept of using Web 2.0 principles and technologies to implement a conversational model within a community.

Why not simply adopt social networking, Web 2.0, or Library 2.0 for that matter? Let us examine each term's limitations:

- *Social networking*: Social network sites such as MySpace and Facebook have certainly captured public attention. They have also proven very popular. In their short life spans these sites have garnered an immense audience and drawn much attention from the press. Some of that attention, however, has been very negative. MySpace, for example, has been typified as a refuge for pedophiles and online predators. Even the television show Saturday Night Live has parodied the site for the ease with which users can create false personas and engage in risky online behaviours. To say you are starting a social networking site in your library may draw either enthusiastic support, vehement opposition or simply confused looks. Add to the potential negative connotations the ambiguity of the term. Is a blog a social networking site? Is Flickr? To compound this confusion, the academic domain of Social Network Theory predates MySpace by about a decade.
- *Web 2.0*: Ambiguity also dogs the Web 2.0 world. For some, it is technology. For others, it is simply a buzzword for the current crop of Internet sites that survived the burst of the.com bubble. In any case, Web 2.0 certainly implies more than just the inclusion of users in systems.
- *Library 2.0*: As stated before, the term Library 2.0 is a vague term used by some as a goad to the library community. Further, this term limits the discussion of user-inclusive Web services to the library world. While this brief focuses on the library community, it also sees the library community as a potential leader in a much broader field.

So, ultimately, the authors propose 'participatory networking' as a positive term and concept that libraries can use and promote without the confusion and limitations of previous language. The phrase 'participatory network' also has a history of prior use that can be built upon. The phrase 'participatory networks' represents systems of exchange and integration and has long been used in discussions of policy, art, and government. The phrase has also been used to describe online communities that exchange and integrate information.

LIBRARIES AS PARTICIPATORY CONVERSATIONS

So where are we? We started with the abstract statement that knowledge is created through conversation. We then looked at the current landscape of technologies that can facilitate these conversations and showed examples of how libraries, other industries, and individuals are using these technologies. In this section we combine the larger framework with the technologies to see how libraries can incorporate participatory networks to further their knowledge mission.

PARTICIPATORY LIBRARIANSHIP IN ACTION

Let us look specifically at how participatory networks can be used in the library's role as facilitator of knowledge through conversation. An obvious example is libraries hosting blogs and Wikis for their communities creating virtual meeting spaces for individuals and groups, just as libraries do in the physical world. Indeed, these are increasingly useful functions for libraries. They meet a perceived need in the community, and can generate excitement both within the library and in the community.

The idea of creating online sites for individuals and organisations makes sense for a library, although it is not without difficulties. Libraries could also use freely available open source software to create library versions of Wikipedia. Another way for libraries to offer these services would be through a cooperative or other third-party vendor.

Such a service can easily be seen as a knowledge management activity capturing and providing local expertise while linking this expertise to that produced at other libraries. Another reason for libraries to engage in participatory networking is that one library can more easily collaborate with other libraries in richer dialogues. We currently have systems that connect our online catalogues and share resources through interlibrary loan. These conduits exist and can be used for the transferal of richer data, as has been proved through collaborative virtual reference systems.

In our current systems, as in traditional library practice, when users are referred to other libraries, they are sent out and not brought back. In a participatory library setting, libraries would facilitate a conversation between the user, the community of the local library, and then through the developed conduits, other libraries and their communities. The end result would be a seamless web of libraries where the user can ignore the intricacies of the library's organisation structure and boundaries, and in which the libraries are using the best local resources to meet local needs. Bringing libraries seamlessly together to participate in conversations with a single user has another significant advantage: the Library would make it easy for users to join the conversation regardless of where they are, through the presentation of a single façade.

There is, for example, only one Google, one Amazon, and one Wikipedia. Why should users have to search from among thousands of libraries to find the conversations they want? Participatory networking will be most effective when libraries work together, when the whole is greater than its parts. We currently see elements of The Participatory Library in the OCLC Open Worldcat project. For example, users searching Google may come across a listing provided by OCLC.

After selecting the entry for the book, the user can then jump to his or her own local library's information about the book. Users do not have to know which library to visit to find a book near them. Extending this concept to conversations, one goal of these participatory networks is to make it easier for the user to enter a conversation with The Library without having to work to discover their own specific entry points. However, ensuring this effective seamless access to the Library will require more than simply adding elements of participatory networking around the edges of the library. Adding services like blogs and Wikis may be seen merely as adjunct to current library offerings. As with any technological advance, scarce resources must be weighed against a desire to incorporate new services. Do we expand the collection, improve the Web site, or offer blogs to students? A better approach for making these kinds of decisions is to look at the needs of the community served in context with the commonly accepted, core tasks of a library, and see how they can be recast as conversational, or participatory tools.

In point of fact, every service, patron, and access point is a starting point for a conversation. Let's start with the catalogue. If the catalogue is a conversation, it is decidedly formal and, more importantly, one way. Think of today's catalogue as the educational equivalent of a college lecture. A formal system is used to serve up a series of presentations on a given topic. The presentations are rigid in their construction. They follow an abstract model and provide minimal opportunities to the receiver of the information to provide feedback or input.

They provide no constructive means for the user to improve or shape the conversation. Even recent advances in catalogue functions do little more than make the presentation of information more varied. They are still not truly interactive because they do not allow user participation; they do not allow for conversation. To highlight the one-way nature of the catalogue, ask a simple question: what happens when the user doesn't find something?

Do we assume that the information is there, but that the user is simply incapable of finding it? Do we assume that the information does not exist? Do we assume that the catalogue itself is limited? What if we assume that the catalogue is just the current place a user is involving in an ongoing conversation...what would that look like? How can such a traditionally rigid system be made more participatory? What if the user, finding no relevant information in the catalogue, adds either the information or a placeholder for someone else to fill in the missing information? Possibly the user adds information from his or her expertise.

However, assuming that most people go to a catalogue because they don't have the information, perhaps the user instead begins a process for adding the information. The user might ask a question using a virtual reference service; at the end of the transaction, the user then has the option to add the question, along with the answer and associated materials, to the catalogue. Or perhaps, the user simply leaves the query in the catalogue for other patrons to answer, requesting to be notified when an answer is posted. In that case, when a new user does a catalogue search and runs across the question, he or she can provide an answer.

That answer might be a textual entry, or simply a new query that directs the original questioner or new patrons to existing information in the catalogue. The catalogue can also associate conversations with any data point. For example, a user pulls up the record for a book s/he feels might be relevant to an information need s/he is having. This process starts a conversation between that user and the library, its users and authors of associated works. The user can see comments and ratings associated with this book from not only users of this library but users of other libraries. Also associated is a list of related works and the full audio of a lecture by the author. The user might also be directed to an in-person or online book group that is reading that book.

The point is that the catalogue facilitates a conversation as opposed to simply presenting what it 'knows' about a topic and then stepping out of the process. The catalogue, then, does not simply present information, but instead helps users construct knowledge by allowing the user to participate in a conversation. There are other means of improving systems in a conversational library. Take the implicit link between the catalogue and circulation. Of course these systems have always been linked in that items found in the catalogue can be checked out and checked out items have their status reflected in the catalogue. But this kind of 'state' information is a pretty meagre offering.

Imagine using circulation data to improve the actual functionality of the catalogue. Take the example of a user who is searching the catalogue for fictional books on magic. Currently, a relevance score between an item's metadata and the query is computed and then all the items are ranked in a retrieval set. This relevance score can be computed in many ways, but is usually based on the number of times a keyword appears in the record and the placement of that keyword in the metadata record. What is missing is the actual, real-world circulation of an item. Wouldn't it make sense, given such an abstract query, to present the user with Harry Potter first? What if we added circulation data to our relevance rankings: how many times this item has been checked out? It turns out that using a simple statistic is amasingly powerful.

It is akin to Google's page rank algorithm that presents sites most linked to higher in the results. Also, for those worried that users would be flooded with only popular materials, studies show that while these algorithms do change the very top ranked material, the effect quickly fades so that the user can still easily find other materials. Another consideration for adjusting a search is to allow the user to tweak the algorithms used to retrieve works. In the example, a user could turn off the 'popularity' feature. The user could also toggle switches for currency, authority, and other facets of relevancy rankings. The conversational model requires us to rethink the catalogue as a dynamic system, with data of varying levels of currency and, frankly, quality, coming into and out of the system. In a conversational catalogue there is no reason that some data can't exist in the catalogue for limited durations. Records of well-groomed physical collections may be a core and durable collection in the catalogue, but that is only one of many types of information that could exist in the catalogue space. Furthermore, even this core data can be annotated and linked to more transient media.

So, the user might see a review from a blog as part of a catalogue record on one day, but when s/he pulls the record up again in a few days, that review might be absent, the blog writer having withdrawn the comment. This is akin to weeding the collection; however, it would happen in a more dynamic fashion than occurs with the content on library shelves. The conversational model can also be used in other areas of the library.

What do we digitise? What do we select? What programmes do we offer? What do we preserve? The empowered user can participate in answering all of these questions but does not replace the expert librarian; rather, the user contributes additional and diverse information and commentary. In fact, the catalogue scenario just proposed already assumes that the library catalogue does more than store metadata. In order for the scenario to work the 'catalogue' must store questions, answers, video, audio...in essence the catalogue must be expanded and integrated with other library systems so that a final Participatory Library System can present a coherent view of The Library to patrons.

FRAMEWORK FOR INTEGRATION OF PARTICIPATORY LIBRARIANSHIP

As has been noted, participatory networks and libraries as conversations are not brand new concepts sprung from the head of Zeus. Instead they are means to integrate past and current innovations, and create a viable plan forward.

Along the left hand of the graph are current library systems. While the terminology may differ from library to library, nearly every system can be found on today's library web sites. By showing the systems together, the problems of user confusion and library management burden become obvious. Users must often navigate these systems based on their needs, and often with little help. Should they search the catalogues first or the databases? Isn't the catalogue really just another database? Which database do they choose? In our attempts to better serve the users by creating a rich set of resources and services, we have instead complicated their information seeking lives.

As one librarian puts it, "don't give me one more system I, or my patrons, have to deal with." From the array of systems on the left hand, we can see that libraries have not been doing themselves any favours either. We are maintaining many systems, therefore making the calls for yet more systems not only impractical but unwise. The answer is to integrate systems, combining the best of each while discarding the complexity of the whole. The library world is in the midst of doing just that. This section seeks to highlight promising developments in integrating library systems well beyond the library catalogue and to highlight not only an ideal endpoint, but also how this ideal system is truly participatory.

Merging Reference and Community Involvement

The functional area furthest along in the integration of participatory librarianship is reference; since, reference is most readily recognisable as a conversation, this comes as no surprise. Over the last decade, reference services have gone online, and have led to shared reference services. More importantly, reference done online creates artifacts of reference conversations: electronic files than can be cleaned of personal information and placed in a knowledge base, and used as a resource for other users.

A new development in reference is the reference blog, in which multiple librarians and other users can be part of a question answering community with conversations that can live on beyond a single transaction. Another functional area of libraries that is already involved with participatory librarianship is community involvement. For decades, public libraries have supported local community groups through meeting spaces. Some libraries are now hosting Web spaces for local groups.

As libraries incorporate participatory technologies into their offerings, they can create virtual places such as discussion forums, Wikis, and blogs for these community groups to use. If there are standards for these discussion areas, then groups from different communities could also easily participate in shared boards; this makes sense for groups such as Weight Watchers or Alcoholics Anonymous that have local branches and national involvement. In an academic setting, these groups can be student, faculty, or staff organisations or courses. In addition to reference and hosted community conversations, the library has been actively creating digital collections of materials. Parallel to the digital collection building of library materials is an active attempt to create institutional repositories of faculty papers, teacher lesson plans, organisational documentation, and the like.

These services are participatory systems in which collections come from users' contributions, and they may evolve into digital repositories that include both user-created and librarian-created artifacts. These different conversations can be archived into a single repository, and if properly planned, the reference conversations can live alongside, and eventually be intermingled with, the community conversations, and the digital repository into a community repository. Community repositories allow librarians to be more easily involved in the conversations of the community and capture important artifacts of these conversations for later use.

Merging Library Metadata into an Enhanced Catalogue

Participatory librarianship can be supported by another functional area of the library: collections. Traditionally, the collection comprises books, magazines, and other information resources paid for by the library. Electronic resources such as databases that are leased instead of purchased make up a large portion of library expenditures. More recently, Web-based resources have been selected and added to the virtual collection. Several kinds of finding aids are used to locate these information resources.

The catalogue and databases both contain descriptions of resources and searching interfaces. In order to improve access, libraries include records for databases within the catalogue. Conversely, federated searching tools combine the records from different databases and could allow the retrieval of both books and articles by combining records from both the traditional catalogue and databases into one tool. If community-created resources are part of the catalogue, then these resources would also be findable alongside other traditional library resources.

The tools for describing information resources can also be participatory. In traditional librarianship, the librarians provide metadata that patrons then use to make selections. By examining this use data, recommender systems can be created to help users locate new materials. In participatory networking, patrons will be encouraged to add comments about items. If standards are used for these comments, then they can be shared among libraries to create larger pools of recommendations. As these comments are analysed, they can be combined with usage databases to create stronger recommender systems to present patrons with additional choices based upon what is being explored.

The end result is an enhanced catalogue that allows users and libraries to find information regardless of which system the information resides in. However, the enhanced catalogue is still just that, a catalogue. It contains surrogates of digital information and is managed separately from the artifacts themselves. In the case of physical items, this may be all the library systems can manage, but in the case of digital content, there is one more step that needs to be taken. Namely, the artificial barrier between catalogue and content must come down.

Building the Participatory Library

At this point in the evolution of distributed systems into a truly integrated library system, the Participatory Library, we have two large collections: one of resources and one of information about the resources. The first collection of digital content, the community repository, is built by the library and its users collaboratively. The second collection, the enhanced catalogue, includes metadata, both formal and user-created. Both the community repository and the enriched catalogue are participatory. Yet to realise the dream of a seamless system of functionality, these two systems must be merged allowing users to find resources and, much more importantly, conversations.

Furthermore the users must be able to add to both metadata and content. The result may be conceived of as a single integrated information resource, which, for the purposes of this conversation, is called the Participatory Library. Users may access the Participatory Library directly through the library, or they may access it as a series of services in Google, MySpace, or their own homepages. The point is that the access to the library takes place at the point of conversation, not at the point the user realises he or she needs information from the library.

CONVERSATIONS AND PRESERVATION

The conversation model highlights the need for preservation. Aside from simply providing systems that facilitate conversation, libraries serve as the vital community memory. Conversations construct knowledge, but someone must remember what has already been said, and know how to access that dialog. Scientific conversations, for example, are built on previous conversations. Capturing conversations and 'playing them back' at the right time is essential.

This might mean the preservation of artifacts but it also means the increasingly important tasks of capturing the digital dialogs. This highlights the need for institutional repositories. Specifically, Web sites, lectures, courseware, articles must be kept. Further, they must be kept in true conversational repositories that capture the artifacts the methods and the process. They must be kept in information structures that make them readily available as conversations: in other words, users must be able to search for materials, and be able to reconstruct a conversation in its entirety from one fragment.

BEING WHERE THE CONVERSATION IS

Imagine the conversations that are going on in your local library as you read this. Imagine the physicist chatting with the gardener, and the trustee talking with the volunteer who is reading the latest best seller. What knowledge can be gleaned from these novel interactions? Can you measure it? Can you enhance it? Can you capture it? Can you recall it when it would be precisely what a user needs to meet an information need? Note also that these conversations do not belong solely to the library. The library is only part of the conversation. Faced with the daunting variety of resources available on the Web, many organisations try to become the single point of entry into it. Remember that conversations are varied in their mode, places and players, and, more importantly, that they are intensely personal.

This means that participants need to have ownership in them, and often in their locations as well. This also means that the library, as facilitator, needs to be varied in its modes and access points. In many cases, it is better to either create a personal space in which users may converse, or, increasingly, to be part of someone else's space. What we can learn from Web 2.0's Mashups is that smaller sets of limited functionalities lead to greater incorporation of tools into people's lives.

In the ChicagoCrime Google Maps Mashup, combining maps from Google and Chicago crime statistics, it was important for the host of the site to brand the space and shape the interface for his conversation on crime. Can your library functions be as easily incorporated into these types of conversations? Can a user search your catalogue and present the results on his or her Web site? The point is that libraries need to be proactive in a new way. Instead of the mantra, 'Be where the user is', we need to, 'Be where the conversation is. 'It is not enough to be at the users' desktops; you need to be in their e-mail programme, in their MySpace pages, in their IM lists, and in their RSS feed readers. All of these examples point to a significant mental shift that librarians will need to make in moving from delivering information from a centralised location to delivering information in a decentralised manner where the conversations of users are taking place.

The catalogue example presented earlier is an example of a centralised place for conversations. What if, Instead of only being in a catalogue, the same data were split into smaller components and embedded in the user's browser and e-mail programmes? Just as Google's mail system embeds advertising based upon the content of a message, The Library could also provide links to its resources based upon what a user is working on. By disaggregating the information within its system, The Library can deliver just what is needed to a user, provide connections into Mashups, and can live in the space of the user instead of forcing the user to come to the space of the library.

CHALLENGES AND OPPORTUNITIES

There is clearly a host of challenges in incorporating participatory networks and a participatory model into the library. This is to be expected when we are dealing with something as fundamental as knowledge and as personal as conversations. We consider four major challenges that must be met by libraries before they can truly get into the business of participatory librarianship.

Technical

There is a rich suite of participatory networking software that libraries can incorporate into their daily operations. Implementing a blog, a Wiki, or RSS feeds these days is not a hard task, and they can easily be used to deliver information about library services and conversations to the user's space.

Furthermore, these systems are often tested in very large-scale environments and are, in some cases, the same tools used in large participatory networking sites such as Wikipedia and Blogger. Some of these packages are commercial, but others are open source software. Open source software is cheaper, easier to adapt, and, in some cases, more advanced.

The downside to open source is that it requires a considerable amount of technical knowledge by the library and does not come with a technical support hotline. The largest technological impediment, however, may be the currently installed base of software within libraries. Integrated library systems have a long history, and include a broad range of library functions. Legacy code and near monolithic systems have restricted the easy exchange of a diverse set of information. Were these systems written today they would use modular code and loosely coupled APIs and allow customers much more customizability of interface.

These changes may come to integrated library systems but it may take years. Several libraries are currently attempting to pick apart these integrated systems themselves. Often, libraries go to the underlying databases that hold the library metadata or create their own data structures, such as the University of Pennsylvania Data Farm project. Once components of this system are exposed, the catalogue simply becomes another database that can be federated into new and unified interfaces. However, such integration requires a great deal of technological expertise.

There is an opportunity for ILS vendors or large consortial groups such as OCLC to move quickly into this space. In the meantime, there is an opportunity for the larger library community. This technology brief was created in response to a perceived need. Whether evidenced in the Library 2.0 community or in conversations at LITA, libraries are now interested in incorporating new Web technologies into their offerings and operations.

The technologies under consideration here present platforms for experimentation. Rather than setting up thousands of separated experiments, however, the library community should create a participatory network of its own. The technology certainly exists to create a test bed for libraries to set up various combinations of communication technologies to test new Web services against pooled data and even to incorporate new services into the current library offerings. By combining resources in a single, large-scale test bed, libraries cannot only get greater impact for the their investments, but can also directly experience life as a connected conversation. These connections, if built at the ground level, will then make it easier for The Library to come into existence. Terminology can be clarified, claims tested, and best practices collaboratively developed, greatly accelerating innovation and dissemination.

Operational

In addition to being in the conversation business, libraries are in the infrastructure business. One of the most powerful aspects of a library is its ability not only to develop a collection of some type of information but to maintain it over time. Sometimes infrastructure can be problematic but more often than not, it provides a stable foundation from which to operate. There are many conversations going on that need infrastructure but have none. Think of the opportunities in your community for using the Web to facilitate a conversation. It might be a researcher wanting to disseminate the results of his or her latest study. It might be a community organisation seeking funding. It might be a business trying to manage its basic operational knowledge.

The point is that such individuals and community organisations are not in the infrastructure business and could use a partner who is. Imagine a local organisation coming to the library, and within a few minutes setting up a Web site with an RSS feed, a blog and bulletin boards. The library facilitates, but does not own, that individual's or organisation's conversation. It does form a strong partnership, however, that can be leveraged into resources and support.

The true power of participatory networking in libraries is not to give every librarian a blog; it is in giving every community member a blog. In addition, the library can play the role of connecting these conversations to other users when appropriate. Participatory libraries allow the concept of community centre to be extended to the Web. Many public libraries have no problem providing meeting space to local non-profits. Why not provide Web meeting space in the form of a Web site or Web conferencing? Many academic libraries attempt to capture the scholarly output of their faculties, why not help generate the output with research data stores? The answers to these questions inevitably come back to time and money.

However, there is nothing in this brief that says such services have to be free. In fact, the best partnerships are formed when all partners are invested in the process. The true problem is that libraries have no idea of how to charge for such services. Faculty would be glad to write library support into grants, but need a dollar figure to include and how long each task will take. Many libraries aren't used to positioning their services on a per item basis, and this makes it difficult to build partnerships. Sometimes it is not a lack of money, but a lack of structure to take in money that is the problem.

Policy

As always, it is policy that presents the greatest challenges. The idea of opening the library functions to a greater set of inputs is rife with potential pitfalls. How can libraries use the technologies and concepts of Facebook and MySpace without being plagued by their problems? How can users truly be made part of the collection without the library being liable for all of their actions? The answers may lie in a seemingly obscure concept: identity management. Conversations can range in their mode, topic, and duration. They can also vary in the conversants.

The library needs to know a conversant's status to determine policy; and requires a unique identifier like a library card, to uphold it. In traditional libraries, that is the extent of identity management. In a participatory model, distinctions among identities become complex and graduated, and require us to consider a new approach. This new model, of patrons adding information directly to library systems, is not as radical as it may first appear. We have become very used to the idea of roles and tiered levels of authority in many other settings. Most modern computer systems allow for some gradation in user abilities. Online communities have even introduced merit systems, by which continual high-quality contributions to a site equals greater power in the site.

Think about Amazon, Wikipedia, even eBay; as users contribute more to the community they gain status and recognition. From participants to editors, from readers to writers, these organisations have seen membership as a sliding scale of trust, and libraries need to adopt this approach in all of their basic systems.

We currently do, to a degree, in the form of librarians, paraprofessionals, and other staff. Yet even these distinctions tend to be rigid and often class based, with high walls between the strata. Some of this is imposed by outside organisations but a great deal is there by inertia of the field. Skillful use of identity management will help libraries avoid the baggage of MySpace and Facebook.

As users grain greater access, greater responsibility, and greater autonomy, libraries need to be more certain of their identities. That is, for a user to do more requires the library to know more. Knowing about a user may involve traditional identity verification, or tracking an activity trail whereby intentions can be judged in relation to actions. These concepts may be expressed as, 'The more we know you, the more control you can have in valuable services such as blogging, or the catalogue."

The concepts are illustrated in Blogger and LiveJournal, both of which require some level of identity information. In another example: to join LiveJournal you must be invited, thus the community confers identity. The common theme is that verifying identity is community based. The difference between the library and MySpace is that the library works in an established community with traditional norms of identity, whereas MySpace is seeking to create a community. Both the library and the services, however, base their functions and services on identity.

Ethical

As knowledge is developed through conversation, and libraries facilitate this process, libraries have a powerful impact on the knowledge generated. Can librarians interfere with and shape conversations? Absolutely. Should we? We can't help it. Our collections, our reference work, our mere presence will influence conversations. The question is, in what ways? By dedicating a library mission to directly align with the needs of a finite community, we are accepting the biases, norms and priorities of the community. While a library may seek to expand or change the community, it does so from within. When Internet filtering became a requirement for federal Internet funding, public and school libraries could not simply quit, or ignore the fact, because they are agents of their communities. School libraries had to accept filtering with federal funding because their parent organisations, the schools, accepted filtering.

We see, from this example, that libraries may shift from facilitating conversations to becoming active conversant, but they are always doing both. Thus, the question is not whether the library shapes conversations, but which ones, and how actively? These questions are hardly new to the underlying principles of librarianship. And nothing in the participatory model seeks to change those underlying principles. The participatory model does, however, highlight the fact that those principles shape conversations and have an impact on the community.

WIRELESS NETWORKS IN MEDIUM-SIZED ACADEMIC LIBRARIES

Wireless networking offers a way to meet the needs of an increasingly mobile, tech-savvy student population. While many research libraries offer wireless access to their patrons, academic libraries serving smaller populations must heavily weigh both the potential benefits and disadvantages of this new technology. Will wireless networks become essential components of the modern academic library, or is this new technology just a passing fad? Prompted by plans to implement a wireless network at the Houston Cole Library (HCL), which serves a student enrollment close to ten thousand, this study was conducted to gather information about whether libraries similar in size and mission to HCL have adopted wireless technology. The study also sought to find out what, if any, problems other libraries have encountered with wireless networks and how successful they have perceived those networks to be. Other questions addressed include level of technical support offered, planning, type of equipment used to access the network, and patron-use levels.

REVIEW OF LITERATURE

A review of the literature on wireless networks revealed a number of articles on wireless networks and checkout programmes for laptop computers at large research institutions. Seventy percent of major research libraries surveyed by Kwon and Soules in 2003 offered some degree of wireless access to their networks.

No articles, however, specifically addressed the use of wireless networks in medium-sized academic libraries.

Many articles can also be found on wireless-network use in medical libraries and other institutions. Library instruction using wireless classrooms and laptops has been another subject of enquiry as well. Breeding wrote that there are a number of successful uses for wireless technology in libraries, and a wireless Local Area Network (WLAN) can be a natural extension of existing networks.

He added that since, it is sometimes difficult to install wiring in library buildings, wireless is more cost effective. A yearly survey conducted by the Campus Computing Project found that the number of schools planning for and deploying wireless networks rose dramatically from 2002 to 2003. "For example, the portion of campuses reporting strategic plans for wireless networks rose to 45.5 per cent in fall 2003, up from 34.7 per cent in 2002 and 24.3 per cent in 2001."

The use of wireless access in academia is expected to keep growing. According to a summary of a study conducted by the EDUCAUSE Centre for Applied Research (ECAR), the higher-education community will keep investing in the technology infrastructure, and institutions will continue to refine and update networks. The move towards wireless access "represents a user-centred shift, providing students and faculty with greater access than ever before." In an article on ubiquitous computing, Drew provides a straightforward look at how WLANs work, security issues, planning, and the uses and ramifications of wireless technology in libraries.

He suggests, "Perhaps one of the most important reasons for implementing wireless networking across an entire campus or in a library is the highly mobile lifestyle of students and faculty." The use of wireless will only increase with the advent of new portable devices, he added. Wireless networking is the best and least expensive way for students, faculty, and staff to take their office with them wherever they go. The circulation of laptop computers is a frequent topic in the available literature.

The 2003 study by Kwon and Soules primarily focussed on laptop-lending services in academic-research libraries. Fifty per cent of the institutions that responded to their survey provided laptops for checkout. The majority indicated moderate-to-high use of laptop services. Positive user response and improved 'public reputation, image, and relations" were the greatest advantages reported with laptop circulation. The major disadvantages associated with these services were related to labour and cost. A study of laptop checkout service at the Mildred F. Sawyer Library at Suffolk University in Boston revealed that laptop usage was popular during the fall semester of 1999. Students checked out the computers to work on group projects.

A laptop area was set aside on one library floor to provide wired Internet access for eight users. However, students wanted to use the laptops anywhere, not one designated place. The wired laptop areas were not popular, Dugan wrote, adding that "Few students used the wired area and the wires were repeatedly stolen or intentionally broken." An interim phase involved providing wireless network cards for checkout to encourage patrons to use their own laptops, and, when a wireless network was put into place in the fall of 2000, demand exceeded the number of available laptops for checkout.

METHOD

A survey was designed to find out how many libraries similar in size and mission to HCL have adopted wireless networks, the experiences they have encountered in offering wireless access, and, most importantly, whether they felt the investment in wireless technology has been worth the effort. The National Centre for Education Statistic's Academic Library Peer Comparison Tool, a database composed of statistical information on libraries throughout the United States, was used to select institutions for this study.

A search on this database retrieved eighty-eight academic libraries that met two criteria: full-time enrollments of between five thousand and ten thousand, and classification by the Carnegie Classification of Higher Education as Master's Colleges and Universities I. The survey was administered to those thought most likely to be responsible for systems in the library; they were selected from staff listings on library Web sites. If such a person could not be identified, the survey was sent to the head of library systems or to the library director.

The survey was divided into the following sections:

- Implementation of wireless network
- Planning and installation stages
- User services
- Technical problems
- Benefits specific to use of network

Surveys were mailed out in March 2004. An Internet address was provided in the cover letter if participants wished to take the survey online rather than return it by mail. An e-mail reminder with a link to the online survey was sent out three weeks after the initial survey was mailed. All letters and e-mails were personalised, and a self-addressed stamped envelope and a ballpoint pen with the JSU logo were included with the mail surveys. In the e-mail reminder, the authors offered to share the results of the project with anyone who was interested, and received several enthusiastic responses.

RESULTS

A total of fifty-three completed surveys were returned, resulting in a response rate of 60 per cent. The overwhelming majority responded that their library offered wireless-network access. Even if the thirty-five surveys that were not returned had reported that wireless networks were not available, more than 50 per cent would still have offered wireless networks. Survey results also pointed to the newness of the technology. Only four of the fifty-three institutions have had wireless networks for more than three years. The majority has implemented wireless networks just within the last two years.

When asked to identify the major reasons for offering wireless networks to their patrons, the three responses most chosen were:

- To provide greater access to users;
- The flexibility of a network unfettered by the limitations of tedious wiring; and
- To keep up with technological innovation.

Least significant factors in the decision to implement wireless networks were cost; use by library faculty and staff; to aid in bibliographic instruction; and use for carrying out technical services. Somewhat to the authors' surprise, wireless use in bibliographic instruction was not high on the list of reasons for installing a wireless network, identified by only 9 percent of respondents. The benefits of wireless for library instruction was stressed in the litreature by Mathias and Heser and Patton. In addition to obtaining an instrument for gauging how many libraries similar in scope and size to HCL have implemented wireless networks and why they chose to do so, questions on the survey were also designed to gather information on planning and implementation, user services, technical problems, and perceived benefits.

PLANNING AND IMPLEMENTATION

Although Tolson mentions that some schools have used committees composed of faculty, staff, and students to look into the adoption of wireless technology, responses from this survey indicated that the majority of the libraries did not form committees specifically for the planning of their wireless networks.

In addition, 49 per cent of the libraries took fewer than six months to plan for implementation of a network, 37 per cent required six months to one year, and 15 per cent reported more than one to two years. Actual time spent on installation and configuration of wireless networks was relatively short, 98 per cent indicating less than one year. One of the most important issues to consider when planning to implement a wireless network is extent of coverage—where wireless access will be available. Survey responses revealed varying degrees of wireless coverage among institutions. 20 per cent had campus-wide access, 55 per cent had some level of coverage throughout the entire library, 37 per cent provided a limited range of coverage outside the building, and 20 per cent offered access only in certain areas within the library.

Institutions vary in their approaches to networking depending on enrollment. Smaller colleges and universities with fewer than ten thousand students are "more likely to implement campuswide wireless networks from the start. Larger institutions are more likely to implement wireless technology in specific buildings, consistent with a desire to move forward at a modest pace, as resources and comfort with the technology grow." Questions on the survey also queried respondents about the popularity of spaces in the library where users access the library's wireless network. Answers revealed that the most popular areas for wireless access are study carrels, tables, and study rooms. 19 per cent indicated that accessing wireless networks in the stacks is popular. Of particular concern to HCL, a thirteen-story building, was how the environment of the library would accommodate a wireless network.

A thorough site survey is important to locate the best spots within the library to install access points and to determine whether there are architectural barriers in the building that might interfere with access. The majority of survey respondents indicated that the site survey conducted in their library for a wireless network was carried out by their academic institution's IT staff. While library staff conducted 35 percent of site surveys, only 17 per cent were conducted by outside companies.

USER SERVICES

An issue to be addressed by libraries deciding to go wireless is whether laptop computers should also be provided for checkout in the library. After all, it might be hard to justify the usefulness of a wireless network if users do not have access to laptops or other hardware with wireless capabilities. While one individual reported working at a 'laptop university' in which campuswide wireless networking exists and all students are required to own laptops, not all college students will have that luxury.

In order to provide more equal access to students, checking out laptops has become an increasingly common service in academic libraries. Seventy percent of this survey's respondents whose institutions offered wireless access also made laptops available for checkout. Comments made throughout the survey seemed to imply that while checking out laptops to patrons is an invaluable complement to offering wireless access, librarians should be prepared for a myriad of hassles that accompany laptop checkout. Wear and tear of laptops, massive battery use, cost of laptops, and maintenance were some of the biggest problems reported. One participant, whose institution decided to stop offering laptops for checkout to patrons in the library, wrote, "It required too much staff time to maintain and we decided the money was better spent elsewhere.

The college now encourages students to purchase a laptop [instead of] a full-sized PC." One participant worried that the rising use of laptops in his library would lead to the obsolescence of its more than one hundred wired desktops, writing, "Our desktops are very popular and we think having them is one of the reasons our gate count has increased in recent years. What happens when everyone has a laptop?" The number of laptops checked out in the libraries varied.

The majority of libraries had purchased between one and thirty laptops available for checkout.

Three institutions had more than forty-one laptops available for checkout. One library could boast that it had sixty laptops available for checkout with twelve pagers to notify students waiting in line to use laptops. When asked about the use of laptops in libraries, 46 percent observed moderate use, while 32 per cent reported heavy use of laptops. Only 3 percent indicated that they hardly ever noticed use of laptops in the library. For those students who chose to bring their own laptop to access the library's wireless network, half of the institutions surveyed required students to purchase their own network-interface cards for their laptops, while 19 per cent allowed students to check them out from the library.

In addition to laptops, personal digital assistants, (PDAs) were listed by 37 per cent of respondents as devices that may access wireless networks. One librarian indicated that cell phones could access the wireless network in his library. 56 per cent of respondents indicated that users are able to print to a central printer in the library from their wireless device. An important consideration for implementing a wireless network is how users will authenticate. Authentication protocol is defined by the Microsoft Encyclopaedia of Networking as "any protocol used for validating the identity of a user to determine whether to grant the user access to resources over a network." Authentication methods listed by the institutions surveyed varied greatly and the authors could not identify all of them.

Methods mentioned were Lightweight Directory Access Protocol (LDAP), virtual private network (VPN), and Media Access Control (MAC) addresses, Bluesocket, Remote Authentication Dial in User Service (RADIUS), pluggable Graphical Identification and Authentication (pGINA), Protected Extensive Authentication Protocol (PEAP), and e-mail logins. Out of the thirty-nine responses to this question, seven individuals indicated that they do not require any type of authentication at the present. Although some individuals noted that they are planning to enable some type of authentication in the future, one participant suggested that there were ethical issues involved in requiring users to authenticate.

This person argued that "anonymous access to information is valued" and praised his institution's current policy of allowing "anyone who can find the network" to use it.

A concern about offering wireless network access in the library is how library staff will be prepared to handle the flood of technical questions that are likely to ensue. The level of technical support offered to users varied among the institutions surveyed. More than half of the respondents indicated that users receive help specifically from IT staff or from the campus computer centre. 39 per cent of users received help from the reference desk, while 19 per cent received help from circulation staff. 33 per cent of the responding institutions offered technical help from a Web site, while 7 per cent indicated that they did not offer any type of technical support to users.

Technical Problems

The technical problems most often encountered with wireless networks centered on architectural barriers that cause black-outs or slow-spots where wireless access fails. This confirms the importance of carrying out thorough site surveys and testing prior to installation of access points. Site surveys may be carried out by companies specially equipped and trained to determine where access points should be installed, the most appropriate type of antennae and how many access points are needed to provide the greatest amount of coverage. Configuration of the network was the second most highly reported problem associated with installing wireless networks, seeming to suggest the need for librarians to coordinate their efforts and rely on the knowledge provided by the IT coordinator within their institution.

Lack of technical support available to users, slow speed, and authentication were also indicated as technical problems most encountered. Integrating the wireless network with the existing wired network was the least-mentioned problem associated with wireless networks. Although security problems, particularly concerning Wired Equivalency Protocol (WEP) vulnerabilities, have been pointed out as one of the major drawbacks of a wireless network, the majority of users had not as yet experienced security problems. Although one participant wrote, "Don't be too casual about the security risks," another individual wrote, "Talk to your networking department," as many of them are overly worried about security.

Perceived Benefits

Respondents reported that the number-one benefit of offering wireless access was user satisfaction. Giving patrons the ability to use their laptops anywhere in the library and do multiple tasks from one machine is simply becoming what more and more users expect.

The second largest benefit revolved around flexibility and ease of use due to the lack of wires. 35 per cent indicated that allowing students to roam the stacks while accessing the network was a significant benefit. Although a few studies have suggested the promise of wireless networks for aiding bibliographic instruction, only 9 per cent of respondents indicated this as a benefit of wireless technology. Use of wireless technology for instruction, it might be recalled, was not a significant factor noted by respondents in the decision to implement a wireless network.

Likewise, use of this type of network to carry out technical services was also low on the scale of benefits. 73 per cent of users claimed that wireless networks have thus far been worth the cost-benefit ratio. While 70 per cent indicated moderate to heavy use of the wireless network, 27 per cent reported low usage. When asked what advice they would give to others considering adopting wireless networks in their libraries, the overwhelming majority of responses were positive, recommending that HCL take the plunge.

As one individual wrote, "Offer it and they will come. It has really increased the usage of our library." Other individuals noted that it is simply necessary to offer wireless access to keep up with technological innovation, and that students expect it. The most significant warning, however, revolved around checkout and maintenance of laptops, which, from the results of this survey, seems be both a big advantage and a headache. Several individuals echoed the importance of doing site surveys to test bandwidth limitations and access.

One particularly energised participant, using multiple exclamations for emphasis, shared a plethora of advice. "Throttle connection speeds! Allow only http access! Block ports and unnecessary protocols! Secure your network and disallow unauthenticated users! Use access control lists! Establish policies that describe [wireless fidelity] Wi-Fi risks and liabilities on your part!".

Useful advice on wireless-access implementation gleaned from this survey fell under the following categories:

- Be aware of slower speed.
- Create a policy and guide for users.
- Do it because more users are going wireless, it is necessary to keep up with technological innovation, and because students love it.
- Provide plenty of access points.
- Install access points in appropriate places.
- Ensure continuous connectivity by allowing overlap between access points.
- Purchase battery chargers and heavy-duty laptops with extended warranties.
- Get support from IT staff for planning and maintenance.
- Offering wireless will increase library usage.
- Perform or have an expert perform a careful site survey and do lots of testing to locate dead or slow spots in the library due to architectural barriers.
- Enable some type of authorisation.
- Be aware of security concerns.
- Although the majority of participants' networks support 802.11b, a few participants suggest using the 802.11g standard because it is 'the fastest' and 'backwards compatible to 802.11b'.

3

Internet

Internet is the network of networks, *i.e.*, a global network which make WWW.

BIRTH OF THE NET

The Internet grew out of an experiment in the 1960s by the U.S. Department of Defence. The DoD wanted to create a computer network that would continue to function in the event of a disaster, such as a nuclear war. If part of the network was damaged or destroyed, the rest of the system still had to work. That network was ARPANET, which linked U.S., scientific and academic researchers.

It was the forerunner of today's Internet. In 1985, the National Science Foundation (NSF), an American research organisation, created NSFNET, a series of networks for research and education communication. Based on ARPANET protocols, the NSFNET created a national backbone service, provided free to any American research and educational institution. At the same time, regional networks were created to link individual institutions with the national backbone service. NSFNET grew rapidly as people discovered its potential and as new software applications were created to make access easier. Corporations such as Sprint and MCI began to build their own networks that they then linked to NSFNET.

When commercial firms and other regional network providers took over the operation of the major Internet arteries, NSF withdrew from the backbone business. NSF also coordinated a service called InterNIC that registered all addresses on the Internet so that data could be routed to the right system. This service has now been taken over by Network Solutions, Inc. and other Internet registration services in cooperation with NSF

NET ANATOMY

The Web physically consists of your personal computer, web browser software, a connection to an Internet service provider, computers called servers that host digital data, and routers and switches to direct the flow of information.

WEB BROWSERS

A web browser is the software programme you use to access the World Wide Web, the graphical portion of the Internet. The first browser, called NCSA Mosaic, was developed at the National Centre for Supercomputing Applications in the early 1990s. The easy-to-use point-and-click interface helped popularise the Web. Microsoft Internet Explorer and Netscape Navigator are the two most popular ones.

NAVIGATING THE WEB

The Web is known as a client-server system. Your computer is the client; the remote computers that store electronic files are the servers. To visit the web site, enter the address or URL of the web site in your web browser. Browser requests the web page from the web server that hosts the requested site. The server sends the data over the Internet to your computer. Your web browser interprets the data, displaying it on your computer screen.

The 'glue' that holds the Web together is called hypertext and hyperlinks. This feature allows electronic files on the Web to be linked so you can jump easily between them. On the Web, you navigate through pages of information--commonly known as browsing or surfing-based on what interests you at that particular moment. Web pages are written in a computer language called Hypertext Markup Language or HTML

W3C

The World Wide Web was originally developed in 1990 at CERN, the European Laboratory for Particle Physics. The original idea came from a young computer scientist, Tim Berners-Lee. It is now managed by The World Wide Web Consortium. The WWW Consortium is funded by a large number of corporate members, including AT&T, Adobe Systems, Inc., Microsoft Corporation and Sun Microsystems, Inc. Its purpose is to promote the growth of the Web by developing technical specifications and reference software that will be freely available to everyone.

WEB ADDRESSES

World Wide Web is a network of electronic files stored on millions of computers all around the world. Hypertext links these resources together. Uniform Resource Locators or URLs are the addresses used to locate the files. Every URL is unique and identifies one specific file.

DOMAIN NAMES

Every computer that hosts data on the Internet has a unique numerical address. For example, the numerical address for the White House is 198.137.240.100. But since, few people want to remember long strings of numbers, the Domain Name System (DNS) was invented. DNS, a critical part of the Internet's technical infrastructure, correlates a numerical address to a word. To access the White House web site, you could type its number into the address box of your web browser. But most people prefer to use 'www.whitehouse.gov.' In this case, the domain name is whitehouse.gov.

THE STRUCTURE OF A DOMAIN NAME

A domain name has two or more parts separated by dots and consists of some form of an organisation's name and a three letter or more suffix. For example, the domain name for IBM is 'ibm.com'; the United Nations is 'un.org.' The domain name suffix is known as a generic top-level domain (gTLD). It describes the type of organisation. Currently in use gTLDs:

```
.aero--For the air-transport industry
.biz--Reserved for businesses
.com--For businesses, commercial enterprises
.edu--For educational institutions and universities
.gov--Reserved for United States government agencies
.info--For all uses
.mil--For the United States military
.net--For networks; usually reserved for organisations such as
Internet
service providers
.org--For non-commercial organisations
```

BOOKMARKS AND FAVOURITES

Bookmarks and Favourites save Web addresses so you can return to them quickly. To save a web page, go to the Bookmarks or Favourites menu or click on its icon and select Add. When you click on the icon again, the title of the page you recorded will appear at the bottom of the list. To access the page, just double-click on the title.

To organise your Favourites, Click on the Favourites button on the toolbar to open the Favourites window. Now select Organise Favourites. Click on the folder icon to create a new folder, then name it. Now click on each Favourite once, hold down your left mouse button and drag the Favourite into the appropriate subject folder.

ABUSING INSECURE FEATURES OF INTERNET EXPLORER

INTERNET EXPLORER SECURITY MODEL

First, let us start with a description of the security framework used by Internet Explorer to classify resources and to enforce security policies when they are processed. Internet Explorer 4 introduced the concept of URL Security Zones as a means to classify web content according to its trustworthiness. Using this, framework security policies are configured for each of five pre-established Security

Zones, then while it is running Internet Explorer dynamically assigns content received from the Web to a corresponding Security Zone based on the content's origin and the settings configured for that Security Zone are then used to enforce the security controls associated to its trust level. Thus, a web application executed by Internet Explorer will be granted authorisation to perform actions depending on the privileges set for the Security Zone to which it was assigned by Internet Explorer.

These are the five Security Zones of Internet Explorer listed by increasing level of trust:

- *Restricted Sites Zone*: Used for Web sites that contain content that can cause problems when downloaded. Use this zone to cause Internet Explorer to alert that potentially-unsafe content is about to download, or to prevent that content from downloading. The user explicitly adds the URLs of untrusted Web sites to this zone,
- *Internet Zone*: For Web sites on the Internet that do not belong to another zone. This default setting causes Internet Explorer to prompt the user whenever potentially unsafe content is about to download. Web sites that are not mapped into other zones automatically fall into this zone,
- *Local Intranet Zone*: For content located on an organisation's intranet. Because the servers and information are within an organisation's firewall, it is reasonable to assign a higher trust level to content on the intranet,
- *Trusted Sites Zone*: For content located on Web sites that are considered more reputable or trustworthy than other sites on the Internet. Assigning a higher trust level to these sites minimizes the number of authentication requests. The user explicitly adds the URLs of these trusted Web sites to this zone.
- *Local Machine Zone*: The Local Machine zone is an implicit zone for content that exists on the local computer. The content found on the user's computer is treated with a high level of trust.

Although the default settings for each Security Zone have varied over time since, their introduction in Internet Explorer 4, the number of Security Zones and their implied level of trust have not changed.

For the purpose of this chapter there are two generic types of attacks to the Security Zone framework that are relevant:

- Security Zone elevation attacks, in which web content that should normally be assigned to a Security Zone with trust level X ends up assigned to a Security Zone with trust level Y where $Y > X$; and
- Security Zone restrictions bypass attacks, in which web content that ended up correctly assigned to a Security Zone successfully performs actions that require privileges not granted to that Security Zone.

WHEN A DOOR CLOSES, A WINDOW IS OPENED

Bad design decisions or flawed design sometimes result in features that leave an open door for different kinds of attacks and under the eternal alibi of backward compatibility, it often seems that they will never be closed. In this section, as suggested, describe some of these weak Internet Explorer features. Keep in mind that, as minimal as the security implications of these features may seem at a first glance, they have proved to be key components of the exploitation scenarios exposed herein, where the attacker can compromise a user desktop system by abusing nothing but these features.

Hiding the Key Under the Doormat

HTTP cookies and web navigation history are stored by Internet Explorer in several files and folders in the local file system. Apparently as a security measure random names are used for both files and folders. However, since, they need to be accessed by Internet Explorer in an efficient manner the names and location of the randomly named files are kept inside different mapping files named index.dat. Here are some examples:

```
%USERPROFILE%\Localsettings\History\History.IE5\index.dat
%USERPROFILE%\Localsettings\IECompatCache\index.dat
%USERPROFILE%\Cookies\index.dat
```

Although the format of these index files is not entirely plain text, the security sensitive content is being stored in plain text. Since, these index files are used to reference content stored in randomly named files, obtaining them would result in obtaining the actual locations of the aforementioned files and folders. Hence, the increase in security gained by storing potentially sensitive information in file system objects with randomly select names is dependent on the ability to prevent read access of index files from an attacker. If an attacker is able to inspect the contents of these indexing files, she can easily determine the exact location of the sensitive content that was protected by storing it in hidden files.

A Chip off the Old Block

Internet Explorer and Windows Explorer use common underlying components and resemble each other in many aspects. They both support access to file systems object on SMB shares and use of UNC (Universal Naming Convention) paths to reference them. The use of common components and the idiosyncrasies of both programmes allow a user to do some tricks with Internet Explorer when accessing special files and folders that yield similar results when done using Windows Explorer.

Furthermore, the fact that Internet Explorer supports UNC and SMB has an important security implication. As this naming conventions and protocols can be used without restrictions inside web pages in the Internet zone or above, a web page in those zones can include an HTML tag such as the following:

```
<img src='\\[WEB SERVER IP ADDRESS]\image.jpg'>
```

When Internet Explorer renders this tag, it triggers an SMB request to a server at the IP address specified in the <img> tag. The NTLM authentication negotiation proceeds as follows: anonymous access is first tried and, if failed, the client starts the challenge-response negotiation. The server sends the client a challenge value and the client automatically responds back with the ciphered challenge.

Thus, as part of the challenge-response negotiation, the client sends to the server the following information about itself:

- Windows user name.
- Windows domain name.
- Windows computer name.
- A challenge value chosen by the web server ciphered with the LM/ NTLM hash of this user's password.

This ciphered challenge could then be brute-forced to obtain the plaintext password for the currently logged user.

This achievement opens a variety of security implications:

- If the victim's computer is directly connected to the Internet, it could be compromised as easy as accessing it trough SMB.
- If the attacker knows something more about the victim, she could try this password for accessing other systems.

Even if the attacker is not able to obtain the plaintext password from that the SMB request, the rest of the information obtained can still be useful for other attack vectors as will be shown later on.

Two Zones, the Same Place

The Security Zones model mentioned at the beginning of this article requires Internet Explorer to determine to which zone it will assign a web resource based on its origin.

The Security Zone assigned to a given object referenced using the UNC convention is:

- The Internet Security Zone if the UNC path contains the IP address to specify the target machine.
- The Local Intranet Security Zone if the UNC path contains a NetBIOS name to specify the target machine.

So far this does not sound bad. It makes sense as NetBIOS names can only be resolved within the scope of the local network segment if not mapped explicitly in the lmhosts file. But what happens with IP address 127.0.0.1? As trivial as it may sound, it is not.

In fact, this is one of the root causes of the problems that Microsoft staff has mentioned for closing the attack scenarios described afterwards in this document. After several discussions with MSRC team members, they agreed that the issue is a kind of dead end, given that due to expected functionality and design decisions forcing this address to belong to one zone or another cannot be done without high impact on either security or backward compatibility with existing applications. Since, Internet Explorer makes extensive use of cached files enforcing access control to them is not a minor issue. The assumptions and constrains of the Security Zones model make things become more complicated. Consider, for example, an Internet web site redirecting the navigation flow towards the following URL:

`\\127.0.0.1\PATH_TO_RESOURCE`

The Security Zones scheme, a web site located in a less trusted zone could never provide content for and redirect its navigation flow towards a web site in a more trusted zone. This behaviour is known as Zone Elevation. However, in the case above Internet Explorer will erroneously apply Zone Elevation restrictions and the redirection will effectively occur. Content will be treated as belonging to the Internet zone, in spite of being stored in the local machine. Let us consider a different way to bypass Security Zones restrictions: suppose that example.com was explicitly added to the Restricted Sites Security Zone. Then the following URI will be treated with the privileges of that zone:

`http://example.com/index.html`

However, if the same resource is requested using the UNC notation:

`\\10.1.1.1\index.html`

it will be treated as belonging to the Internet Security Zone. As can be seen Internet Explorer fails to apply zone restrictions to a given resource if it is accessed using a different protocol.

Ways to Put Arbitrary HTML/Script Code in the Victim's Computer

While not straightforward there are at least three different ways for remote servers to write arbitrary HTML/script code in the local file system of clients running Internet Explorer:

- Navigation history files;
- Cookies; and
- History tracking files.

Even though these features are common to every modern web browser, the problem is not in the features themselves but in the way they are implemented:

- The content that a remote server sends to the client is written to various files on the local file system as they are received with little or no transformations/overhead;
- Internet Explorer allows rendering of HTML content read from local files that are not pure HTML. The non-HTML portions that cannot be rendered are simply ignored.

Due to this a remote server that managed to write arbitrary but partially controlled HTML/script code inside these files could eventually force Internet Explorer to treat them as such.

Everything That Glitters is Not Gold

The way Internet Explorer determines how to process the contents of a given file is based on what is known as MIME type detection. This is basically a best-effort heuristic used to determine the content type of a given resource and then launch the corresponding object server/application to process it. Security problems may arise if type detection fails. In some cases, unknown content type is defaulted to be treated as HTML which could, obviously, include scripting code also. Besides, this mechanism has been proved not to be consistent when accessing the same resource through different methods. For example, the proof of concept code for the vulnerability reported in the CORE-2008-0826 Security Advisory took advantage from the fact that Internet Explorer was reacting different when an unknown MIME format resource was directly accessed from an <object> tag than when it was invoked from a script.

OVERALL IMPACT

As can be seen from what has been discussed so far, by chaining the exploitation of a series of weak features an attacker is able to store HTML and scripting code in the victim's computer and then force the victim's browser to load and render it. Even though 127.0.0.1 is in the Internet Zone an attacker can still do some other interesting things: as code is actually stored in the victim's computer, it has enough privileges to access other files in the same origin allowing blind but full access to every file in the victim's local file systems. Thus, interesting files such as the SAM backup file, all of the user's HTTP cookies and history files or any other file on the local system may become available to the attacker.

For example: if the computer compromised has IIS running, an attacker could get the source code of files stored in the Inetpub\wwwroot folder. Even more, as many applications store sensitive information inside configuration files, an attacker could gain complete access to these files if they exist. These attack scenarios have been proven to work in the past in at least three different cases. In each of those cases the same generic approach was applied with the only variations in the way to use Internet Explorer to render internal tracking files as HTML.

For each new attack scenario Microsoft addressed the specific way in which Internet Explorer internal files can be used to deliver malicious HTML/ script content but it is very likely that as long as all the other components of the attack scenario could be chained together using the other individual weaknesses of Internet Explorer, an attacker will be just a single step away from successfully compromising the victim's system.

CORRIGENDA

Contrary to what has been stated in the Common Vulnerabilities and Exposures database for the CVE-2009-1140, it is not just a cross-domain information disclosure vulnerability. That is just a subset of the information you could get. In fact, CVE-2008-1448 description says something more precise: allows remote attackers to bypass intended access restrictions and read arbitrary files. And both of them are the same set of features abused by different means.

SOLUTIONS AND WORKAROUNDS

By the moment of the publication of this document official hot fixes will not be available for the latest variant of the attack exposed herein. Then, users could apply the following workarounds so to protect them from exploitation of these vulnerabilities in the wild.

Internet Explorer Network Protocol Lockdown

Internet Explorer can be configured to lock down HTML content from particular network protocols in additional zones besides the Local Machine zone. This feature allows an administrator to extend the same restrictions of the Local Machine Zone Lockdown to be applied to any content on any arbitrary protocol in any security zone. In this case, in order to prevent this attack from occur, an administrator can configure Internet Explorer to lock down HTML content hosted on the file: protocol if it is in the Internet zone. Since, the file: protocol's most common use is for either Local Machine or Local Intranet content and not Internet content, this mitigation should not imply huge compatibility issues.

Set the Security Level setting for the Internet and Intranet Zones to High

This setting will prevent Internet Explorer from running scripts or ActiveX controls in both Security Zones. Nonetheless, the impact on existing applications could render them unusable.

Disable Active Scripting for the Internet and Intranet Zone with a custom setting

This means to manually adjust the security level for that particular item instead of switching to an entirely different preset as in the previous workaround. Anyway, this could also have a considerable impact in multiple applications.

Only Run Internet Explorer in Protected Mode

If it is available on the operating system you should enable Protected Mode to mitigate this vector. However, as some applications stopped working properly when this working mode was introduced, many users have opted for disabling it.

Use a Different Web Browser to Navigate Untrusted Web Sites

As will be explained next, other browsers different than Internet Explorer can not be exploited the same way. Even so, using other browsers implies that users will be exposed to other risks those browsers are vulnerable to. It is up to the users to evaluate which is the best option.

SEARCH ENGINES

A web search engine is designed to search for information on the World Wide Web. The search results are generally presented in a list of results often referred to as search engine results pages (SERPs). The information may consist of web pages, images, information and other types of files. Some search engines also mine data available in databases or open directories. Unlike web directories, which are maintained only by human editors, search engines also maintain real-time information by running an algorithm on a web crawler. During the early development of the web, there was a list of webservers edited by Tim Berners-Lee and hosted on the CERN webserver.

One historical snapshot from 1992 remains. As more webservers went online the central list could not keep up. On the NCSA site new servers were announced under the title 'What's New!' The very first tool used for searching on the Internet was Archie. The name stands for 'archive' without the 'v'. It was created in 1990 by Alan Emtage, Bill Heelan and J. Peter Deutsch, computer science students at McGill University in Montreal.

The programme downloaded the directory listings of all the files located on public anonymous FTP sites, creating a searchable database of file names; however, Archie did not index the contents of these sites since, the amount of data was so limited it could be readily searched manually. The rise of Gopher led to two new search programmes, Veronica and Jughead. Like Archie, they searched the file names and titles stored in Gopher index systems. Veronica provided a keyword search of most Gopher menu titles in the entire Gopher listings. Jughead was a tool for obtaining menu information from specific Gopher servers.

While the name of the search engine 'Archie' was not a reference to the Archie comic book series, 'Veronica' and 'Jughead' are characters in the series, thus referencing their predecessor. In the summer of 1993, no search engine existed yet for the web, though numerous specialised catalogues were maintained by hand. Oscar Nierstrasz at the University of Geneva wrote a series of Perl scripts that would periodically mirror these pages and rewrite them into a standard format which formed the basis for W3Catalog, the web's first primitive search engine, released on September 2, 1993. In June 1993, Matthew Gray, then at MIT, produced what was probably the first web robot, the Perl-based World Wide Web Wanderer, and used it to generate an index called 'Wandex'.

The purpose of the Wanderer was to measure the size of the World Wide Web, which it did until late 1995. The web's second search engine Aliweb appeared in November 1993. Aliweb did not use a web robot, but instead depended on being notified by web site administrators of the existence at each site of an index file in a particular format. JumpStation used a web robot to find web pages and to build its index, and used a web form as the interface to its query programme.

It was thus the first WWW resource-discovery tool to combine the three essential features of a web search engine. Because of the limited resources available on the platform on which it ran, its indexing and hence, searching were limited to the titles and headings found in the web pages the crawler encountered. One of the first 'full text' crawler-based search engines was WebCrawler, which came out in 1994.

Unlike its predecessors, it let users search for any word in any webpage, which has become the standard for all major search engines since. It was also the first one to be widely known by the public. Also in 1994, Lycos was launched and became a major commercial endeavour. Soon after, many search engines appeared and vied for popularity. These included Magellan, Excite, Infoseek, Inktomi, Northern Light, and AltaVista. Yahoo! was among the most popular ways for people to find web pages of interest, but its search function operated on its web directory, rather than full-text copies of web pages.

Information seekers could also browse the directory instead of doing a keyword-based search. In 1996, Netscape was looking to give a single search engine an exclusive deal to be the featured search engine on Netscape's web browser. There was so much interest that instead a deal was struck with Netscape by five of the major search engines, where for $5 million per year each search engine would be in rotation on the Netscape search engine page. The five engines were Yahoo!, Magellan, Lycos, Infoseek, and Excite. Search engines were also known as some of the brightest stars in the Internet investing frenzy that occurred in the late 1990s. Several companies entered the market spectacularly, receiving record gains during their initial public offerings.

Some have taken down their public search engine, and are marketing enterprise-only editions, such as Northern Light. Many search engine companies were caught up in the dot-com bubble, a speculation-driven market boom that peaked in 1999 and ended in 2001. Around 2000, Google's search engine rose to prominence. The company achieved better results for many searches with an innovation called PageRank. This iterative algorithm ranks web pages based on the number and PageRank of other web sites and pages that link there, on the premise that good or desirable pages are linked to more than others. Google also maintained a minimalist interface to its search engine.

In contrast, many of its competitors embedded a search engine in a web portal. By 2000, Yahoo! was providing search services based on Inktomi's search engine. Yahoo! acquired Inktomi in 2002, and Overture in 2003. Yahoo! switched to Google's search engine until 2004, when it launched its own search engine based on the combined technologies of its acquisitions. Microsoft first launched MSN Search in the fall of 1998 using search results from Inktomi. In early 1999 the site began to display listings from Looksmart blended with results from Inktomi except for a short time in 1999 when results from AltaVista were used instead. In 2004, Microsoft began a transition to its own search technology, powered by its own web crawler. Microsoft's rebranded search engine, Bing, was launched on June 1, 2009. On July 29, 2009, Yahoo! and Microsoft finalised a deal in which Yahoo! Search would be powered by Microsoft Bing technology.

HOW WEB SEARCH ENGINES WORK

A search engine operates in the following order:

- Web crawling
- Indexing
- Searching

Web search engines work by storing information about many web pages, which they retrieve from the HTML itself. These pages are retrieved by a Web crawler— an automated Web browser which follows every link on the site. Exclusions can be made by the use of robots.txt. The contents of each page are then analysed to determine how it should be indexed. Data about web pages are stored in an index database for use in later queries. A query can be a single word.

The purpose of an index is to allow information to be found as quickly as possible. Some search engines, such as Google, store all or part of the source page as well as information about the web pages, whereas others, such as AltaVista, store every word of every page they find. This cached page always holds the actual search text since, it is the one that was actually indexed, so it can be very useful when the content of the current page has been updated and the search terms are no longer in it.

This problem might be considered to be a mild form of linkrot, and Google's handling of it increases usability by satisfying user expectations that the search terms will be on the returned webpage. This satisfies the principle of least astonishment since, the user normally expects the search terms to be on the returned pages. Increased search relevance makes these cached pages very useful, even beyond the fact that they may contain data that may no longer be available elsewhere. When a user enters a query into a search engine, the engine examines its index and provides a listing of best-matching web pages according to its criteria, usually with a short summary containing the document's title and sometimes parts of the text.

The index is built from the information stored with the data and the method by which the information is indexed. As early as 2007 the Google.com search engine has allowed one to search by date by clicking 'Show search tools' in the leftmost column of the initial search results page, and then selecting the desired date range. Most search engines support the use of the boolean operators AND, OR and NOT to further specify the search query. Boolean operators are for litreal searches that allow the user to refine and extend the terms of the search. The engine looks for the words or phrases exactly as entered. Some search engines provide an advanced feature called proximity search which allows users to define the distance between keywords.

There is also concept-based searching where the research involves using statistical analysis on pages containing the words or phrases you search for. As well, natural language queries allow the user to type a question in the same form one would ask it to a human. A site like this would be ask.com. The usefulness of a search engine depends on the relevance of the result set it gives back. While there may be millions of web pages that include a particular word or phrase, some pages may be more relevant, popular, or authoritative than others. Most search engines employ methods to rank the results to provide the 'best' results first.

How a search engine decides which pages are the best matches, and what order the results should be shown in, varies widely from one engine to another. The methods also change over time as Internet usage changes and new techniques evolve. There are two main types of search engine that have evolved: one is a system of predefined and hierarchically ordered keywords that humans have programmed extensively. The other is a system that generates an 'inverted index' by analysing texts it locates. This second form relies much more heavily on the computer itself to do the bulk of the work. Most Web search engines are commercial ventures supported by advertising revenue and, as a result, some employ the practice of allowing advertisers to pay money to have their listings ranked higher in search results.

Those search engines which do not accept money for their search engine results make money by running search related ads alongside the regular search engine results. The search engines make money every time someone clicks on one of these ads.

SEARCH ENGINE BIAS

Although search engines are programmed to rank web sites based on their popularity and relevancy, empirical studies indicate various political, economic, and social biases in the information they provide. These biases could be a direct result of economic and commercial processes, and political processes.Google Bombing is one example of an attempt to manipulate search results for political, social or commercial reasons.

CUSTOMISED RESULTS AND FILTER BUBBLES

Many search engines such as Google and Bing provide customised results based on the user's activity history. This leads to an effect that has been called a filter bubble. The term describes a phenomenon in which web sites use algorithms to selectively guess what information a user would like to see, based on information about the user. As a result, web sites tend to show only information which agrees with the user's past viewpoint, effectively isolating the user in a bubble that tends to exclude contrary information. Prime examples are Google's personalised search results and Facebook's personalised news stream. Eli Pariser, who coined the term, users get less exposure to conflicting viewpoints and are isolated intellectually in their own informational bubble. Pariser related an example in which one user searched Google for 'BP' and got investment news about British Petroleum while another searcher got information about the Deepwater Horizon oil spill and that the two search results pages were 'strikingly different.'

The bubble effect may have negative implications for civic discourse, Pariser, but there are contrasting views suggesting the effect is minimal and addressable. Since, this problem has been identified, competing search engines have emerged that seek to avoid this problem by not tracking or 'bubbling' users. One example is DuckDuckGo.

INTERNET SEARCHING

In 300 B.C., the Library of Alexandria held some half million scrolls and served as a cultural centre for the world, uniting the thoughts of Greek, Egyptian, Macedonian and Babylonian culture. The Letter of Aristeas, the library had "a large budget in order to collect, if possible, all the books in the world." Whole fields of study such as geometry and grammar grew from the scholars who had the fortune to travel to and study at Alexandria.

In 2003 A.D., the Internet forms a distributed library of billions of pages, one that is accessible to anyone, anywhere in the world, at the click of a mouse. Every day hundreds of millions of 'trips' to the library start with a query to an Internet search engine. If I want to research a topic such as 'Library of Alexandria,' I can type those words to a search engine and in less than a second have access to a list of 14,000 pages, sorted by their usefulness to the query. This unprecedented ease of access to information has revolutionised the way research is done by students, scientists, journalists, shoppers, and others. It opens up an online marketplace of products, services, and ideas that benefits both information providers and seekers; sellers and buyers; consumers and advertisers.

How is it that an Internet Search engine can find the answers to a query so quickly? It is a four-step process:

- Crawling the Web, following links to find pages;
- Indexing the pages to create an index from every word to every place it occurs;
- Ranking the pages so the best ones show up first; and
- Displaying the results in a way that is easy for the user to understand.

Crawling is conceptually quite simple: starting at some well-known sites on the web, recursively follow every hypertext link, recording the pages encountered along the way. In computer science this is called the transitive closure of the link relation. However, the conceptual simplicity hides a large number of practical complications: sites may be busy or down at one point, and come back to life later; pages may be duplicated at multiple sites and must be dealt with accordingly; many pages have text that does not conform to the standards for HTML, HTTP redirection, robot exclusion, or other protocols; some information is hard to access because it is hidden behind a form, Flash animation or Javascript programme.

Finally, the necessity of crawling 100 million pages a day means that building a crawler is an exercise in distributed computing, requiring many computers that must work together and schedule their actions so as to get to all the pages without overwhelming any one site with too many requests at once. A search engine's index is similar to the index in the back of a book: it is used to find the pages on which a word occurs. There are two main differences: the search engine's index lists every occurrence of every word, not just the important concepts, and the number of pages is in the billions, not hundreds. Various techniques of compression and clever representation are used to keep the index 'small,' but it is still measured in terabytes, which again means that distributed computing is required. Most modern search engines index link data as well as word data.

It is useful to know how many pages link to a given page, and what are the quality of those pages. This kind of analysis is similar to citation analysis in bibliographic work, and helps establish which pages are authoritative. Algorithms such as PageRank and HITS are used to assign a numeric measure of authority to each page. For example, the PageRank algorithm says that the rank of a page is a function of the sum of the ranks of the pages that link to the page. If we let PR(*p*) be the PageRank of page *p*, Out(*p*) be the number of outgoing links from page *p*, Links(*p*) be the set of pages that link to page *p* and N be the total number of pages in the index, then we can define PageRank by,

$$PR(p) = r / N + (1 -_r) \sum_i \subset Links(p)^{PR(i)/Out(i)}$$

where r is a parameter that indicates the probability that a user will choose not to follow a link, but will instead restart at some other page. The *r*/*N* term means that each of the *N* pages is equally likely to be the restart point, although it is also possible to use a smaller subset of well-known pages as the restart candidates. Note that the formula for PageRank is recursive— PR appears on both the right-and left-hand sides of the equation.

The equation can be solved by iterating several times, or by standard linear algebra techniques for computing the Eigen values of a matrix. The two steps are query independent—they do not depend on the user's query, and thus can be done before a query is issued with the cost shared among all users. This is why a search takes a second or less, rather than the days it would take if a search engine had to crawl the web anew for each query. We now consider what happens when a user types a query. Consider the query, where the square brackets denote the beginning and end of the query, and the quotation marks indicate that the enclosed words must be found as an exact phrase match. The first step in responding to this query is to look in the index for the hit lists corresponding to each of the four words 'National,' 'Academies,' 'computer' and 'science.' These four lists are then intersected to yield the set of pages that mention all four words. Because 'National Academies' was entered as a phrase, only hits where these two words appear adjacent and in that order are counted. The result is a list of 19,000 or so pages. The next step is ranking these 19,000 pages to decide which ones are most relevant. In traditional information retrieval this is done by counting the number of occurrences of each word, weighing rare words more heavily than frequent words, and normalising for the length of the page.

A number of refinements on this scheme have been developed, so it is common to give more credit for pages where the words occur near each other, where the words are in bold or large font, or in a title, or where the words occur in the anchor text of a link that points to the page. In addition the query-independent authority of each page is factored in. The result is a numeric score for each page that can be used to sort them best-first. Traditionally this is done by listing a short description of each result in rank-sorted order. The description will include the title of the page and may include additional information such as a short abstract or excerpt from the page.

Some search engines generate query-independent abstracts while others customise each excerpt to show at least some of the words from the query. Displaying this kind of query-dependent excerpt means that the search engine must keep a copy of the full text of the pages at a cost of several more terabytes. Some search engines attempt to cluster the result pages into coherent categories or folders, although this technology is not yet mature. Studies have shown that the most popular uses of computers are e-mail, word processing and Internet searching. Of the three, Internet searching is by far the most sophisticated example of computer science technology. Building a high-quality search engine requires extensive knowledge and experience in information retrieval, data structure design, user interfaces, and distributed systems implementation. Future advances in searching will increasingly depend on statistical natural language processing and machine learning techniques. With so much data—billions of pages, tens of billions of links, and hundreds of millions of queries per day—it makes sense to use data mining approaches to automatically improve the system. For example, several search engines now do spelling correction of user queries.

It turns out that the vast amount of correctly and incorrectly spelled text available to a search engine makes it easier to create a good spelling corrector than traditional techniques based on dictionaries. It is likely that there will be other examples of text understanding that can be done better with a data-oriented approach; this is an area that search engines are just beginning to explore.

4

Designing Instruction for Technology-Enhanced Learning

INTRODUCTION

Libraries across India, as in other parts of the world, are facing sweeping changes on account of the media in which information is generated, transmitted, disseminated and archived due to the increasing presence of electronic formats. There is no doubt that information in electronic form is a potential asset, and that it can be vigourously applied in any environment. The advent and spread of electronic formats has made a major difference in the information processing and service environments in libraries, especially after the emergence of the Internet and Web as the dominant pathway and repository of electronic information resources.

In an increasingly networked world, it is possible that universities may be able to take back control of scholarly information, and libraries may risk being cut out of the author-publisher-dissemination loop. Libraries act as facilitators to provide the right information to the right user at the right time. Users visit libraries to borrow identified documents, or to take photocopies/printouts of those documents from reference collections or journals not issued out normally.

The advent of Web-enabled information resources, such as e-journals, e-books and e-reference sources, and their access through networks has taken the library to the users and a significant amount of information access is now taking place beyond the four walls of the library. In many cases users want a 'pinpointed precision' in the information search process whereas the library attempts for an 'exhaustive recall' to comply with the various ways in which an information source is approached and to satisfy each user's diverse interests. This information overload may cause doubts in the users regarding the relevance of information services as perceived from a professional angle. Along with quantifying use, it is equally important to assess the qualitative attributes of implicit and explicit use and examine the difficulties of users in properly framing their requests for information.

The limitation on the part of library professionals to perceive and represent what is demanded by users in information systems, and the dilemmas of information organization and retrieval to handle these demands must be effectively addressed. Libraries and professionals are equally concerned about the emergence of Internet as an information repository beyond the library's walls, as amply demonstrated by enhanced citations of Web resources. As library acquisitions are falling, information sources are increasing, and a single site library satisfying the user's needs is a doubtful proposition; users are forced to look beyond the library for their information needs. Thus the only option for the libraries is to enter into collaborations, networking and consortia and to reorient their roles as information services and access centres from their previous roles as information warehouses.

At the same time, the technical advances resulting from enhanced research in science and technology have made it possible to reduce drastically the time involved in information collection and identification. Also the extra time required in adapting printed information to client service through cumbersome manual routines of classification and cataloguing is considerably reduced by the availability of electronic information, leaving the professionals to concentrate more on tasks to support the extensive teaching and intensive research environment.

ACADEMIC AND RESEARCH LIBRARIES

The application of computing to library work in India has a history of at least three decades because since the time the computer entered premier academic institutions and selected R & D facilities, it has been explored for improving information processing and management routines. *Information technology* (IT) enriched library services arrived initially for *science and technology* (S&T) information handling and for the special libraries attached to *research and development* (R&D) centres and academic libraries in higher education institutions.

In comparison to other libraries, academic and research libraries have better infrastructure and skilled manpower in greater numbers, making them able to offer information services comparable to advanced countries. Like qualified teaching and research personnel and well-equipped laboratories, the right information service is another vital element in the trinity which completes a fruitful academic or research environment.

MARKET-DRIVEN COLLABORATION

Academic and research libraries, especially in developing countries, are passing through a very challenging phase in their existence due to unfriendly trends in the emerging information market. On the one hand, these libraries are still left with many of the old problems such as poor budgetary support and weak infrastructure, as well as staff in fewer numbers and often with less expertise. But the new information marketing techniques, like the possibilities of delivering and accessing electronic information in diverse channels, force these libraries to be very vigilant and cautious in their approach towards information acquisition and services. Libraries and professionals in India were quick to understand the emerging information environment was forcing their users to depend largely on those resources, which are becoming more expensive day by day due to the rise in production costs, fall in subscriptions and inflationary trends of Indian currency.

When individual libraries found that alone they are not in a position to satisfy the information requirements of their clients, they formulated various collaborative arrangements with other libraries such as,

- *Interlibrary loan* (ILL) services,
- *Document delivery services* (DDS),
- Resource-sharing, and
- Consortia-based subscriptions.

PRESENT PRACTICES AND EMERGING GOALS

The special libraries attached to research and higher education were lucky enough to garner resources to automate their in-house routine operations and for hosting online public access catalogues (OPACs); some of them also set up facilities to search electronic databases. A few of them evolved the desired infrastructure for Internet surfing, for hosting of full-text database access, and for setting up digital libraries. The major advantage of the progress in computerization is a considerable increase in the amount of information available online. We have experienced that at the start of computer applications only the surrogates (metadata) existed online, but some full-text content has been made accessible online in recent years.

These libraries are experiencing the virtues of electronic information in different forms such as e-journals, e-books, bibliographic/full-text electronic databases on CD-ROMs and through Web access. Due to publishers' 'electronic plus' policies, libraries are able to access electronic versions of printed sources such as journals either for free or by paying an additional fee. However the goal these libraries in specialized research and academic centres should have set for themselves is to enhance their information facilities to fully functional digital libraries, comparable with similar facilities in the developed countries.

CULTURES AND CONFLICTS FACED BY LIBRARIES

The fixed roles suggested by Levy for researchers, publishers and libraries are either overlapping or changing in the electronic scene. There are cases where an author or a library is acting as electronic publisher, and there are publishers providing a wide variety of information packages beyond the contents of printed journals. The real question is: has the library really lost ground in the emerging information scene? Even the critics will not say so.

The concerns expressed are only to revitalize the professional skills of librarians, rejuvenate the style of working and reorient the library towards its rightful place in effective dissemination of information. Maybe the common feeling that the library is a central place in the institution visited everyday by large numbers of users, like any public utility, has lost some ground in the electronic scene. Nonetheless, apart the continuing provision of information services for print sources, the electronic revolution has reaffirmed the library more as an information service and access centre than as an information storehouse.

TECHNOLOGY-ENHANCED LIBRARY SERVICES

TECHNOLOGY ADVANCES

The major technology breakthroughs in the context of libraries include:

- Advent of printing press and mass production of printed documents enabled democratization of information. Libraries had a major role in the print era, as no one can own a large number of books on a particular subject whereas libraries by their very purpose concentrated on doing so.
- Microforms helped to preserve less used information in a compact space and as a smoother delivery option for voluminous sources. Libraries had their unchallenged role even in the microform era as the special purpose readers for microfilms and microfiche were costly and exclusively housed in the library.
- The economical and affordable copying technology revolutionized the concept of information use as it spearheaded the trend of owning copies of relevant portions of library resources. The copying technology freed the user from sitting in the library for long duration for reading, since one can simply get a copy quickly and leave.
- Computing is the biggest technology revolution so far, as it is a major enabler in the information dissemination chain; also it is not a stand-alone technology unlike earlier technologies and can be networked and integrated with a whole lot of other devices and technologies. It not only revolutionized the production of books and microforms but also brought the arrival of online and CD-ROM databases, electronic information resources, Internet and the digital revolution.

PRODUCTS AND SERVICES

Adapting IT for library applications is an ongoing process, right from procuring or developing IT enabled information products through computer aided processing and management to delivering IT-enriched services. Library professionals in India are already exposed to the different offshoots of IT for library organization and information services.

LIBRARY AUTOMATION PACKAGES

The availability of a wide variety of library automation software to suit the varied needs of libraries themselves is a reflection of the progress libraries have made in automating the operations of procuring, processing and providing information sources. Procurement is the end of the story for many other software/databases used in a library, whereas library automation systems will open a floodgate of issues. What the vendor provides is a structure to build information concerning the collection and users, to conduct various aspects of organizing the collection and offering information services.

Thus software needs to be evaluated for its suitability for the target library before purchase. This may include case studies from other libraries using the software, evaluation of hardware and operating system required, computer awareness among staff and users, network as well as computer infrastructure in the institution, and above all estimation of cost and charges for after-sales support. Using suitable software for library automation will significantly reduce manual operations and enable professionals to dedicate more time for professional jobs.

CD-ROM AND ELECTRONIC DATABASES

Due to the poor communication infrastructure prevalent in India and to the immense costs involved, online database services were used only by few institutions. The distribution of the same content of online data repositories subsequently in CD-ROMs made it affordable to a larger number of institutions. While the library automation package gave search-and access facility to information sources present in the local collection, CD-ROM databases attempted consolidated access irrespective of holdings to the bibliographic data of publications in a discipline. CD-ROM databases have also freed library professionals from conducting searches and allowed the end user to conduct the searches. CD-ROM is so common nowadays that a library holds a good number of them not only for bibliographic, numeric and full-text databases, but also those received along with printed books and other reference sources. Managing and serving these high capacity discs was a problem earlier due to the stand-alone software required, whereas the onset of networking and hard-disk cached solutions provides an effective and functional way to enable access to them through the intranet.

WEB

Since the 1990s, the Internet has changed the dissemination of information, such as electronic copies of traditional paper-based journals and conference proceedings, free electronic-only refereed journals, haphazard copies of all kinds of material on home pages and a handful of electronic preprints archives. Most libraries in India now have a website and they use the site to present the basic strengths of the library and to host services such as the OPAC and

Web access to electronic information. The 'size of the catalogue card' and the field lengths of primitive database technology are surpassed in the Web era. Types of information resources on the Web also vary from authentic primary information about the latest research results to ephemeral product catalogues. Issues worth consideration are often the content of the sites that are deleted, modified or changed to new machines without proper redirection and the extraction mechanism through search engines, when a flood of sources is retrieved against a query, of which few are relevant. The Internet and Web demonstrate that a large amount of electronic information can be hosted in a decentralized fashion in a cost-effective manner. The Web has also freed the user's dependence on library resources for finding information related to address and contact details of a person/institution, contents pages of books, journals, etc.

As far as possible, especially for reference and information services, looking at the Web has become an innovative trend in the reference service to complement dated print sources. Many publishers visibly feel the benefits and reach of the Web, and have considered it as an alternate medium for delivering information sources; some publishers even permit unrestricted access of tables of contents and abstracts of their primary journals. As a result of these initiatives, the 'print and distribute' paradigm is challenged by 'distribute and print' paradigm.

CONSORTIAL LICENSES

The term 'consortial licenses' designates library groupings to negotiate access rights to electronic information with publishers and vendors aiming at enhanced access to more resources at better pricing. "Consortia can be a means to introduce products to a previously untapped market" for vendors and "consortia provide shared expertise, access to new electronic and print resources, professional development, new sources of funds, and safety in numbers" for libraries. In contrast to earlier library collaborative arrangements such as ILL and resource sharing, the publisher and trade community are parties in the consortial agreements.

In resource-sharing, libraries concentrate on collaborative subscriptions by avoiding duplication, where as in consortial licenses, the emphasis is to strike the 'best deals' even if the library suffers some duplication. The publisher community experience is that increased subscription costs lead to a reduction in the total number of subscriptions, further raising the subscription cost every year. Publishers also found it difficult to enforce ownership rights with electronic sources, even after adopting the latest technology tools and forcing libraries to sign the toughest of the legal clauses.

The good marketing wisdom of the publisher and trade community prevailed to open up information access rights through consortial licenses for a large part of the product spectrum to at least those libraries or groups of libraries which procure products beyond a certain threshold value. The *Indian National Digital Library in Engineering Science and Technology* (INDEST) is the first and the major consortium in India. It is under the aegis of the *Ministry of Human Resource Development* (MHRD). Before the creation of the consortium, access to electronic journals in these institutions remained at 60% of subscribed titles, but the number of online journals has increased 10 times after the establishment of the consortium.

The rates for access offered to the consortium are lower by 50% to 90% depending upon the category of institution and the consortium paid only 11% of the list price to access these resources. Info net, another consortium, floated by the *University Grants Commission* (UGC) for Universities, is also gaining strength. Similar consortia are also operational for research institutions under the Council of Scientific and Industrial Research (CSIR) and the Department of Atomic Energy (DAE).

DIGITAL LIBRARIES

Libraries in India are engaged in the development of prototypes of digital information resources, as influenced by developments in other countries. There are certain types of content which lie inaccessible or less used in their present physical forms that can be put to more visible and enhanced use through digitization. Also heavily used content presently available in limited numbers of copies can be identified for conversion to electronic format. The linear text in many of the print sources presents difficulties for providing a hypertext approach or a multimedia feeling, for simulating learning by doing; sustaining attention and interest for long duration calls for using electronic technologies to enable content to be more functional.

The static content in printed sources fails to attract users who are increasingly exposed to the widely appealing features of broadcasting and IT-intensive presentation tools. Multimedia-enabled digital information will be useful to a large percentage of illiterate and older population also. There are cases such as papers in journals and conferences in print form that never get their deserved visibility and often end up with out reaching the target population. The digital dissemination of this content may lead to very effective teaching and more focused research in most areas.

To demonstrate the efficacy of digital libraries and collections, libraries must be able to identify materials in the public domain, sources generated in-house, and similar materials to overcome the constraints of copyright. Digital library (DL) development needs a two pronged strategy to digitize local content as well as to devise options for providing access to external resources obtained as free or as part of existing subscriptions or access licenses.

The typical academic or research library in-house digital library on an Intranet must include the following components:

- Consortial access to electronic journals and electronic databases;

- Free/paid Web access to journals subscribed in print format;
- Subject gateways and virtual libraries;
- Free/paid e-books from publishers and portals;
- Intranet access to bibliographic and full-text databases, and CD-ROM publications;
- Local archiving of free and paid e-books;
- LAN serving of e-supplements of purchased books;
- In-house digitization of copyright-owned and copyright- free printed books in the collection;
- Born-digital in-house publications such as research reports, annual reports, convocation reports, teaching materials, theses and dissertations, in-house journals, proceedings of conferences, seminars, workshops, etc., conducted by the institution;
- Preprints and post-prints of research papers sent for publication to journals, conferences, and books, especially with respect to the Open Archives Initiative gaining ground to provide further access to research published in toll journals and to make the results of publicly funded research available to those who need them;
- Publications in the public domain, such as government publications, publications from non-profit institutions, etc.

But many libraries are unable to provide these components due to lack of awareness or due to the hurdles invariably faced by libraries in India. The lack of interest on the part of parent institutions and the absence of action plans or priorities is the major hindrance. Though computer and communication infrastructure is improving, their availability for information work is not appreciated in many organizations. Paschoud commented how several of the speakers and many of the delegates at the International Conference on Digital Libraries (ICDL) 2004 conference in New Delhi focussed on addressing what most European libraries would consider very basic issues such as network/Internet connectivity and management.

Even in places where infrastructure is available, there is an acute shortage of competent labour to take up the task of digitizing local content and evolving digital information repositories. The students, faculty, curriculum and training methodology at the disposal of library schools have to be improved visibly to meet this challenge. Coupled with this is the need for continuing education for retraining the working professionals. Institutions, individuals, or private publishers have rights over content, and motivating them to ease these rights when they are not inclined towards digitization is not a simple task. Levying charges for access is a distant proposition; instead sponsorships from institutions, government bodies and library suppliers can be explored.

Even when hosted as a free facility, enough security mechanisms must be evolved to prevent any trespassing by hackers. Selecting useful content requires careful review and evaluation by subject experts, as digitization will only help to preserve the record, and not its enhanced and continued access. Internet bandwidth in India has to be sufficiently augmented to allow faster access to Web content as more content is being hosted on the Web. The different funding agencies, research councils and institutions are not currently offering monetary support to the desired extent for digital library development.

CULTURE AND CONFLICTS FACED BY USERS

MANUAL AND ELECTRONIC SEARCH

Searching for manual sources required scanning catalogue cards or indexing and abstracting sources. As cross-references often increase the number of cards or pages, there was a difficulty in being very exhaustive. Conducting selective dissemination of information (SDI) services had been extremely difficult as the document profiles must be matched with user profiles with the aid of semi mechanical systems. Most of these limitations are easily eliminated in the electronic environment due to the very nature of information processing and organization in electronic form.

The inherent advantages of indexing electronic information help the user to search for any or all the fields in a timesaving manner. Since document profiles are already stored in the database and search software supports creation of user profiles, current awareness services (CAS) and SDI services are achieved more easily. The concern for end-user searching was dominant right from the beginning of early CD-ROM database systems since the time spent for searching does not involve communication costs as is the case with online searching. Also with the universe of knowledge getting increasingly complex as a result of continuing advances in research in intra and inter-disciplinary areas, vitiating the search conducted by a generalist like a librarian may not be effective in amassing the user's information requirements completely or not achieving the desired results expected by the user.

The convoluted information requirements of present day researchers require sufficient knowledge of their disciplines and since the users are increasingly exposed to the computerized work environment, they feel very confident to conduct information searching on electronic systems. The professional ethos and egos also plays a part as users find more satisfactory results from electronic systems than manual systems, and in a relatively easy and convenient way. The librarians should recognize the confidence and maturity of users to conduct searches on their own as they have better knowledge of their disciplines, more exposure to the different keywords and their relationships and because of the inherent advantages of locating related sources serendipitously while scanning the retrieved results.

There should be closer interaction and effective communication between library professionals and users to understand each other's views about information needs and use. Library user meetings, orientation sessions for new users, special help for research scholars, training programmes about usage of print and electronic resources, a help desk at reference counter, holdings locator services, interacting with users through phone and e-mail, encouraging users to approach the librarian, ask a librarian, and user friendly websites are some options practiced in libraries in India.

INFORMATION USE

Information services provided by a library are primarily based on subjective input from users and hence justify users commenting about misses or noise in electronic information service outputs. An information need is what an individual *ought* to have; an information want is what an individual *would* like to have; an information demand is what an individual *asks* for; an information use is what an individual actually *uses*; and an information requirement denotes what is *needed*, what is *wanted* or what is *demanded*. Information needs are affected by a variety of factors such as the range of sources available, the uses to which information will be put, individual characteristics of the user, social, political and economic systems surrounding the user, and the consequences of information use.

Accessibility of information resources is usually assumed to depend on a range of cognitive, social, and physical factors, such as whether a person is aware of a resource, has the knowledge and skills needed to access it, and has the resource close at hand. Scientists spend 50–60% of their time communicating. The computerised environment has increased the quantum of information available nearby, but it has not enhanced a person's information consumption skills. There is a burden of effort in information storage and retrieval that may be shifted from author to indexer to index language designer to searcher to user. Though the user is exposed to more microfilms, Xerox copies, and electronic information on desktop/ Intranet/Web, ready to display at the touch of a button, the more time one spends in searching and collecting information, the less time s/he gets to use the information. Scholarly articles are identified for reading in five basic ways: browsing, automated searches, citations found in the literature, mentions by other people, and current-awareness tools.

How much information one requires to work on a particular problem is also subjective as human beings observe the 'principle of least effort'. Perhaps one may easily deal with an information crisis by identifying a part of the total references and by using few of what is identified.

USER BYPASSING

Though libraries in India are progressing well on the automation and information access front, there is a definite case of fewer users present in the library due to different reasons. The real question is whether electronic services of libraries have in any way affected the user interests or have the users found more confidence in an information superhighway beyond the library. The same proportions of scientists still browse to identify scholarly articles to read, but more are using online searches and the proportion of readings identified through online searches appears to be increasing. Library acquisitions suffered a serious setback in recent years unable to withstand the price rise and these budgetary constraints forced users to look beyond the library for their varied information requirements.

Hence research publications in some disciplines now cite more Web resources. Librarians are not yet acting as true consumers and hence cannot blame predatory publishers for taking advantage of the situation. Another issue involves the very large and rapidly increasing number of articles obtained through photocopying, interlibrary loan, document delivery, preprints, and reprints. The right step in assessing whether there is a depleted user interest in libraries is to study use patterns over the years and, in a populous country like India, just going by the numbers will not address the qualitative aspects. There has not been much reduction in book issues in an academic library, but are the new acquisitions being used to the same extent? But what is seen is the fall in library attendance, as observed and reported by many library managers.

It is evident that fewer users actually visit the library, and very few still spend more time, a lot of others use the library through lending, photocopies, electronic access through networks, etc. It becomes difficult to quantify use as the library has statistics only about explicit use, but there are also implicit uses through browsing or reading inside the library, which are difficult to quantify. There are also vital questions about whether mere issuing a book or taking a photocopy of a journal article attribute to use and hence comes the need for a qualitative assessment of use. Perhaps professionals are afraid to look at these issues as the results of such assessment may force the authorities to examine critically the investments in a service institution like the library. Like Reenen's comment about false consumers, it seems that librarians fear self-assessment of library usage or to undergo a performance audit.

THE LIBRARIAN'S IDENTITY CRISIS

EDUCATION AND TRAINING

As stated previously, the students, faculty, curriculum and training methodology at the library schools have to be visibly improved to meet the challenges posed by electronic information and impatient, highly demanding users. There are also problems of infrastructure and a directionless attitude in the teaching and research sector often forgetting the interdisciplinary aspect of the subject. Working librarians have good exposure to new databases, their acquisition and use, pragmatic implementation of various routines etc., which are not accessible to library schools.

Thus apart from teaching faculty, expert practitioners in the discipline would also be involved in education programmes to bridge the gap between preaching and practice. The existing courses must always look at the sweeping changes in the library workplace and adapt well to enable the students to face the challenges with confidence, giving ample opportunities for improving reasoning, communication skills, general awareness, and other characteristics identified for a multi-tasking service organization. The age-old teacher-centric teaching has to be circumvented by student oriented and professional (job)-centric teaching.

JOB OPPORTUNITIES

Though the major employer, the government is not recruiting many, more and more universities/institutions are offering library courses in the regular and distance modes. And this upheaval in quantity does not contribute in any way to the quality of these courses. For a prospective student/parent, the job advertisements provide an impression of plenty of jobs in the field, as library jobs at different levels in different institutions do not follow standard designations.

But only when one finishes the course and looks for job openings, does the actual state of affairs come to light. Actually the increase in library-related jobs is merely additive, and not multiplicative, like computers, management or engineering, and should not show an exponential rise at any point of time.

CONTINUING EDUCATION

Since the mode and rate at which information is generated, organized and used is witnessing sweeping changes in the perfectly wired information age, a continuously evolving discipline like LIS is meant to tackle the intricacies of information for societal development; thus it shall not be learned effectively and practiced perfectly by exposing students to a framed curriculum in formal education only.

The discipline has changed drastically from being based totally on print sources; aware of the increasing richness of information in electronic forms and available over networks thus is leading to embracing vigourously other disciplines like computers, management, and information and communication technology.

It is imperative for the information practitioners to continuously monitor and augment their professional skills through continuing education (CE) to discharge their duties to users, employer and profession. The present initiatives on CE are generally being made by national institutions and suffer limitations such as: they are of short duration, generally infrequent, claiming comparatively high fees, working professionals finding it difficult to get sponsorship from their institutions, involve travelling to far off destinations hampering their regular work, etc.

CULTURES AND CONFLICTS FACED BY LIBRARIANS

Gone are the days of close-minded librarians and the quality of candidates entering the profession is continuously improving. As technology-intensive librarianship is gaining ground in the country, working librarians are getting much exposure to new technology tools for providing better information products and improved information services. Working librarians in at least the major academic and research institutions have better computer infrastructure and possess better expertise on the latest information products and services.

It is quite natural in the emerging print plus electronic hybrid library scenario that a library professional right from first job is expected to be conversant with the electronic apart from the manual means of information collection, processing, management and servicing. But there are also apprehensions about the level of technology appropriate to conducting well in the challenging and demanding academic and research setup. A library professional must be distinct from a computer professional due to the very nature of their profession and the expected deliverables. But the acute emphasis on technology has created a situation that a professional can hide many of his/her professional ignorance by a little computer knowledge which is not going to be good either for the profession or for the libraries. Google cannot and will not be replacing libraries because both can co-exist with their diverse functionalities catching the attention of users at different occasions.

The professional nature of the librarian's job always motivates him or her to help the users unlike administrative staff in the institution who are always rule-based; sometimes this may lead to not so proper upkeep of administrative procedures and records, and in some cases cause unnecessary rivalry with the administrative staff. There are also personnel problems as the librarians fail to command a leadership role in many institutions thereby eclipsing their role in strategic planning. Institutions attach prime importance to libraries but are they doing the same towards the personnel in their libraries? It is a strange case of all the virtues are of the system and the problems are due to the staff. Largely a service wing in many institutions, not enjoying the power, visibility, service conditions, and career prospects of the research and teaching staff, the status of library professionals in many of these institutions is not a morale booster, leaving many of them underperforming.

It is not uncommon to see non-professionals heading many libraries, maybe just because they are senior teachers or good administrators or researchers and not because they are good as librarians. There are also problems of the lack of a peer group in the profession resisting such attacks on the profession as many senior professionals have become self-centred, and professional associations compete for minor issues. The professional staff members working in many libraries in developing countries are totally engrossed in administrative and routine jobs related to library operation and administration. Many institutions do not demand their library professionals to pursue an offensive role. The users always need quick services and they never respond to any of the reasonable operational or managerial delays.

The real situation is that the libraries have very little control over their suppliers whereas their consumers have too much control over them. Users are not patient enough to interact constantly with the library staff to tune their profiles to improve the relevance of information services, maybe due to time constraints on their parts. Again by a rough assessment, it seems that less than 10% of the users usually respond to SDI results and the remaining are either using it as it is or rejecting it straightaway. Out of those responding, only a few show their willingness to give feedback to modify their keywords to improve the utility of such services. Users may sometimes get so arrogant with the helpful nature of library staff and doubt it as their weakness.

CONCLUSIONS

Like building collection and providing services, improving access to information should be the guiding criteria for libraries in the electronic era. Apart from hosting external information, they should also evolve local digitization ventures to give more visibility to internal information. We have to design a new set of parameters to judge operational efficiency and performance effectiveness of libraries. Traditional libraries boasted that they attracted a lot of users to stay inside their premises for comparatively longer duration whereas a modern librarian will be more concerned about carrying information to users' desktops. No library, no matter how rich its budget allocation and collection may be, is in a position to satisfy all the information needs of its users. As a person well versed in the intricacies of the emerging information market, the librarian should be frank enough to admit that the information needs of all users are not met by the library alone. Collaboration with other libraries through consortia or networks increases the amount of resources available to users. Most academic and research libraries spend a lot of public money for information needs of a small percentage of the population and optimizing that spending for the benefit of more number of users is the need of the hour. Library professionals have a major role in the emerging print plus digital hybrid information environment that is looming large in many academic and research libraries.

This role can be properly identified and refined only through constructive interaction of administrative heads of institutions, library professionals and professional associations. There is no doubt that we are passing through a severe phase and this is the right time to have a close introspective and critical look at collections developed, services offered and professional skills required in the light of complex user needs, hazy use patterns and the ever-increasing spread of Internet, electronic databases and digital libraries.

5

Library Consortium, Resource Sharing and Networking

INTRODUCTION

In the present era of Information technology, the information needs of the users have been increased so enormously that no single library on its own can meet their information needs. This has necessitated the need for effective linkages and cooperation between libraries and information centers for sharing of available resources and information through networking. The consortia for library can be considered as a major step towards library cooperation in sharing electronic resources. The consortium should take lead role in the development of a national strategy for information provision for research in higher education.

LIBRARY RESOURCE SHARING AND NETWORKING

The term resource applies to a thing, person or action to which one resorts to in times of need and sharing indicates allotting, apportioning or contributing something that is owned, to benefit others. Resource sharing, therefore, refers to reciprocity, implying a partnership where each member has something useful to contribute to others and which each is willing and able to make available when needed.

Resource sharing is an empty concept, but for the approach permitting resource sharing to work is that which:

- Entails having resources to share
- Having a willingness to share them, and
- Having a plan for accomplishing resource sharing

Resource Sharing is an integral part of modern library services. In the developed countries, no library services can be thought without sharing of resources. In the past, ₹ was limited to the interlibrary loan system. In the modern age, with the development of science and technology and innovations of techniques and devices, resource sharing has become easier and fruitful due to the availability of databases, information network, and online sharing facilities. Thus, the resourcesharing system helps one library to access to resources of other libraries.

When resource sharing is agreed upon by participating institutions, then the following aspects must be planned:

- Identify and locate major collections, sources and materials
- Assemble, publish and distribute collective information for all participating bodies
- Workout the basis for sharing, reference service, lending service, copying service, access to materials, delivery service, and lists of holdings
- Establish means of sharing ideas, development and problems in the form of a newsletter
- Plan for new developments in the knowledge of what others are doing
- Developing a National Information Policy

The following are the most important benefits of resource sharing to participating institutions:

- Easy access to materials
- Enables co-operating institutions to extend limited resources
- Allow greater staff specialization
- Improve services to users
- Avoids unnecessary duplication
- Reduces the number of places which will need to go for services
- Improves working relationships between cooperating libraries.

Resource sharing refers to a joint use of resources available on a system or a network by user or peripherals. In the language of information management, when we talk about resource sharing we simply mean collective use of information of all types by various end users from a control coordinating unit or from within a network component at a reduced cost with easy accessibility.

Library cooperation and resource-sharing activity can take place in several forms and can happen at many levels, which include:

- Interlibrary loans/reciprocal borrowing privileges
- Exchange or sharing of expertise, resources, and facilities
- Exchange of publications and photocopies and other reprographic services
- Sharing of bibliographic information
- Cooperative acquisition, cooperative cataloguing, and cooperative collection development preparation of union list of holdings
- Cooperative relationship and network development

The implementation of resource sharing is largely depends on library networking. It gives an easy and wider access to information as members have an expanded information-base and service. A network is a form of arrangement or an administrative structure that links a group of individuals or organizations who have agreed to work together and/or share resources. Information networking entails the sharing of resources so that the information needs of both actual and potential users of information—from the local to national level—of all network participants are met.

The network enables the participating bodies to facilitate and expand their users' access to literature and information without corresponding investment in purchase, and processing of information is exchanged through the network on a formal basis.

The network may be responsible for coordinating, organizing and providing information and literature support at the national and international level.

The main activities and functions of the network are as follows:

Acquisition of materials:

- Joint purchasing of materials
- Assignment of specialization in material acquisition
- Coordinated subscription
- Exchange of duplicate holdings

Technical services:

- Co-operative cataloguing
- Abstracting and indexing services
- Interlibrary loan
- Reciprocal borrowing privileges
- Reference and/or referral services

Publication programme/repackaging information:

- Union catalogue/list of periodicals
- Mutual notification of purchase through lists of new arrivals or acquisition list
- Bibliography development
- Newsletters
- Joint directories of personnel, projects, consultants, resource persons, etc.
- Manuals

Coordination services:

- Clearing house functions
- Retrieval and storage function
- Referral center

Delivery/mailing service:

- Research, training and other special services
  - User interest surveys
  - Joint research projects
  - In-service personnel training
  - Workshops and meetings
  - Translation services

RESOURCE SHARING AND NETWORKS INITIATIVES IN BANGLADESH

In Bangladesh several Resource-sharing and networks initiatives was taken by different organizations in different sectors to launch Resource sharing and networking systems.

Some of these are as follows:

- *National Agricultural Information System (NAIS)*: The Agricultural Information Centre (AIC) was taken an initiative to develop a network of agricultural institution.
- *Social Science Research Council (SSRC)*: Social Science Research Council, Dhaka was taken an initiative to develop a social science information network in Bangladesh.
- *Health Literature, Library, and Information Service (HeLLIS) Network*: The HeLLIS network was developed by SEARO (WHO), New Delhi, India and National Health Library and Documentation Centre (NHLDOC), Dhaka. All the health libraries of Bangladesh were brought under this network.
- *Development Information Network on South Asia (DEVINSA)*: The DEVINSA network was organized by CSCD (Committee on Studies for Cooperation for Development in South Asia) through the Marga Institute, Colombo, Sri Lanka. All SAARC countries, except Bhutan, were the participants of this network.
- *Information Network on Rural Development (INRD)*: Centre on Integrated Rural Development for Asia and the Pacific (CIRDAP), Dhaka was taken an initiative to develop a regional network on rural development.
- *Women Information Network (WIN)*: Centre on Integrated Rural Development for Asia and the Pacific (CIRDAP), Dhaka was taken another initiative to develop a network on women information.
- *Bangladesh Development Support Information and Communication (BDSIC) Network*: Bangladesh Academy for Rural Development (BARD), Comilla was taken an initiative to launch a network of rural development institutions in Bangladesh
- *National Science and Technology Information Policy (NASTIP)*: Under this policy, a four-tier science and technology information networking system has been recommended.
- *The Association of Management Development Institutes in South Asia (AMDISA) Library Network*: The Association of Management Development Institutes in South Asia was launched a library network on management development. The Headquarter of this network was located at the Administrative Staff College of India, Hyderabad. One institute in each SAARC country was selected as a focal point. The Institute of Business Administration Library, Dhaka University was selected as the National focal point for this network.

- *University Libraries*: Dhaka University Library took an initiative several years' back to develop a network of the university libraries, initially by preparing a union catalogue of the holdings of the university libraries.
- The University Grants Commission of Bangladesh (UGC), in collaboration with the Asia Foundation, took an initiative to compile a union catalogue of the collections of different universities of Bangladesh and to establish an information network within the universities.
- *Bangladesh National Scientific and Library Information Network (BANSLINK)*: Bangladesh National Scientific and Technical Documentation Centre (BANSDOC) was taken an initiative to build up a Network, known as BANSLINK, to develop a resource-sharing network having dial up connectivity with 15 libraries and information centres of the country.
- *Sustainable Development Network Programme (SDNP)*: SDNP is a UNDP funded programme, which started a union catalog services in 2002 in their virtual library programme. The SDNP virtual library prepared this union catalog of 13 libraries, all of which are using CDS/ISIS software for bibliographic record keeping. The SDNP virtual library union catalog is a webbased Online Public Access Catalog.

Bangladesh being a developing country cannot effort to waste its resources. To avoid this, an effective resource sharing and networking system is necessary.

At present the following resource sharing and networking systems are working in the country:

- *Population Information Network (POPIN)*: The National Institute of Population Research and Training (NIPORT) has taken an initiative to establish an information networking system in the field of health, population, family planning and maternal and child health in collaboration and cooperation with the government and non-government organizations, autonomous bodies, voluntary organizations, and international organizations.
- National Health Library and Documentation Centre (NHLDOC), (Ministry of Health, Government of Bangladesh) and International Centre for Diarrhoeal Disease Research, Bangladesh (ICDDR,B) signed in 1976 an agreement to facilitate library cooperation through an interlibrary loan system and agreed to cooperate with each other to avoid duplication of journal subscriptions. Subsequently, some other library named, BIDS, BIRDEM, USAID, Dhaka, Aga Khan Community Health Programme, Dhaka, and the Bangladesh Rural Advancement Committee joined this programme by signing interlibrary loan agreements. The system has been working well.

- *United Nations Library Network in Bangladesh (UN L-Net BD)*: In March 2002 United Nations Information Centre (UNIC) Library has taken an initiative to establish the UN Library Network in Bangladesh (UN L-Net BD). Initially the Network consisted of twenty major libraries of different government, NGOs, including the UN agencies in Bangladesh. At present there are 26 members in this network. It was agreed that UNIC library would act as a focal point and secretariat of the network.

It is not possible for one libraries or information centers to hold the full stock of information resources or to procure all information, which may be in demand by its clientele. Even not a single library or information centers can meet the thrust of knowledge of all the readers from its holdings.

To solve this problem, library cooperation started long ago, such as Inter-library loan, document delivery, library networks etc. At present the more accepted system of resource sharing is library consortia. Consortia approach is one of the many ways of maintaining cooperation and coordination among the libraries and in fact it has emerged as the 'state of the art' in library cooperation in recent years.

The word 'consortia' was originated from the Latin in early 19th century in the sense of partnership. Oxford Advanced Learners Dictionary describes Consortia as 'a group of people, countries, companies, etc. who are working together on a particular project'.

A library Consortia is an association of a group of libraries that agree to share their resources to satisfy the needs of users. Consortia may be formed on a local, regional, national, or international basis; on a functional or format basis; or on a subject basis.

BENEFITS OF CONSORTIA

The benefits of Consortia are many:

- A comprehensive collection is possible
- Building communication among different libraries
- Avoid duplication of core collection specially for core journals
- Scope of electronic archives
- Easy access to resource sharing on Internet by developing common resources databases
- Effective document delivery systems
- Better scope for developing a union catalogue
- Reduce cost of information
- Time saving
- Improved resource sharing
- More professional services to users
- Help to develop a competitive professionalism among LIS professionals

INTERNATIONAL EFFORTS FOR LIBRARY CONSORTIA

The development of library consortia is the outcome of the desire for resource sharing and consortia seem to be getting bigger. The global development of OCLC is prime example. Due to escalating cost of documents, decreasing budgets, inadequate storage area and competent staff, LIS professionals of the world are coming together to form consortia.

There are several International efforts for library consortia are:

- Consortium of University Research Libraries (CURL)
- Consortium of Academic Libraries in Manchester (CALIM)
- Colorado Library Information Network,
- Washington Research Library Consortium (WRLC),
- BIBSYS (Shared University, Research and National Library of Norway)
- Queensland University Libraries Office of Cooperation (QUOLOC)
- China Academic Library and Information System (CALIS), China,
- Takatsu University Library Consortium (YULC), Japan
- Tokyo Western Regional Academic Library Consortium, Japan,
- Yamatesen Ensen Private University Libraries Consortium, Japan
- Korea Resource Sharing Alliance (KORSA), Korea,
- CONsortium on Core Eletronic Resources in Taiwan (CONCERT),
- Ministry of University Affairs (MUA). ThaiLIS.

INDIAN INITIATIVES FOR LIBRARY CONSORTIA

In India at present there are many consortia being run successfully by different organizations. Some of them are as:

- CSIR e-Journal Consortia,
- INDEST (Indian National Digital Library in Science and Technology) Consortia
- FORSA (Forum for Resource Sharing in Astronomy)
- UGC-INFONET
- IIM Library Consortia,
- ICICI Knowledge Park,
- DAE Library Consortium,
- ICMR Library Consortia,
- HELINET (Rajiv Gandhi University of Health Sciences, Karnataka).

BANGLADESH INITIATIVES

The information revolution has brought radical changes to the functions and services in all types of libraries. Many libraries in Bangladesh till today are not in a position to afford to procure all documents and subscribe to core journals in major discipline due to financial constraints. As a result, with the aim of ensuring rapid resource sharing among the major libraries and documentation centers in Bangladesh, many library networking and resources sharing efforts were started to help each other. The objectives of these consortia are for better resource sharing, to reduce information costs, for speedy delivery of documents, to keep abreast of new developments etc. Much emphasis should be given at the national level in Bangladesh for the development of documentary information resources, because it is considered as vital resources to promote the development of economy, science, technology and culture etc. University Grants Commission of Bangladesh (UGC) and Dr. Javed I. Khan of Kent State University have taken an initiative to develop a digital library system for Bangladesh. A 4-member committee was formed by the UGC to draft a concept paper on forming Consortia in Bangladesh, and the committee has already submitted the report to the UGC for their approval.

CONSIDERATION NEEDED TO FORM CONSORTIA

The following issues need to consider before building the consortia:

- Technology infrastructure
- Resources identification
- Budget and funding
- Pricing issues
- Subscription payment issues
- Access related issues
- Licensing and copyright issues
- Archival issues
- Usages and usability issues
- Coordination among partners
- Availability of efficient staff
- Overcoming political objections
- The egos of individuals and institutions
- Adequate professional training on ICT for the LIS professionals
- Sustainability issues

RECOMMENDATION

In this era of global communication, networks and consortia are highly important. A library consortium in the country is needed to achieve cost effectiveness and bridging of the digital divide. To develop library consortia in Bangladesh we have to overcome many hurdles such as inappropriate ICT infrastructure, inadequate funding, limited trained personnel, technological capability, lack of understanding of the concept of consortia. But anything new comes up with new challenges and opportunity, it is up to the individuals to take up the challenge and accept the opportunity.

So, we can recommend the following suggestions for establishment of library consortia in Bangladesh:

- The Government and LIS Professionals bodies should take initiative to conduct some workshops on Consortia.

- The Government and LIS Professionals bodies should start a forum to bring the librarians/ Information professionals and the publishers/ vendors together for better communication and interactions.
- The Government should also make attempts to provide the necessary ICT infrastructure such as high-speed links and a stable network to access the e-journals.
- Policy makers, both in national and international levels together with Internet Service Provider (ISP) should have a shared obligation to seek ways to achieve the wide spread use of the internet.
- Bangladesh should have a separate ministry to coordinate the overall development of the library and information system in the country.
- LIS professionals must market their services to the private sector for sponsorship and support.
- The government should encourage and must recognize the role of librarians and information professionals in building an information society for the development of the nation.
- Involvement of management of the parents organization for sustainability

CONCLUSION

Consortia in Bangladesh are still in table talk and there is a need to study the consortia models and guidelines and methodologies. It is recommended that the concept of Consortia can work well among similar organizations having similar situations such as sufficient additional funds available for the libraries of the consortia members and above all the committed mindsets of the library administrators. On the other side the subscription of e-journals are increasing day by day and the library budgets are shrinking, so it is needed for the library professionals to work together and formulate consortia for subscription to e-journals. Bangladeshi LIS professionals should seriously think and take initiative for consortium movement like western countries for maximum utilization of resources at the reduced cost, time and space.

6

Information Systems Security in Special and Public Libraries

INTRODUCTION

Digital Library systems are the computerized information storage and retrieval systems connected to computer networks and have maximum flexibility, durability, immunity, stability, scalability, accessibility and compatibility with other media at minimum cost, space and maintenance. Library network provides transmission of information dissemination of catalogues; abstract and full text formats as well as various basic functions of libraries like acquiring, digitizing and archiving of contents. The networking of library resources means that users or patrons can access the information from their desktops irrespective of their physical location. The library networks provides library without walls.

TRADITIONAL LIBRARY NETWORK MODEL

Traditional library network setup was established with Ethernet technology and fewer clients and server machines. Ethernet has become the most commonly used LAN (Local Area Network) technology worldwide. More than 85% of all installed network connections are using Ethernet technology, according to International Data Corporation. As a transport protocol, Ethernet operates at 10Mbps data transmission speed and Layers 1 and 2 of the 7-layer OSI networking model, delivering its data packets to any device connected to the network cable. This type of network have very limited infrastructure.

The hardware and software is used make library network it includes one server machine and 5 to 10 client machines connected to gather. The server is responsible for all library related activities and like storage and retrievals. The same server runs library management software like SOUL and provides resources to the clients.

The other hardware requires is hub/switch, network interface card (NIC) etc. while software need is generally network client software and network card drives. This setup has only one server, which provides library management information, database storing and retrieving, running library software for library with limited support for services.

GENERAL NETWORK MODEL

Traditional library networks model operate at 10Mbps speed. At these speed libraries that use extremely large files such as transferring audiovisual contents to desktop, can experience long delays when sending such data across the network. This model uses the extended version of Ethernet called fast Ethernet, which is simply, an extension of existing Ethernet technology, running 10 times faster at 100 Mbps. This setup model has two servers one for library applications and the other is for Internet access through remote location. These two servers provide information to switch, which is of 100Mbps.

Both the server NIC are of 100Mbps, which is little, bit higher then the traditional network setup. The Windows NT server provides user authentication and library management services to the various clients connected to it. While Internet server provides Internet services with remote online libraries, and Internet services.

HIGH SPEED NETWORK MODEL

Traditional and general setup model operates at 10/100Mbps speed, while high speed network operates at gigabit 1000Mbps speed. Easy and straightforward migration to higher performance level without disruption, low cost of ownership including purchase and support cost and flexibility in network design are prime criteria for the high speed network model. This model is 100 times faster than regular 10 Mbps Ethernet and 10 times faster than 100Mbps fast Ethernet.

This also employs the same protocol, same frame format and same frame size as its predecessors like 100Mbps fast Ethernet. This model setup has three main server connected to central switch with 1000Mbps gigabit data transmission speed. All three-server has gigabit Ethernet card Installed. The high speed network switch has 1000Mbps network link and distributes network traffic to four hub/switch segments like Internet services, digital content reading room, audiovisual learning and finally library management. Out of four hub/switch segments three are working at 100Mbps speed with 100Mbps fast Ethernet cards installed on each desktop machines.

The hub connection has also 100Mbps link support. The fourth segment named audiovisual self-learning. Transferring this high bandwidth intensive file on the shared Ethernet makes network busy or low so that this segment must of 1000Mbps. This high-speed network segment provides simultaneous access to all the clients with streaming audio and video without any hustle form network speed. The high-speed performance is possible because the traffic is segmented. User authentication etc. services from windows-NT sever while NAS (Network Attached Storage) server provides database, digital books, thesis, journals audio and video learning material storage.

The NAS server has very large capacity storage with 1000Mpbs gigabit card installed on it. This server provides automatic storing and transfer of data on network with supporting domain server. IIS server provides Internet access and web services of any other digital library from Internet.

NETWORK SECURITY

The process of securing your library network begins with realizing what the library stands to lose if security is not pursued. Network security is not just "another thing to do." Its importance lies in protecting the library's network resources. Network resource means the equipment, software, and data that make up a networking system, including the user data that is shared over the network.

In terms of network communication, this includes the servers, workstations, hubs, switches, routers, firewalls, and telecommunications links that make up a network. In terms of usage, this includes shared printers, database systems, shared software, user accounts, the shared or user-specific files stored on a central server, and the keystrokes and form information that travel across the network.

IMPLEMENTING NETWORK SECURITY

We divide the realm of network security in libraries into seven main categories: physical security, password security, hardware security, server security, workstation security, perimeter security, and financial security These areas are expanded in the *Checklist* by separating out specific configuration issues related to web servers and general administrative issues related to budgeting, planning, and policy development.

There are many sections in the security checklist:

- General security.
- Physical security of computers and network equipment.
- Password security.
- Hardware security.
- Workstation security.
- Network server security.
- Network equipment security.
- Switch/Router/Hub security.
- Web server security.

LOCAL AREA NETWORK SECURITY

Securing any computer in a library must be achieved without any compromise to these three basic concepts: public service, user privacy and legal access. In an office or business environment, security is a matter of making sure those documents and transactions haven't been tampered with, corporate information is protected, personal employee information is kept private, and data is available when the business wants it to be. Network and computer security in a library setting faces these same challenges and a few additional ones. The major local area network security points are: Password Security, Hardware Security, Workstation Security, LAN/Domain Server Security, and Network Equipment Security. As a librarian we have to protect these levels of security in the network.

PASSWORD SECURITY

The least expensive and most important aspect of network security is the use of appropriate passwords.

Password protection is inherent in various aspects of the network:

- Administrative access to server functions
- Workstation access to various files and services (such as the Internet)
- Administrative access to network hubs, switches, routers, and firewalls
- Access to administrative files, such as confidential personnel files or reports

Here are the checklist items related to password security:

- Develop written password policy and provide to all staff and patrons using specific user logons
- Develop written instructions in creating strong passwords and provide to all staff and patrons using specific user logons
- Document passwords for all network equipment, servers, and workstations
- Store password documentation in secure location known only by library director and one other person

HARDWARE SECURITY

Hardware security is a convenient category used to classify miscellaneous items related to your computer and network hardware. The first set of items relate to the BIOS (the Basic Input/Output System) of your servers and workstations. The BIOS is a well-known feature on all Intel/AMD PCcompatible servers and workstations. It performs basic tests of internal components to be sure they are working satisfac-torily. It also stores and manages the configuration of many of the parts inside the CPU case.

WORKSTATION SECURITY

Properly securing workstations is a very important part of the overall network security in a library. There are a large number of configuration issues to address when securing workstations. Using the Windows NT Workstation/ 2000 Professional operating system provides a better security foundation than does Windows 98.

Those libraries using Windows 98 on public workstations are highly encouraged to install special software to secure many of the workstation functions:

- Configure NT Workstation/2000 Professional partitions with NTFS file systems.
- Windows NT/2000, unlike Windows 98, includes a feature known as file system security.

LAN/DOMAIN SERVER SECURITY

This paper assumes the use of Windows NT/2000 as the library's server operating system. In most small library local area networks, there will be one or two servers: a main server, usually a *domain controller* under Windows NT/2000, which verifies the logins of all users, and a file server used with the library automation system. In some libraries, these two services are combined on one server. It is possible to operate in a very small environment with just Windows NT Workstation/2000 Professional-based computers and no server at all, but it is more difficult to maintain security in this environment. So this base level of security assumes the presence of at least one server.

The following items are needed to secure the local area network servers in the library:

- Configure all NT Server partitions with NTFS file systems.
- Configure separate operating system and data partitions (both NTFS).
- Mirror server drives (or implement RAID), if funding allows, for redundancy.
- Configure servers with private IP addresses (LAN-wide recommendation).
- Remove unnecessary services.
- Remove unnecessary files/programmes.
- Configure file system with proper file/folder access permissions.
- Restrict access to the Network Monitor Agent.
- Disable anonymous user logons.
- Disable caching of user logons.
- Configure account policy to restrict unauthorized logon attempts.
- Create logon-warning message (a warning against unauthorized logon or access and use of restricted resources).
- Create alternative Administrators group and restrict membership.
- Restrict privileges of default Administrators group
- Create alternative Administrator account (with new name) with full privileges.
- Disable default Administrator account.
- Configure auditing of Administrator account logon attempts (to track hacking attempts).

- Set a strong password for current administrator account.
- Use different passwords for domain/server accounts than for local workstation accounts, or use different account names.
- Restrict access permissions for the everyone group.
- Disable Guest account if enabled.
- Create appropriate user and group accounts (minimum of three groups: Patrons, Staff, and Administrators).
- Set appropriate group access permissions.
- Implement procedures for file backups according to backup plan.
- Restrict access to backup programme.
- Create and maintain current Emergency Repair Disks, and store in a controlled location.
- File all server component documentation (papers/manuals/disks) for use by service technicians.

NETWORK EQUIPMENT SECURITY

Network equipment refers to all the devices required to get data signals from one computer to another. Generally, these include hubs, switches, routers, and firewalls. Libraries should be purchasing network equipment that provides management capabilities. This provides the possibility of remote management of the network even if the library does not contract for that service initially:

- Set appropriate network management protocol (SNMP) passwords/ community strings
- Record and secure any password settings created by staff or contractors

These two items minimize the risk of network equipment configurations being altered by unauthorized personnel. When the library hires a vendor to install and configure network equipment, be sure to document all passwords used to secure the equipment. It is the library's responsibility to secure these passwords by documenting them and storing the documen-tation in a secure (preferably locked) location.

- Configure audit logs properly, if available
- Implement procedure for monitoring audit logs
- Schedule periodic installation of firmware updates
- Document equipment settings for future use in reconfiguring equipment
- File all network equipment documentation (papers/manuals/disks) for use by service technicians.

CONCLUSION

A Library network service is an assemblage of digital computing, storage and communication machinery together with the software needed to reproduce, emulate and extend the services provided by the conventional libraries. The analysis of depicted models indicates that scalability in the increasing processing capabilities of digital computing of workstations and servers providing services to the clients, larger and larger storage needs and effective management of storage and increasing requirements of network bandwidth and high speed data transfer are the prime issues of infor-mation technologies. The library network once established is not secured from the administrators' point of view but must provide network security policy for servers, clients and other connectivity devices to provide satisfactory level of network security.

7

Characteristics of Online Cataloguing and Library Networking

LIBRARY AND INFORMATION NETWORKS IN INDIA

The explosion in the amount of literature that is available, increases among the number of users and their different needs, and the application of electronic media are forcing libraries to construct and participate in networks. Magnetic tapes, floppy disks, and CD-ROMs provide enough data storage capacity. Retrieval through telecommunications networks and access to international databases are available for searching for information on various subjects. With the advent of networks, remote transmission of texts and graphics, video clips and animated clips are also possible.

DEFINITIONS

- A library network is broadly described as a group of libraries coming together with some agreement of understanding to help each other with a view to satisfying the information needs of their clientele.
- UNISIST II working document defines Information Network as
  - A set of inter-related information systems associated with communication facilities, which are cooperating through more or less formal agreements in order to implement information handling operations to offer better services to the users.
- The National Commission on Libraries and Infor-mation Science in its National Programme Document defines a network as
  - Two or more libraries engaged in a common pattern of information exchange, through commu-nications for some functional purpose.

OBJECTIVES

- To promote and support adoption of standards in library operations.

- To create databases for projects, specialists and institutions to provide online information services
- To improve the efficiency of housekeeping opera-tions
- To coordinate with other regional, national and international network for exchange of information and documents
- To generate new services and to improve the efficiency of existing ones

NETWORK DEVELOPMENT IN INDIA

Some factors that are responsible for the development of library and information networks in India are:

- The report of the working group of the planning commission on modernization of library services and informatics for the seventh five year plan, 1985-90
- The National Policy on Library and Information systems document accepted by the ministry of HRD, Government of India.
- The report on national policy on university libraries prepared by the Association of Indian Universities
- The UGC report on information systems for science and technology under the Department of Science and Industrial Research (DSIR) Government of India has been vigourously promoting an integrated approach to library automation and networking.

LIMITATIONS IN NETWORK DEVELOPMENT

A network may fail in the early stages if there is not proper planning or if adequate funds are not available. Moreover, a common memorandum of agreement signed by the partici-pating libraries at the institutional level is essential for the success of a network venture. On a more practical level, catalogue data must be in a standard, machine readable form for it to be shared and exchanged. And, finally, a continuous flow of external assistance is crucial for the network's survival.

TYPES OF NETWORKS

Presently, there are three types of computer networks:

- LAN;
- MAN and
- WAN.

Local Area Network (LAN)

A LAN is a number of related computers and electronic devices that share information over a transmission media. A typical use of LAN is to tie together personal computers in an office so that they can all use a single printer and a file server. The LAN can be within a building or a campus wide network.

Metropolitan Area Network (MAN)

Attempts are being made to develop this type of network in metropolitan areas such Delhi, Calcutta, Bangalore, Madras, etc.

Wide Area Network (WAN)

A large-scale network, involving offices in different cities and countries is referred to as WAN, which is specially designed to interconnect data transmission devices over wide geographical areas.

CATEGORIES OF NETWORK

Library networks have been divided into two categories: general network and specialized network. The latter can further be divided into metropolitan network and countrywide network.

GENERAL NETWORKS IN INDIA

NICNET:

- *Title:* National Information Center Network
- *Sponsor:* Planning Commission, Govt. of India.
- *Membership:* Four national and regional nodes, 32 state and union territory nodes; seventy cities and towns
- *Services:* Bulk file transfer; teleconferencing; full text and bibliographic retrieval services
- *Application:* ICMRNIC Center; MEDLARS in India; Chemical Abstracts database

INDONET:

- *Title:* INDONET data Network
- *Sponsor:* CMC Ltd = Informatics India Ltd
- *Membership:* Commercial computer network
- *Services:* Database services such as DIALOG, COMPUSERVE; IP; SHARP
- *Applications:* ACME; file transfer; international gateway

I–NET (VIKRAM):

- *Title:* I–NET
- Sponsor: Dept. of Telecommunications, Govt. of India
- *Connectivity:* Packet switched public data network covering nine cities
- *Services:* Information exchange through e-mail/FTP; Bibliographic databases

SPECIALIZED NETWORKS

Metropolitan Networks

CALIBNET:

- *Title:* Calcutta Libraries Network

- *Sponsor:* NISSAT–Govt. of India
- *Applications:* Cataloguing; serials control; acquisitions; circulationediting and retrieval of records;delivery; library automation; CALIBNET INFO Services

BONET:

- *Title:* Bombay Library Network
- *Sponsor:* NISSAT & NCST
- *Objective:* To promote cooperation among libraries in Bombay
- *Services:* online catalogue; online document delivery; IRS; interlibrary loan; dissemination of information

DELNET:

- *Title:* Developing Library Network
- *Sponsor:* NISSAT & NIC
- *Objective:* To promote resource sharing; develop a network of libraries; collect, store, disseminate information
- *Members:* 165 Institutions, 600 Libraries, 15 States in India, 5 from outside India
- *Services:* resource sharing; free Software; ICE online facility; books database; thesis database; Indian specialists; database

ADINET:

- *Title:* Ahmedabad Library Network
- *Sponsor:* NISSAT, DSIR & INFLIBNET
- *Objective:* To bring cooperation among its regional libraries; to develop databases; to integrate scientific and technical information systems
- Members: nine libraries
- *Services:* library automation; library holdings; database in progress

MYLIBNET:

- *Title:* Mysore Library Network
- *Sponsor:* NISSAT
- *Objective:* Developing software tools; conducting seminar; workshops/training programmes; conduct surveys
- *Host Site:* CFTRI, Mysore
- *Members:* 116 Institutions
- *Services:* MYLIB Database; E-journals; food patents; CFTRI Library Bulletin; public services.

Countrywide Area Network

DESINET:

- *Title:* Defence Science Information Network
- *Sponsor:* DESIDOC, Delhi
- *Activity:* Focus on scientific, research and defence communities

ERNET:

- *Title:* Educational and Research Network
- *Sponsor:* Dept. of Electronics, Govt. of India; UNESCO
- *Members:* eight institutions
- *Services:* Communication services such as e-mail, file transfer, remote log on, database access, bulletin board etc.,

SIRNET:

- *Title:* Scientific and Industrial Research Network
- *Sponsor:* CSIR (Commissioned Agency-NCST, Bombay)
- *Members:* 40 labs and R&D Institutions
- *Applications:* scientific communication; leather technology; natural products; food technology; medicinal Plants

VIDYANET:

- *Title:* VIDYANET (Dedicated Communication Computer Net)
- *Sponsor:* TATA Institute of Fundamental Research, Bombay
- *Objectives:* To provide rapid means of communi-cations by linking computers at various institutions in India to similar networks outside the country; to stimulate corporate research, the day-to-day exchange of research information and the execution of joint projects and publications
- *Services:* File transfer facility; sharing of computer resources and access to remote applications, data-bases, libraries, etc.

BTISNET:

- *Title:* BTISNET (Specialized Information Network)
- *Sponsor:* Dept. of Biotechnology, Govt. of India.
- *Connectivity:* 10 Specialized Information Centres in genetic engineering, plant tissue culture; photosynthesis and plant molecular biology; cell transformation; bio-process engineering.
- *Services:* Data processing using applications software; online communication access; facsimile facility

INFLIBNET:

- *Title:* Information Library Network
- *Sponsor:* UGC
- *Connectivity:* computer communication network of universities and R&D; libraries and bibliographic information centers throughout the country
- *Members:* 200 Universities; 400 College libraries; 200 R&D libraries
- *Services:* catalogue service; database Services; document supply services; e-mail; BBS: audio and video conferencing, etc.

BALNET:

- *Title:* Bangalore Library Network
- *Sponsor:* JRD;. Tata Memorial Library
- *Members:* 100 Libraries

MALIBNET:

- *Title:* Madras Library Network
- *Sponsor:* INSDOC and NISSAT
- *Members:* 15 Libraries
- *Activity:* Two important databases, a directory database of current serials in Madras and a contents database covering articles published in 300 journals available in Madras libraries.

DIGITIZATION PERSPECTIVE OF MEDIEVAL MANUSCRIPTS

Medieval Manuscripts are rich sources of tradition, history and culture. These ought to be preserved, organized and disse-minated to make them available to the world at large. The western countries have taken a lead in starting digital initiatives to preserve the manuscripts but such initiatives in India are either poorly organized or in primitive stage of development.These rich treasures of our country are distributed in private and public institutions in variety of media (parchment, vellum, palm leaves, paper ètc.), languages, scripts, collection sizes and in different conditions. Hence there is a scope to address the problem and focus it from different dimensions to suggest solutions. The information technology has come with a promise to develop digital initiatives for manuscripts for preservation, dissemination and delivery.

It is further desirable to initiate digital libraries for medieval manuscripts (DLMM) to achieve following goals:

- A cost effective bibliographic control of manuscripts.
- An unhindered access to contents over computer and communication network without any barrier (political, geographical, social etc).
- The effective retrieval is possible in digital format because surveying and cataloguing them manually has not been carried out in a scientific, systematic and uniform way and that has resulted in their poor recall and precision etc.
- The medium, generally paper, used in these manuscripts is old and not of superior quality. Most of the manuscripts are moth eaten, torn out, water stained etc. Thus digitization is a viable alternative to enhance the longevity of its life and preserve them from different hazards.
- The digital format can serve as an electronic archival copy accessible in the network from where users can make multiple copies at different points.
- Modern times witness new weapons of warfare and destruction coupled with escalating terrorism having inbuilt tendency to devastate treasures of culture and scholarship. Therefore, it is significant to address the problem and use image technology advances to preserve the manuscripts from such hazards.

- Manuscripts are not fully exploited by the scholars and researchers and to make them available in digital form around the globe via internet and fully searchable through search engines will make their diffusion much wider and give more visibility to cultural heritage of ancient and medieval scholarship.
- The revival of culture, moral values and traditions eroded by technological and industrial developments is desired these days. Hence, MMDL may help to rediscover it by making manuscripts (containing rich culture and traditions) more transparent, accessible to one and all. The attention of world towards rich past will help to have better understanding of each others values and traditions and will generate a fresh quest for knowledge among scholars who are already well set for making increasing use of computers and communication networks.

DIGITIZATION PROCESS

The main focus of digitization is preservation and access of manuscripts. The digitization confronts many problems and requires utmost caution and research and exploration.

The project chain normally consists of:

- Instigate the project
- To assess and select the material
- Prepare for digitization
- To digitize
- Edit
- Delivery
- Support

Most archival programme begin as an idea which may stem from a new funding opportunity or it may be a part of institutions overall strategy in managing its rare collections. Thus the initiative can be either reactive digitization in response to external request or proactive digitization when authorities target an archive of manuscripts. In reality, many institutions in India operate in reactive manner when catching a new call or opportunity for sponsorship. This immediately follows to perform an initial assessment of the manuscripts under consideration and select material from it which could be digitized.

The medieval manuscripts are normally copyright free but need adequate information about the manuscript for its retrieval which involves expertise of orientalis, scholars, codocoligists, linguists etc at one or the other stage of the project. However, 'cherry-picking' is acceptable proposition (*i.e.* focusing a sized item within chosen archive when funds are limited and extended when funds are available) by using a matrix covering all varying categories by which an item can be assessed. This matrix needs to devise to meet diverse situation when many such examples can be located. Digitization is the core of an archival project which need source item, capture device, computer with required storage to house the digital image and necessary software interface. The picture is clear when one focuses on three components *i.e.* anatomy of image, image formats and digitization hard-ware and software.

The anatomy of dots, pixels, resolution, bit depth, shade etc effect the quality of image. For example one major problem arise when resolution concerning the size of the image scanned compared with the original dimension of the manuscript but the resolution at which one chooses to scan is not always the "effective" resolution. This creates more problems especially in surrogate like microfilm but technology seems to remedy such problem in future.Bit depth and dpi are probably important factors which influence quality and dynamic range (Dmax-Dmin) all depending upon the hardware used. However it will be everyone's interest to opt for high quality though affected by many constraints and pressures. The most frequently cited reason for not choosing maximum resolution is resulting file size.

Simple formula for calculating the file size is:

- Resulting file size= dpi x dpi x bit depth x dimension/8

Let us assume one page of 10 inch square item scanned at 24-bit colour at a resolution of 600 dpi Applying formula it comes to:

- 600 x 600 x 24 (10 x10)/8
- = 864,000, 00/8
- =108, 00,000 bytes
- 108,000 Kb or 108 Mb

It clearly shows the file size extremely large—equivalent to 75 floppy disks and nine such images would fill 1 GB hard drive. There could be other reasons as well for sacrificing higher quality for better speed. However, one solution to the balancing of quality versus size is to employ some form of compression using encoding/decoding algorithm to make it much smaller. Ideally this would mean no loss of information but many file formats provide 'lossy' compressions although not necessarily obvious to human eye, do involve degradation in quality. Therefore TIFF is generally used for master images of bi-tonal documents for being 'lossless'.

Interpolation is also used in connection with compression but it is best to avoid it in capturing or resizing to maintain quality true to its original. Good number of file formats (.TIFF;.JPG;.GIF;.PCD;.PNG;.PIC;. BMP;.PDF;.DJVU; AND PYRAMID File) have their relative qualities and limitations but still TIFF is widely used as cross–platform and archiving format for high quality images to be saved without any loss in original capture but alone not tied to any particular scanner or displayed and conversion from TIFF to other formats is relatively straight forward.

However JPG and GIF prove ideal for displaying via web in all browsers. The others may have advantage for compression, printing etc but remains to be seen how far these may go. The digitization process has complexity in deciding about many problems of utmost importance which influences are curatorial concerns on how source material is to be digitized.

For example, handling of a rare and delicate item like manuscript or painting may be restricted regardless of digitization, one could not be able to run ones' fingers across an original copy and therefore certain types of scanning will be prohibited and this contact digitization (using flatbed scanner with bright light from CCD) is often prohibited for handling fragile manuscripts, as against non–contact digitization (like camera) at a distance with employing facilities (ultraviolet or infrared) illumination for controlling light to reduce heat. So a survey of digitizing hardware (flatbed scanner; sheet feeders; drum scanners, slide scanners; microfilm scanners; different variety of digital cameras; oversized document scanners and scan backs) need to be undertaken so to arrive at right type of software for different types of manuscripts. Outsourcing to the reputed and well established firms can be another alternative for bigger archives, of course, with extreme care and vigilance. The digital software (covering capturing, processing and delivery of images) is required though much hardware comes bundled with a range of imaging software but as referred to earlier, many decisions are to be undertaken regarding file formats etc. Processing may involve many things like cropping, fine tuning, colour schemes, applying filters etc and creating of derivatives.

After understanding hardware and software requirements, the archival body responsible for digitization should be able to perform digitization assessment as under:

- Suggest digitization procedure to meet objectives of the archive/ library and satisfy needs and recommen-dations of curators/ conservation experts
- Establish digitization from original material/or surrogate
- Place of digitization: In-house or out sourcing
- Establish cost of conversion (*i.e.* unit cost for digitizing each unit)

The next step is in the practical issue of actual digitization and steps involved therein before capturing image are:

- Material is to be checked and prepared
- Sample shots taken to allow for accurate bench-marking (process at the beginning of digitization project to set levels in the capturing process to ensure that the most significant is captured. It is a dual process involving not only the study of the source document itself but also sample shots and the bench marker should have full knowledge of present/future needs of the user)
- Cameras calibrated accordingly when digitalization is under way.
- Quality Assurance (Different from Benchmarking being post process check to verify decisions made earlier were right ones) checks to be undertaken to assure digital files match all applications.

ORGANISATION

Without a brows-able or searchable catalogue, end users will struggle through to find manuscripts in the collection they may seek. This descriptive information attached to digital archiving may be commonly referred to as metadata. This needs to be a thorough understanding and debate as one third of overall cost of a project of digitization is involved in it. Text based cataloguing provides most straightforward approach to recording of information about digital manuscripts and the director/manager has to decide the structure of its catalogues and its resultant format–an appropriate metadata system which should meet the current and future requirements of the library and its users.

Metadata as term crept into standard Vocabulary of IT related projects has invited much discussion, confusion and problems that a single accepted standard have not evolved and yet user requirements are eluded out of sight. However a successful metadata system should satisfy needs of cataloguers, users, technical experts and administrators. Thus it should be flexible, extensible and forward looking which allow easy searching and browsing by the user at different points of access to collection preferably as a part of online catalogue.

Many large digital projects looked elsewhere leaving MARC or Dublin Core and RDF systems out strapped to cope up with the complexities. The solution that has been adopted is that of SGML/XML. However RDF is also used in combina-tion and has proven more logical and practical policy. The findings of the CEDARS (The CURL Exemplars for Digital archives) are extremely influential on future digital initiatives. Like many other projects, CEDFARS has recognized the need for a comprehensive metadata system and currently looking at open archival system.

JIDI (JISC image Digitization initiative) project has set out a lengthy set of definitions for metadata categories and has segmented cataloguing into five levels via Collection, Work, Visual document, Person and Organization. But RLGs working group on preservation issues on metadata has taken 16 categories under which digital image should be recorded. The CEDARS/JIDI/RLG is extensive, complex and overlapping and XML approach seems to offer best possible solution for the present.

Assuming that one accepts XML as the metadata system of choice, the next step is to decide the Flavour of XML i. e. which DTD is used. One may write ones own DTD, though most digital imaging project select an off the shelf DTD and at present two DTD that are greatly used are TEI and EAD. The Text Encoding Initiativer (TEI) was established in 1987 and reviewed in 1998 as TEI-lite. Besides its complexity, people have looked to other DTDs for their projects on account of the literary and linguistic background of TEI. The notable example being of EAD (Encoded Archival Description) seems to be attractive to both curator and librarians as it emanated from background of archival description. Most digital archival projects chose TEI flavour (DTD) of XML; EAD occasionally or a combination of both. Some are started to embed Dublin Core metadata or others with XML and write their own DTD. The other aspect is describing content, file naming and creation of metadata. The knowledge about a manuscript, its relation with traditional knowledge, history and scholarship, lack of standard terms in vocabulary tools are problems which crop up very significantly and may affect the retrieval system especially at delivery stage.

The uniformity, consistency and expertise of the catalo-guers under the supervision of orientalists well versed in different languages will be of utmost importance. However, secondary tools (descriptive catalogues/Directories etc) will be of immense help at this stage especially in varied cultural and linguistic diversity of Asian subcontinent. One may have to follow different extremes—simply dealing with broad description of the manuscript and other to decipher the depth matter about the nature, significance and importance of the document.

The file naming of manuscripts is very useful especially if Meta get lost and thus should be meaningful and/or mnemonic conveying information about file and its relation to other files besides persistent and consistent. The first one need to convey is some form of meaning to a file name. The most obvious example would be using a file naming system that reflects the shelf mark/accession numbers of the volume under digitization e.g. The filename "ms25fir.jpg" would suggest that it is an image of folio one, recto from manuscript number 25.

Similarly.jpg suffix may indicate that this is derivative of master image (.TIF). Some users are frequently frustrated by the fluid state of WebPages and their sudden disappearance, rendering URL obsolete. It is therefore important that the identifiers one uses for digital file are persistent-hence the notion of persistent URLs (PURLS).

DELIVERY AND DISSEMINATION SYSTEMS

Flat–file Browsing (series of Linked files) can be a quick and easy solution to many programmes but it is also extremely unsophisticated from both cataloguers and users perspective. Complicated searches are not available besides updating the site is always cumbersome. The structured approach is seen as desirable and database programme can be used to store the metadata and link it to image files. The simplest way is to use a standard desktop database system such as Microsoft access link aging images and can interface relatively easily with the web (using Microsoft ASP).

The second option is to choose a system designed specifically for image database—an option that has been chosen for many projects. These have limitations due to high cost, lack of interoperability and focused on museums and galleries. A third option is SGML/XML route to treat the catalogue as a text base. It will allow one to catalogue all the material in XML, place XML file or files on a server and allow user search the texts.

The user would probably do this in web form. Then, through CGI scripts the system could convert the users input (i. e search or browse) to syntax usable by XML search engine on the server. This search engine in turn would analyse the catalogue files and return the hits; with further set of scripts converting material back to HTML for web display (although with XML this intermediate conversion process will eventually will not be necessary). Experience shows that the solution works well and is customizable to such an extent as to satisfy the most demands of users.

This, however, needs knowledgeable and experienced staff. The first digital image the user sees is the thumbnails image-*i.e.* a small derivative of around 100 pixels high created from a larger image. The thumbnail is usually small enough (PFG file of up to 40:1 compression) to allow to download quickly and convey at the same time meaningful graphical information about full image. From Thumbnail, the user could be allowed to download an image of sufficient resolution (say 72 dpi–a screen resolution) to fit a low end monitor of 640x480 resolutions.

Some difficulty arises when one considers the next level of image for advanced analysis or study (e. g. 150-200 dpi). The files would be larger in terms of file size (and slower to network) and one may not be keen perhaps to allow such images to be freely available. Besides creating, delivery of the full text has invited decisions to choose between transcriptions or by OCR. Having done so, it is surrounded with some form of structural make–up using a recognized SGML/XML DTD, with level of encoding to be chosen by the project management.

Future copyright decisions, if any and image protection decisions are to be made at an institutional level. It will vary from collection to collection and importance and policy of the parent institution. However employing banners and water-marks may cut right across the image and always be visible and defeat the entire purpose of the programme of digitations. The dissemination programme can be offline using CD_ROM technology and need to save as a backup for future use and transfer to other media keeping the life span of the medium in consideration.

However to make the cultural and historical assets more visible on-line access will be the viable solution but proper organization and management is to be taken into account in keeping large size of the collection in view in each country of Asia. It is reported by National Commission of Manuscripts in India that there are 50 million manuscripts about India available in many media, languages and scripts. Thus such diversity in a particular country can't be managed by a single organization but needs to be organized according to the region, language, script and available expertise in the institution etc. However coordinating bodies in particular country can coordinate and monitor in order to achieve possible unifor-mity, consistency and maintaining of accepted standards so that overlapping is avoided and interoperability is achieved in a cost effective manner. This will also solve the web-hosting problems to a greater extent and a Portal can be maintained by the coordinating agency so to serve a Gateway for important resources of Asia with links to global digital archives in the coming future.

DIGITIZATION INITIATIVES

Western Countries

Western countries have taken a lead in undertaking digital library projects for medieval manuscripts resulting in development of various lists, union catalogues of manuscripts in various libraries in the region or country. These have evolved into OPAC's of the manuscripts with many fields for their retrieval and displaying images of manuscripts with different resolutions.

The prominent among them is the prestigious programme of Laurentius digital library of the Lund university, MASTER (Manuscript Access Standards for electronic Records), "Medieval manuscripts of Bodleian Library", The Digital scriptorium, Oxford university manuscripts, Medieval Manuscripts Of Syracuse University Library, The Bibliotheque National De France, "Medical Manuscripts in NLM", "European Manuscript server Initiative" (EMSI), "Unesco Memory of World", "The Humanities Text Initiative (HTI)" and "Manuscript digitization Demonstration Project of LC".

These projects have used photographic and digital methods to develop a full or partial archival copy of the manuscripts available on-line using different software with JPEG format for image processing in association with different metadata initiatives. These attempts could be very useful in evolving a common strategy for digitization of vast manuscripts resources.

Indian Initiative

Khuda Baksh Oriental Public Library

It is one of oriental libraries having rich collection of Persian, Arabic, Urdu and other language manuscripts. The descriptive catalogue is in 30 vols which appeared in 1923 and reprinted in seventies, besides other catalogues and publications compiled by different authorities. Now the institution has launched a website and a link is given to the whole catalogue of the library in a tabular form.

The table has hyperlinks to different volumes of the catalogue which can be browsed as JPEG files and browsed from as a file from top to bottom. The whole project has been undertaken by National Informatics Centre. It has not introduced any retrieval mechanism as the document is treated as collection of image files in JPEG format. The catalogue, ironically, can't be accessed under metadata or any useful descriptor.

Raza Library, Rampur, Uttar Pradesh

The library developed under the patronage of "nawabs" contains a collection of about 10,5000 vols. has appeared recently on the web with an interface for the manuscripts. It displays information of two manuscripts on a single screen, giving brief bibliographic information in Romanized form along with a folio of the manuscript scanned. However the collection is limited to few manuscripts only and further work is in progress. The retrieval engine for the data is missing as they have not structured the data nor made use of any digital library software.

Kashmir University Project

The Department of Library and Information Science, University of Kashmir, Srinagar, JandK has undertaken a project sponsored by the UGC for designing a database of medieval manuscripts available in Kashmir. The work is in progress and is made accessible on web after proper test and assessment.

ISSUES

- High band communication with computer networks which support efficient image document transfer
- Data storage
- Data compression and interpolation
- Scanning and conversion technologies
- Planning and execution (in house, outsourcing, financial implications, funding etc)
- Data image file format(.TIF..JPG.GIF..PCD.PNG,and others like.PIC..PDF.BM)
- Text encoding initiative (TEI)
- Single interchange standard for both First level (abbreviated)and full description of the manuscript
- Development of the software for simple descriptive records and provide means for fully detailed records
- Link manuscript images and full text transcript
- Adaptation of Unicode for different scripts and languages and research thereof for developing multilingual databases.

NEED FOR DIGITIZATION: PROBLEMS AND PROSPECTS IN COLLEGE LIBRARIES

Information technology and networks are the major tools to shape our society in future. The application of information technology has the largest impact on library and librarianship. It has changed the way we perceive and disseminate information and has even threatened the traditional approaches to library and library professionals.

The impact of such technologies (Computer network, Internet, Hypermedia, Multimedia, CD-ROM etc.) has led to a paperless society. The convergent of computational storage and networking technologies now have a wider impact on society. The computers can record any information/document at high speed and disseminate information wherever required to the users. It is possible now to digitize and store information in the form of high quality graphics, network texts, colour images, voice signals and video clips at a relatively affordable cost.

DIGITAL LIBRARY

The term "Digital Library" in a broad sense is a compu-terized system that allows obtaining a coherent means of access to an organized, electronically stored repository of information and data. It is a relatively new concept. The term digital library explains the nature of its collection. This term became familiar towards the end of the 20th century. Resources in digital library are electronic store and access of information. Access to digital library is therefore, not based on space or time. The Berkeley Digital Library Project, University of Cali-fornia "the digital library will be a collection of distributed information sources, producers of information will make it available and consumers will find it perhaps through the help of automated agents". The Stadford Digital Library project states "the integrated digital library will create a shared environment linking everything personnel information collection to collection of conventional libraries to large data collection shared by Scientists". Digital Libraries do not mean libraries in the classical sense but a network of multimedia systems.

NEED FOR DIGITIZATION

With the rise of information explosion libraries facing manpower and monetary constraints are able to acquire every document published under one roof and thus evolve the concept of resource sharing and network. Automation has helped libraries in improving library activities and accelerates their working. It saves the effort, time and manpower of libraries. In an automated system the information can be altered and updated without the repetitive work involved in the manual system.

With the development of computer, any information can be turned into sequences. So, any user can access into the sequence without any trouble and delay. It saves the time for the users, staffs and increases productivity and reliability. As a series of development the concept of digitization evolved in the field of libraries. The process of library culture is and shall be as follows– the traditional libraries shifted towards automated libraries; the automated ones towards electronic ones; the electronic ones towards digitization ones and ultimately to virtual libraries (libraries without walls).

CHARACTERISTICS OF DIGITAL LIBRARY

The important characteristics of digital libraries are as follows:

- Digital library is a digital object.
- Digital library provides faster access to information

- Digital library enables easy management of large amounts of data
- Digital library collections are fixed and permanent.
- Digital library support formal and informal learning procedures
- Digital library can be accessed by any user from any workplace.

FUNCTIONS OF DIGIRAL LIBRARY

The most important functions of digital libraries are:

- To provide friendly interface to users.
- To avail network facilities.
- To support library functions.
- To improve the cost effectiveness of library operations.
- To enhance advanced search, access and retrieval of information.
- To support in editing and publishing annotations and integration of information.
- To digitize documents for preservation and for space saving.

SCOPE OF THE STUDY

The scope of the study entitled "Need for Digitization: Problems and prospects in college libraries of Manipur" is limited only to some leading colleges of Manipur. In this paper an attempt has been made to study the problems and prospects of Digitization.

METHODOLOGY

The study was conducted through questionnaire and interview method.

Major Findings Colleges in Manipur

The development of college libraries in Manipur was very late and started only from the 1940s, when the first college of the state, the D.M. College, Imphal was instituted with a well furnished library. At present there are 32 affiliated government colleges and 8 government aided colleges, 22 affiliated private colleges and 8 permitted private colleges in Manipur. Libraries have been set up in all the colleges of Manipur. Majority of them are, however, facing financial problems for the development of resources manpower, money and collection etc. Application of modern technology in the work of college libraries still remains bizarre in Manipur.

PROBLEMS

The manpower, money and collection in college libraries of Manipur are in a pitiable position. Without proper infrastructure and well-trained staffs, digitization of college libraries is not possible. The most important aspect in this regard is financial resources from the concerned authorities. Some burning problems in college libraries of Manipur may be noted as follows:

- Library facilities in the college libraries of Manipur are inadequate and disorganized.

- Training for manpower-development (library staff) is not yet seen in Manipur.
- The earmarked plan and non-plan fund allotted to the libraries are insufficient.
- Lapses in the management of the fund allotted to the libraries can be seen from time to time.
- Information technology is lacking far behind in the colleges of Manipur.
- Creation of posts and consequent appointment of trained staffs are not done.
- Lack of cooperation among the libraries in colleges of Manipur.
- Lack of reading habit in the libraries by the students.
- Non-application of modern advanced technology in college libraries of Manipur.

PROSPECTS

The changing information and communication tech-nologies have brought the creation, handling, delivering and storage of information in digital forms. In this changing environment using digital technology in the college libraries is of utmost importance. The college authorities (Principal, Libraries and Staffs) of Manipur are also aware of the same in the state.

The following points may be recommended/suggested in this connection for the College Libraries particularly in Manipur and in India as a whole:

- The government should take steps for providing library facilities with well-equipped modern tech-nology at par to the colleges.
- The concerned authorities should not grant affiliations and permissions to the private colleges until and unless they can keep the requisite library norms.
- Information technology may be facilitated for making network among the libraries.
- A committee consisting of library authority, staffs and user community may be constituted to initiate joint efforts introducing computerized service in the library.
- Availability of information technology facilities (like internet) should be considered and encouraged.
- E-resources training/awareness programme may be organized from time to time by the concerned authority.
- College management committee should take steps to take help/ assistance from the UGC (INFLIBNET) for the successful implementation of modern technology.
- Earmarked grants for the college libraries should be given.
- Libraries must be encouraged to renovate themselves in the modern trends.
- Adequate funds may be provided and utilized properly.

DIGITAL ARCHIVING: INDIAN SCENARIO

Before the advent of digital video storage analog recordings on films and video tapes were placed on the shelves with a card catalogue. Whenever the library has to make room for the inclusion of new material, some of the old materials were removed and stored off-site, which is properly viewed as an archive. These analog and physical archives had limited shelf life depending on the medium on which the content is stored. In the digital age archiving is in the digital form-that is migrating the content electronically to new media for the purpose of preservation.

The classic meaning of archiving is:

- To place the documents in a secure place for presentation.
- To remove the data or documents from common use and conserve for future use.

The word *'Archive'* derives from the Greek word *Arkheia* meaning "Public records". The word denotes local, regional and national government collections of documents and other records kept for consultation and research purposes. One of the earliest digital-archives was a use-net news group called Talkorigins, which was devoted to mainstream theories in geology, biology, cosmology, theology etc. Contributions arguing the Darwinian evolutionary line were posed and often sent to bear all the hallmarks of serious research arguments and bibliographic referencing.

DIGITAL ARCHIVING

Digitization is sometimes recommended as a preservation strategy for materials that are in fragile formats and which are not in frequent use. Images and audio-visual materials are being stored in digital formats more than ever before, for example, digitizing pages of delicate manuscripts, preserving images of texts which are important for scholars. The primary goal of digital archiving is the storage, retrieval and access of rare documents with the aid of electronic technology for image capturing and reproducing.

The aim is to create conditions, whereby the researcher can consult the manuscripts without physically handling the individual items and at the same time the artistic quality of the calligraphy and decoration of the manuscripts could be preserved for future generation. In each and every country of the world the *National Archives department* is responsible for the preservation of important documents of that particular nation. Digital Archives can be defined as Repositories of digital information, that are collectively responsible for ensuring through the exercise of various migration strategies, that the integrity and long term accessibility of the nation's social, economic, cultural and intellectual heritage is preserved in digital form.

ADVANTAGES OF DIGITIZATION

The most promising strategy for saving the intellectual and artistic content of endangered volumes is to transform or convert it to a different medium by copying it to a film or digital form. Digital archiving is a recent work of digital libraries and ensures long term storage and access. By digitizing the documents, lots of space can be saved-a stack of CD's will take much lesser space compared to the space occupied if the same information was to be stored as hard copies. In addition, Electronic-files can be accessed from any where, at any time and at a cheaper price.

MIGRATION OF DIGITAL INFORMATION

Refreshing digital information by copying it from medium to medium and the possibility of maintaining a complex set of emulators describe two distinct points on a continuum of approaches to preserving digital information. It is a periodic transfer of digital material from one hardware and software configuration to another or from one generation of computer technology to a subsequent generation.

CREATION OF INFORMATION IN DIGITAL FORM

Information objects in digital form have to be created, edited described and indexed, annotated, revised, re-created, modified, disseminated and retained for future use, by a complex interwoven community of creators and other owners, value-added services and institutional and individual users. The process of preserving digital information will vary with different kinds of objects like textual, numeric, image, video, sound, multimedia simulation etc.

ORGANIZATION OF DATA

Before scanning the documents for digitization, one has to organize the data, that is to be archived, so that the process will go on in a smooth way and the scanned data can be retrieved properly.

The most important steps which are to be followed are given below:

- Organize the data that is to be archived in to files.
- Decide how to organize the scanned file, for example-by subject, by code number, by chrono-logical order, by keyword, by author, by title etc.
- File names should be clearly identified, so that one can easily recognize the contents of the file.
- All the files or documents which are to be scanned should be kept in order.
- All the staples and paper pins, if present, should be removed.
- The paper folds and creases in the paper should be smoothened out.

Scanners

Different scanners are available for scanning the docu-ments but one has to select the scanner on the basis of materials, like

- Vacuum-fed belt scanners–can be used for fragile and odd shaped material.

- Plane-protected wide-angle scanners–can be used for book scanning.
- High-volume scanners can be used for–architectural drawings and other oversize materials.
- Flat-bed scanners can be used for–delicate and fragile materials.

METHOD OF SCANNING

After deciding the type of scanner and type of material to be used, one has to decide whether to scan the documents as images or with OCR (Optical Character Recognition).If the document is scanned with OCR, the files need to be saved in the form of application for easy editing. The benefit of OCR is that the documents are converted to an editable format. If the document is to be archived to maintain the integrity of the records for preserving, they should be scanned as images. The documents should be scanned at a minimum resolution of 150 ppi, through 300 ppi, for future use or print.

The choices available for saving the documents as images are:-

- *BMP:* Bit Map is the native image format for the windows operating system and will provide high quality images.
- *TIFF:* Tagged Image File Format is very detailed and it is supported by many operating systems.
- *JPEG:* Joint Photographic Experts Group format comprises the data, but it is enough for normal use.

STORAGE METHOD

When all the documents are scanned, they should be saved on CD zip disks or floppy disks or tape drives. For storing the files on the disks, labeled folders should be created, the disks as well as the disk cases should be labeled. In digital archives there may be many levels of storage on the basis of expected use for the retrieval. Seldom-used material may be stored offline, usually in tape media, which is less expensive. The data which is in high demand and where retrieval time is at a premium, online storage in magnetic media may serve best.

An intermediate solution is near-line storage, where the data can be stored on optical or tape media and loaded in jute box, which is more responsive to users demand than offline storage. The most promising strategy for saving the intellectual and artistic content of endangered volumes is to transform or convert it to a different medium by copying it to a film or digital form. Paper documents can be transferred to microfilms, DVD's (Digital Video Data) and CD-ROM's (Compact Disk Read Only Memory).This process is known as Archiving. Digital archives can use any of the three methods.

RETRIEVING DIGITAL ARCHIVES

Digital archives must maintain the information in a form, so that the users can access the information over the net through search engines, print, audio etc. If the archives are saved on CD's, floppies or tape mediums they should be checked periodically for content redundancy. If the digital archives need to be accessed in a distributed network environment, the digitized data should be connected to networks using proper protocols and bandwidth suitable for retrieving the information.

ARCHIVING IN INDIA

Preservation of Indian culture and literature is one of the oldest traditions of India. Thousands of years ago, Indian philosophers, scholars and poets have expounded their knowledge through treatises, sacred songs, commentaries on scriptures etc. which were recorded on specially treated palm leaves and birch barks, in the form of engravings on brass and copper plates etc. for future use. Before the invention of the printing press, the texts were handwritten by the craftsmen so that the universal knowledge can be preserved for future use. This proves our theory that Archiving has existed since long in India.

Indian National Archives

Indian National Archives department, which is located in Delhi is making efforts through various conservation methods and photo duplication processes to preserve the important documents of Indian cultural art, political and economical and literature. Department of Indian National Archives is using a unique method of rejuvenating and repairing the old documents with the help of "Cellulose acetate foil and tissue paper", which is known as "Solvent of Hand lamination". The Conservation Research Laboratory is a department of Indian National Archives has been successful in retrieving palm leaves that have gone dry since the last three decades. The National Archives is trying to ensure the longevity of documents by microfilming and reprographing.

Preservation of Indian Art

C-DAC–Center For Development of Advanced Compu-ting is trying to digitally preserve and disseminate Indian Art in the form of paintings. By using HP (Hewlett Packard) equipment to capture, store and make available via internet to the researchers and art lovers.

In this project, using comprehensive suite of H.P. Technologies, the scientists capture images in extraordinary details using digital cameras to store and process the images on workstations and to develop new colour pallets and drivers to make the individual works and print realistic reproductions on large prints. By digitizing Indian art in this way not only the art is preserved but is also made available to a larger audience.

Muktabodha Institute-Archiving of Indian Manuscripts

Muktabodha institute is working in collaboration with libraries and institutions around India to make digital images of specific, rare manuscripts and texts. The institute recognizes the importance of saving the spiritual knowledge and preserved around 871 works in microfilm format. Around 262 of these works were converted to digital image format. The institute is launching the "On-line digital library" website with 74 volumes of the Kashmir series of texts and studies. These volumes were originally published in Sanskrit language.

The main contribution of this institute is in the preser-vation and accessibility of photographic images of rare manuscripts and religious scriptures, so that the valuable information is more easily available to scholars around the world. At present Muktabodha discontinued the practice of microfilming the manuscripts and started producing digital images directly from the manuscripts. Since the main objective of the institute is in the dissemination of old religious literature by digitizing and preserving them, the institute decided not to face the hassels of microfilming and adopted the process of digital imagery.

COMMERCIAL ARCHIVING ORGANIZATIONS

Many commercial organizations have come up and made it easy to have any time anywhere, to access to information. These organizations provide electronic publicizing, content management, digital archiving etc. for the E-Publishers, individual purposes and institutions like libraries etc. Some of the organizations of India are the following.

DPS (Digital Publishing Solutions)

The Digital Publishing Solutions (DPS) is a Pune based organization, which has digitized so far 3.5 million pages and made digital archiving a reality. It scans the data from paper, photographs, negatives, microfilm, microfiche, transparencies and then the data digitized using the OCR and stored the digitized data in E-book format. Now the data is sold online using DX Reader, online XML reader. This organization is a approaching the libraries interested in preserving the rare books, manuscripts etc. In India DPS is working for 15 libraries, National research Institute, Indian national science academy etc.

JALVA

Mumbai based Jalva Media provides solutions for media management, indexing, content archiving data distribution, with partnership of other companies like mediasite, Ibeam Broadcasting, Madge.web, microsoft, Real and Apple. Jalva and SGI are offering better technologies like MPEG2 (moving picture experts group 2) which allows archiving data in DVD (digital versatile disk) by providing longer storage like and cross-platform compatibility.

Sampradaya

SAMPRADAYA Which means *handling down of tradition*. It serves as a resource centre by documenting the various aspects of the South Indian

(Karnatic) music. It was founded in 1980, by two students of South Indian music Michael, Nixon of Veena and Ludwig, Pesch of Flute, under the guidence of late Savitri Rajan with the purpose of documenting Sampradaya Sangeetam. The main contribution of this organization is to bring to light and preserve this music tradition by documen-tation, archiving of recordings, music books, journals, manuscripts etc. This organization is conducting in-depth taped interviews of eminent Carnatic musicians, and organizing seminars and workshops on important topics of South Indian Music. Sampradaya Audio listening library is only one of its kind in South India, where the public has free access to music recordings and archival collections. It has 8 separate music listening stations.

PROBLEM AND PROSPECTS OF DIGITAL LIBRARY

The world has become a global village due to the development of information technology especially computer technology. Computer technology plays a vital role for gene-rating and disseminating information in the network environ-ment.

The rise of digital libraries has also brought phenomenal changes in the progress of collection, storage, preservation of rare documents, retrieval and dissemination of information. Computer technologies not only create and develop some modern libraries but also transform many existing libraries on the modern lines. A digital library is a global virtual library. And it can be defined as library with all the information available in the digital form. Data accessible through digital library system in addition to full text information includes non text information. With the advent of digital technology the possibility of horizontal and vertical integration of knowledge and information has increased significantly. As such there is every reason that the role and the status of traditional library will change.

DIGITAL LIBRARY AND DIGITIZATION

Perception of the term "digital library" is a bit like perception of the elephant in the poem 'The Six Blind Men and the Elephant" where each of six blind men gives different descriptions of the elephant according the elephant's body part they touch. The library communities have also used different terms over the years to denote this concept. The idea of easy and fingertip access of information conceptualized as digital library begins with Vannenar Bush's MEMEX MACHINE and has continued to evolve with each advances in information technology.

Today people give different definitions of digital library in arrays of terms such as electronic library, virtual library, hybrid library, library without walls, cybrary, spatial library, digitize collection, library of the future etc. While these are not necessarily synonyms of digital library, they do have some aspects in common and the term digital library is one most widely accepted. Digital library may be treated as repositories of massive amount of information content in digital form in different servers on diverse format permitting access over different electronic networks.

According to Edward Fox (Editor of ASIS and commu-nication of ACM) a digital library is an assemblage of digital computers, storage and cummunication machinery together with the context and software needed to produce emulate and extend those services provided by conventional libraries based on paper and other material means of collecting, cataloguing, finding and disseminating information... A full service digital library must accomplish all essential services of traditional libraries and also exploit the well advantages of digital storage, searching and communication.

Digital Library Federation in USA define digital library as "organizations that provide the resources, including the specialized staff, to select, structure, offer intellectual access to, interpret, distribute, preserve the integrity of ensure the persistence over time of collections of digital works so that they are readily and economically available for use by a defined community or set of communities".

A digital library "is that set of global internet worked libraries" that includes the following criteria:

- A collection of text, images, or data in digitized form
- A set of systems for indexing and navigating or retrieving in that collection.
- One or more defined community of users.

Christine Borgman opines that the term digital library has various meanings.

However, for her, it clusters around two themes:

- From research perspective, digital libraries are content collected and organized on behalf of users' communities,
- From library-practice perspective; digital libraries are institutions or organizations that provide information services in digital forms for the enhancement of information storage and retrieval system.

Similarly, Levy points out that "notably for librarians, digital library refers most directly to institutions that oversee digital collections. For the other professionals like computers and information scientist digital library refers to digital collections without regard to institutional settings in which they might be managed. More comprehensively, in digital libraries the information arrives as needed at the users' screen like the attending waiter ever filling the water glass before the glass is empty. However, these defined perceptions are likely to evolve as activities move research development endeavours to full scale practice.

Digitization, now a day, has become one of the key activities in libraries. These two terms Digital library and Digitization goes hand in hand, like the two sides of a coin, the elements that form both concepts can not be separated.

Digitization can be defined as the digital conversion of library and other archival materials. Digitization is also a technique for data transmission at a very high speed.

It is the conversion of any fixed analog media – books, journals, and photos, paintings into electronic form through scanning, sampling, or even re-keying. Digitization provide solution to traditional library problems such as conservation, preservation, storage space, remote access to information collection, acquisition of original digital works created by other publishers, agencies, access to external digital materials and resources.

WHY DIGITAL LIBRARIES

Libraries have changed with time to time from mere static storehouse to dynamic service centers, serving all professionals and non-professionals utilizing useful need base collection. The emphasis of the users has also shifted from micro document to micro piece of information with the changed of the medium from clay tablets to paper and now to electronic and optical media. The worlds of both communication and production of information are changing at a very fast pace and the conver-gence of these had huge impact on libraries.

All this changes in libraries is due to the impact of information technology and this impact is seen in the form of digital library. Due to information explosion during the last few decades many techniques and technologies have emerged for handling the information more readily, speedily and effectively. Many computer specialists also succeeded in integrating text, graphics, audio, animations, and video converted into a digital media. People feel enthused to read from computer screens.

Varieties of software are now available which are capable of manipulating and rendering information. At the same time price of personal computers are getting cheaper and cheaper to a very affordable cost. Besides allowing remote access, bringing the diverse material together from scattered locations, solving space problems, raising the profile of institution, enhancing preservation, increasing in retrieval and dissemi-nation of information in digital libraries system, people in the library professionals shows increased concern in building digital library. Dwindling budgets of library and high information demand are also another factor.

NEED AND IMPORTANCE OF DIGITAL LIBRARY

We are in the midst of information explosion and information technology revolution leading to the emergence of electronics information era. Rapid advances in information processing, storage and communication technologies have revolutionized the role of libraries worldwide in disseminating information services to their users. Libraries therefore, are reconsolidating their services and information products, incorporating new technologies of upgrading information resources, changing information objects, models of communication and information delivery in order to add value to their services and to satisfy the changing information needs of user community.

In fact, impact of information technology on libraries and its users is an important factor for transformation of traditional organizational structure into new institutional entities. Infor-mation seekers are also no longer statisfied with the printed materials alone. As a result the users demand for information delivery in digital form, considered more dynamic in electronics multimedia documents, at their desktop are increasing day by day.

Thus, there is a need to develop digital library and to adopt electronic media for its collection development so that it can fulfill the requirement of users. Libraries and other library professionals should make efforts for setting digital libraries and conversion of resources into a digitized format.

Some important features of Digital library can be summarized as:

- To introduce new service and material
- To provide remote access to information resources that are expensive and rare and easy searching that are impractical manually;
- To facilitate in the management of digital content
- To minimize in handling of rare and unique collection of traditional library
- To improve access to the latest information at a very high speed
- To support search and retrieval
- To provide users friendly interface
- To support formal and informal learning
- To reduce errors that would have occurred in the manual systems scientifically because of bar code
- Cost effectiveness and affordable and
- To raise library profile
- Digital libraries as global multilingual expository of data must attract people from all walks of life regardless of geographical locations.

Technical Architecture

Technical architecture is another factor that need enhance-ment for digital information service system. Therefore, libraries need to upgrade current technical architecture to accommodate digital materials.

The architecture includes the following components:

- Local Network with high speed and fast connection to internet
- Full text search engines to index and provide access to resources
- Variety of servers (FTP and Web server)
- Electronic documents management functions that will support digital resources
- A variety system functions to coordinate mange the entry and retrieve data

- Local Library system with adequate PCs having LAN
- Well trained and manpower
- Relational databases that support a variety of digital formats

Present Status of Library in Manipur in the present technological environment

In library information system, information technology has had a clear and persuasive impact in almost every area of the library. The most significant development in information technology over the last few years or so is digital technology. Digital technology is revolutionizing the traditional concepts of preservation and access in library and archive communities. The applications of digital system and computing system in the libraries have been a subject of interest to present day professional librarians.

More recently the libraries have sought to implement increasingly complex solution that involved distributed networking and access to remote information resources. During the eighties, the whole focus of the librarians shifted towards library automation but in the nineties it has shifted towards digitization. The phrase library automation has been generally accepted within the profession to encompass early automation activities, yet it does not do justice to the current state of affaires as libraries have move well beyond the automation of internal procedures. In Manipur, however, applications of technologies in libraries are lagging far behind.

There are two university libraries, 74 affiliated colleges, nine public libraries, one state central library at Imphal and others at different districts of Manipur and many high and higher secondary schools libraries. But most of the libraries function in the traditional way with conventional printed shelf collection except some libraries like Manipur University library, Central Agricultural Library, RIMS Library, DOEACC Library etc. These libraries have initiated automation. Manipur University Library started automation since 1989 in the areas such as cataloguing, serial control, information retrieval and circulation recently.

This library provides internet facility, OPAC and has become one of the important nodes in the academic libraries system. As far as college libraries are concerned collections of information resources which support the faculty and students are not up to the mark because of lack planned systematic approach to the development of resources. Many of college libraries built up their collection of printed materials as activities and services are yet to be automated. Only one college library *i.e.* Modern College library has started Data entry using CDS/ISIS.

Books are still the only important channel for dissemi-nation of information. The librarian and other supporting professional staff are not well qualified and trained with the new modern technology. As far as infrastructures are concern a large majority of libraries have not yet automated their activities as they are handicapped to switch over to computeri-zation and modernization because of lack of infrastructural facilities like computer hardware, software, and human-ware. And most of the libraries are not provided internet facility.

Regarding school and higher secondary school libraries, majority of school libraries are not able to provide even the facilities of a traditional library. From the discussion it is evident that the libraries in Manipur, except some, automation of the operations and services progressing very slowly. Automation as well as conversion of digital library will not be possible within five year though plan for automation exist.

In Manipur it is not an easy task to develop digital library system as automation in the library is totally absent. Keeping in views of the reasons, authority should take initiative for promoting library automation by implementing new IT in the libraries of Manipur so that users from different communities can get the universe of knowledge available in the digital format.

PROBLEMS

Problems faced while entering into a digital libraries systems in Manipur can be summarized as:

- Libraries exist only in the traditional form and there is no electronic library/digital resource;
- Most of the libraries function with inadequate number professional staff required for smooth functioning and there is a general unwillingness to develop digital library system;
- Even if the librarian and some professionals are qualified they certainly lag behind because of lack of awareness about value of information, cooperation and coordination in the resource building and sharing of information and poor communication skill;
- Libraries lack standardization of methods due to unwillingness to adapt to new requirements;
- Presently large majority of library have no computer and no internet facility and other infrastructural facilities required to exploit the opportunities provided by electronic media. Therefore, the best use of electronic publication on-line and network access are not possible;
- Total absence of hardware, software and trained human power is another reason;
- A highly irregular and unpredictable power supply; and
- Lack of financial support due to the acute financial problem the state is facing.

In fact, the main problems faced seem to be lack of financial resources and lack of computer education without which automation in the libraries are not possible.

PROSPECT

The dawn of information revolution is considered to be one of the marvelous achievements of the 20th century. The rapid growth and development of IT has resulted in the development of digital library, tools and skill relating to encoding information objects in digital format. The application of digital technologies within the library comes along with the development of computer technology. Keeping the points in view it is necessary to consider some perspective of digital library.

Digital library not only creates and develops modern libraries but also transforms many existing libraries. Digital Library introduced the concept of hypertext, facilitates networking in order to communicate and exchange digital information from source location to destination.

It also facilitates preservation, storage, and communication of diverse multimedia objects but also provides intensive access from multiple locations and enrich teaching and learning environment which is not possible with the traditional library. Due to information explosion and existence of information society, everybody is aware of the newly developed technologies. This new developments are reflected in LIS education and in those libraries with existing infrastructure, services and network.

In fact, there is a complete change in activities, role of library, librarians and other professionals (staff). Most of the librarians in Manipur have now entered in the technological era of communication dominated by film and electronic media. The libraries are expected to be an automated information system having pervasive impact in almost every areas of library-be it the online catalogue, online database, online searching, document delivery, inter library loan, circulation etc. Clearly, the impact of automated system in libraries has been pervasive and significant.

DIGITAL PRESERVATION OF MANUSCRIPTS: A CASE STUDY

During the history extending over 5000 years, India has produced a large wealth of literature. This vast knowledge treasure was written on different kinds of material like birch bark, palm leaf, cloth, wood, stone and paper etc. India perhaps has one of the oldest and largest collections of manuscripts in the world. They are in the custody of different institutions like libraries, museums, monasteries, mosque and individuals. Many of them have disappeared and a large number are in a state of damage/decay. We already have lost huge manuscript collection in Buddhist monasteries like Nalanda, Taxila and Vikramshila.

Taxila at the North West front of India was destroyed by foreign aggression. Nalanda library known as Dharmganj had three sections Ratnadodhi, Ratnasagar and Ratna Rajak. Ratnadodhi was a nine storied library. First Hun king Michirkul damage the library in AD 450-470. In AD

1205 Bakhtiyar Khilji destroyed it completely and his soldiers use the manuscripts for boiling water. Let us hope no more Khilji is born in modern time and let us take step to save these manuscripts for further decay and damage that will destroy them. The public access of older manuscripts also leads to substantially quicker disintegration of the originals.

An appropriate alternative that could be the solution to the existing problem is preservation by way of microform or use of modern computer technology which is digitization of the manuscripts. The manuscripts, besides having information (the image data) also have visual information (secondary image data).

The information regarding physical form, binding, paper, history of manuscript, source of acquisition, its present market value which is often high, is called physical data. All these are very important in manuscripts.

There are many libraries in the world where rare manuscripts of Indian origin are preserved and some of them are:

- Copenhagen Royal Library (Denmark);
- Bibliotheque Nationale (France);
- Preussiche States Bibliothek,
- Universitats Bibliothek,
- Staats Bibliothek,
- Bayershe Staats Bibliothek(Germany);
- British Library,
- Royal Asiatic Society,
- Bodleian Library,
- India Institute,
- Cambridge University Library (United Kingdom);
- Darbar Library (Nepal);
- Punjab University Library (Pakistan);
- Museum Library (Sri Lanka).

HISTORICAL BACKGROUND OF UJJAIN CITY

Ujjain is an ancient, historical pilgrimage city of India. It is known as cultural capital of India. Ujjain was called by ancient people Vishala, Kanak Shiringa, Amaravati, Pratikalpa Awantika, Ujjaini, etc. It is situated on the fertile land of Malwa. Ujjain which has always been known for its sanctity stands on the right bank of river Shipra. This city is one of the seven sacred cities of the Hindus. Where one of the Jyotir-lingMahakal rests and during 'Simhstha Mela' or 'Kumbh Mela', a festival held in every twelfth years, people went there to have a dip in the holy water of 'Shipra' on the auspicious days.

Also known as city of Mahakavi Kalidasa is also famous for Guru Sandipani Ashram where lord Krishna completed his education. Historically, this city was the capital of the famous king Vikramaditya who was famous for his judgment and Navratna of scholars. Sawai Jaising of Jaipur had erected here an observatory which is still standing.

Scindia Oriental Research Institute (SORI)

Scindia Oriental Research Institute, Ujjain a pioneer manuscript library of India, was ranked 11th in India as per the Indian National Trust for Art and Cultural Heritage (INTACH) survey.

Establishment

The history of Oriental Institutes begins with establish-ment of Asiatic Society of Bengal in 1789. Royal Asiatic Society of London was established much later to it in 1823. Its Bombay branch was established in 1829. These institutes were established with an aim to collect manuscript. After that many institutions started colleting rare manuscripts in India and abroad. In India Baroda, Mysore, Kashmir, Kochin and Travancore etc., started collecting manuscripts. Bhandarkar Oriental Research Centre, Poona was established. In Madhya Pradesh, Bhelsa (Vidisha), Maheswar, Mandesaur, Ujjain, Dhar and Chanderi had rare manuscript collections but in neglected state.

The manuscript from Ujjain were being sent out of Ujjain, a few of them to Oritental Institute, Baroda. In 1931, king of Baroda, Maharaja Siyaji Rao Gaekwad wrote to Regency Council of Gwalior State about scattered manuscripts in Ujjain and recommended its colletion and preservation. On this, a manuscript library named Oriental Book Collection was established on 20th October, 1931. It was started with only 11 manuscripts in a rental house in Pan Dariba. This was increased to 2000 by July 1933. On 1st July, 1933, it was transferred to Madhav College, Ujjain.

A galery was constructed for their display which is still in very good condition. Dr. Divakar started caring these manu-scripts. In 1936 and 1941 the manuscript catalogues were published. Maharaja Jiwaji Rao Scindia set up a committee in 1938 under the Chairmanship of Sir Manu Bhai Desai with Dr. Radhankrishnan, Dr. Amarnath Jha and Professor Paranjbe as its members to establish permanent memory of Maharaja Vikram celebrating Vikram era festival. The committee recomm-ended establishment of Vikram University, Vikram Kirti Mandir including Archeologoical Museum, Scindia Oriental Research Institute and a Conference hall.

During independence movement, it was delayed. In 1941, Vikram Bi-Centinary festival was organised in Ujjain when the earlier oriental book collection was renamed as Scindia Oriental Institute and was included in normal budget of education department of Gwalior State for financial help. President of India Dr. Rajendra Prasad lay fouindations of Vikram Kirti Mandir on 8th May, 1951. But due to delay in its progress, the Scindia Oriential Research Institute was transferred in a rental house-Nawab Saheb Bangla near Madhav Club.

After state reorganisation in 1956 and establishment of newly carved Madhya Pradesh, the SORI was transferred to the control of Deputy Director of School Education in M.P. Government. Finally Vikram University was established in 1957 and on 06/11/1960 an Memorandum of Understanding (MoU)was signed between M.P Govt. and Vikram University. On 26/06/1961 the institute was transferred to the Vikram University. In 1966, it was shifted to newly constructed Jiwaji Rao Library building. In August 1968, after construction of some parts of Vikram Kirti Mandir, the institute was shifted to its own place.

Staff

In the beginning (till 1956) the institute has the post of one Curator, one Shastri, one Librarian, one assistant cataloguer and one clerk.

Collection

Collections of this institute are very rare and important. Only a small portion of the present collection of manuscripts was made available from Ujjain. Remaining collection was brought from different places mainly from Lashkar, Gwalior, Mandsaur, Poona, Jalgaon, Sagar, Ratnagiri, Banaras, Jalone, Indore and Srinagar (Kashmir). Here we can see that only 473 manuscripts have been added since 1986.There are various kinds of manuscripts in the institutes. More than enough manuscripts are collected in Sanskrit language but the other manuscripts are written in many languages like Marathi, Hindi, Gujrati, Aarabic, Persian, Bengali, Maithali and Telegu etc.

Many kinds of writing materials cab be seen here like:

- Papers,
- Palm leaves,
- Brich barks,
- Metal plates etc.

There are also manuscripts which are written in different kind of scripts. The scripts are:

- Devanagari,
- Brahmi,
- Gupta,
- Jain,
- Maithili,
- Modi,
- Sharada,
- Muriya,
- Farasi,
- Bangla,
- Telegu,
- Tamil, etc.

Acquiring Manuscripts

Whether it becomes known that a particular manuscript is being sold the 'Sastri' and other staff members of the institute goes to the place to purchase and study the manuscripts. The 'Sastri' knows about the collection of manuscripts in the institute and after seeing the catalogues it is decided whether or not the manuscript is useful for the institute. The pages are checked if found useful. It is checked whether the pages are in agreeable state and written by a single person or two or more persons. Thereafter, meeting is convened and the draft for purchase is proposed before the committee. If the proposal is assed then the cost of the manuscript is assessed and after due assent of the seller and the manuscript.

Types of Manuscript Available in SORI

- *Palm Leaf Manuscript:* In India maximum manuscripts of ancient period are written on palm leaves. Palm leaves are usually 37 inch in length and three inch in width. The palm leaves were boiled and then were rubbed by couch shell for smoothness. Then with the help of iron pen, letters were scratched and ink was pasted on them-simultaneously. This method was popular in South India. Hot atmosphere is harmful for palm leaves. The palm leaf manuscripts if kept in paper or cloth, is mutilated. In SORI only three palm leaf manuscripts are available.
- *Birch Barks Manuscripts:* Birch tree is found in Himachal Pradesh. Its inner bark is just like papers which were used for writing. Some times its length is found to be 60'. These were cut into pieces as per requirement and then were written with different inks. The manuscripts written on birch barks are generally found in Kashmir and north India. In SORI only 3 manuscripts of this type are available.
- *Paper Manuscripts:* It is said, that first of all, the paper was made by Chinese peoples. In ancient India also the paper was made. In our country, many types of papers are famous for writing, like Kashmiri, Moghulai, Ahmadabedi, Daulatabadi, etc. The paper used, was prepared by hand using different raw material like bamboo, cotton, etc. In SORI most of the manuscripts available are on paper. Leather, Cloth and Wooden manuscripts are not available at SORI.

Publications of Scindia Oriental Research Institute

The institute has published the following titles under the 'Scindia Oriental Series'

- *Tattvasara* (Marathi), 1936, 414p.
- *Alankara Manjusha* (Scindia Oriental Series no.1), 1940, 384p.
- *Ancient Jaina Hymns* (Scindia Oriental Series no.2), 1951, 178p.
- *Sastrattva Vinirnaya* (Scindia Oriental Series no.3), 1952, 136p.
- *Chikitsa Manjari* (Scindia Oriental Series no.4), 1959, 206p.
- *Journal of Scindia* Oriental Institute, Vol. I (1955) and Vol. II (1956).

- A descriptive catalogue of manuscripts in the Scindia Oriental Institute, Vol. II, (literature),
- Part-I, 1983, 282p. 8. A descriptive catalogue of manuscripts in the Scindia Oriental Institute, Vol. II, (literature), Part-II, 1985, 414p.

It may be noted that for some reasons Volume I (Vedic Sahitya) is not published and Volume III to XII ready but yet to publish.

In addition the following three Vikram volumes have been published in commemoration on the completion of 2000 years of Vikram era:

- Vikram Volume (English), 768p.
- Vikram Smriti Grantha (Hindi), 927p.
- Vikram Smriti Grantha (Marathi), 568p.

Micro-filming of Manuscript

Some 4190 manuscripts of importance have been microfilmed by Indira Gandhi National Centre for Arts (IGNCA) at SORI. One copy of the microfilm is available with SORI. The IGNCA has microfilmed 2,50,000 manuscripts in 66 libraries running to 11 million folio. Other manuscripts at SORI are yet to be microfilmed due to lack of staff though a microfilm processing unit is available. Department of culture, Govt. of India has started National Mission for Manuscripts which will convert manuscripts into electronic record as one of the activities.

Besides preparation of catalogue, search of manuscript in society through surveys and building up of a National Manuscript Library. The institutions have been provided fund to start the mission. ₹10 millions has been allocated to launch the mission. A total of ₹265 million is estimated for building, cataloguing, conservation, microfilming, and digitization starting from the year 2002-2007.

Besides ₹25 million will be spent on purchase of manuscript from the customers. SORI is recognized as Manuscript Resource Centre (MRC) for all Madhya Pradesh for the preparation of accession catalogue, launch awareness programme in society. In total 23 such MRCs have been recognized in India. Under the project SORI is getting grants and the preliminary work has started.

MANUSCRIPTS DIGITAZATION PROCESS

The digitization process at SORI is yet to start. In this section we have studied technologies available at present so that options can be selected at final stage. There are various options available for digitization of reading material. The re-typing is not possible in case of manuscripts. Scanning is the only possibility in case of manuscripts. It is nothing more than a picture of printed page in digital form. Digital imaging technology convert manuscripts into digital images and can be made available over electronic networks-a digital image is composed of set of pixels. The text can be retrieved, printed and modified using appropriate software. The scanning of manuscripts using computer image scanner is done carefully due to variations in text and colour and images. Aperture of can also be made by digital camera or other feasible imaging devices. The digital images can be captured at varied of density or bits pixel. Simple binary scanning in black and white is not always complete in digitizing manuscripts as coloured illustrations are also valuable with texts. Light and darkness of document is to be considered before digitization.

Colour images are more complex because they need encoding of shades. Resolution of image is measured in dot per inch (dpi). Higher dpi leads to better resolution and quality of image but larger image file. 300 to600 dpi are recommended for better resolutions. File compression is another important aspect because image capturing takes more space. Various types of scanners such as Flatbed, sheet feed, drum scanners and digital cameras are available to scan manuscripts. Mircofilm scanners are used to convert roll film, fiche into digitized form. Video Digitizer are also available now a days which may be also used for scanning.

DIGITIZATION EXPERIENCES

There have been few manuscripts digitization projects in the world to point problems and solutions of digitization of manuscripts. The experiences may be helpful in deciding technological options. A few experiences are given here. UNESCO project entitled "The Memory of the World" aim to initiate to support the safeguarding of existing document for future. Under the programme in 1993 first memory disk was published on two CD ROMs having digital form of two entire manuscripts that National Library of Czech Republic to test the possibility of digitization of manuscripts.

Latter more CDs were made. These two projects studied the problems of manuscripts digitization. Each image 2.40 MB and display of original image was very time consuming. More such experience was made to get high resolution. The present technology has enabled approximately 100 on a CD-ROM with full preservation of colour and passed resolutions. Manuscript digitization demonstration Project sponsored by Library of Congress is carried out in cooperation with National Library Digitization act. Digitization of Manuscript of the National Library of India undertook a pilot project entitled "Down Memory Lane" to digitize its rare and brittle books in 90's.

A local private agency was given the responsibility to scan and clean the documents. Between the year 1999 and 2001 approximately 6601 books/ manuscripts containing 2.5 million pages were scanned and archived in 548 CD-ROMs. National Library has 3000 volume of paper manuscripts and 334 palm leaf manuscripts in Arabic, Persian, Urdu, Bengali, English, Hindi, Tamil and Sanskrit language. Many of them with beautiful illustrations fine epigraphy and elegant bindings. The sample project was undertaken for the digitization of these manuscripts. The project was undertaken in collaboration with Trinetrix Technologies, Calcutta.

A Persian Manuscript – Tutinamah was sample project. The image was captured by a digital camera (Nikon D100 with bayonet mount 28-70mm f/ 2.8 ED–IF AF-S Zoom-Nikon lens) mounted vertically on the photographic copy stand (Bojen System 800 Repro Copy Stand W/bb 1740), with side illumination through 40 watts incandescent lamp. The background was chosen to be slightly lighter than the document colour in order to minimize shadow and optimize digital transfer. The digital camera had special colour metric filter that enabled the camera to capture a broader spectrum of colour than most digital scanners.

The lighting was also provided selectively from by two 1000-watt Elinchrome Strobe lights (daylight balance) at 45% angle to copy surface, with multiple diffusion filters between copy surface and light to soften shadows and reduce glare for specific pages with illustrations. The image processing station was a HP Brio, PC with Pentium IV processor, 128 MB DDRAM. The workstation had the image processing software like Kodak Imaging, Abode Photoshop 6. There was an image transfer device connected to the USB port, which gathered images from the memory card of the digital camera. The lighting environment was adjusted as per the specific requirement document using light meter.

The manuscript was set on the Photography copy stand bed opening it at angle of 120 degree to avoid the stress to the binding of the manuscript. The image was captured from the manuscript at the different aperture, focal length and shutter speed and the captured images were transferred to the image processing Station. Final images were at suitable Aperture Focal length shutter speed. First for all right hand side pose and then for all left hand side pages in colour as uncompressed 8 bit per channel (24 bit RGB) TIFF files at 300 dpi. The images were then transferred to the Image Processing Station. The files were converted to three basic formats as per the requirements namely, PDF, TIFF and JEPG.

The individual image PDF files were tagged and a composite PDF file was prepared as per the original document pagination and sequence. The images were stored in CD-ROMs and were made resident in hard disk of the central server. The images produced have minute tonal variations due to shade of colour and illustration. A white light is more helpful to minimize tonal variations. Software Adobe Photoshop version 6 is very resource consuming. From the experiment it is clear that digitization of manuscript is not as simple as one can understand as photocopying and scanning.

It is much more complicated need expertise, costly and time consuming. It requires costly digital cameras, work stations and high quality hardware and software. The images need to be as close to the original as possible, with removal of worm marks, stain marks. The images need to be clear and the details of the illustrations of pages have to be captured to the best possible extent. Cost-benefit analysis on the project with the long-term view on the scope of project in large scale is to be considered. The project estimations and determination of the time frame of completion of digitization of the entire collections of manuscripts is to be decided.

INSTITUTIONAL REPOSITORY OF INFLIBNET CENTRE USING DSPACE

INFLIBNET Information and Library Network is an Autonomous IUC of the University Grants Commission (UGC) started in 1991 with its Headquarters located at Gujarat University campus, Ahmedabad.

The Programme is directed towards modernization of libraries and Information centres, and establishment of a mechanism for information transfer and access, to support scholarship, learning and academic pursuits. It also aimed at establishing a National Network of Libraries and Information Centres in Universities, institutions of higher learning and R & D Institution in India. It is basically a co-operative endeavour in resource development, sharing and its utilization at national level.

The main objective being to evolve a National Network, interconnecting various Libraries and Information Centers in Universities, deemed universities, colleges, UGC information centers, Institutions of National importance and R&D institu-tions, the centre has taken the initiative of building Dspace INFLIBNET an Institutional Repository using the open source software Dspace to support the long term preservation of the digital material for the Academic community.

So far the centre has already hosted the CALIBER proceedings, Course materials, Newspaper clipping etc. The Academic community can also submit their resourceful articles in this repository centre and preserved it for future use. The building of an Institutional Repository is needed in the present scenario of digital world because of the following certain changes:

- Technological changes.
- Significant increase in the overall volume of research.
- Increasing dissatisfaction especially on the part of Librarians with traditional print and electronic journals price and market model that have become less relevant and more difficult to sustain in a period of rapidly escalating prices and relatively flat library budgets.
- Increase uncertainty over who will handle the preservation archiving of digital scholarly research materials.

All these factors have evolved and combined to create new expectations in the Academic community for the production, distribution and interchange of scholarly communication and to force a rethinking of the relative roles of authors, librarians and publishers as well as the possibility of entirely new actors who will emerge as the publishing model. In such an environment Institutional repository might act well to preserve an Institutional intellectual work product.

INSTITUTIONAL REPOSITORY

An Institutional repository is a digital archive of the intellectual output of an Academic Institution. It makes the quality and breath of scholarship produced at that Institution accessible to others world wide over the internet. It is a set of services that a University/Organization offers to the members of its community for the management and dissemination of digital material created by the institution and its community members. It is most essentially an organizational commitment to the stewardship of the digital materials including long term preservation.

An effective Institutional repository of necessity represents collaboration among librarians, Information technologies, archives and record managers, faculty and University administrators and policy makers. At any given point in time, an Institutional repository will be supported by a set of Information technologies but a key part of the services that comprises an Institutional repository is the management of technological changes and the migration of digital content from one set of the technology to the next as a part of the organizational commitment providing repository services.

The basic and fundamental level of an Institutional repository is that it is a recognition that the intellectual life and scholarship of an University will increasingly be represented documented and shared in digital form and that a primary responsibility of our University is to exercise stewardship over these riches both to make available and to preserve them. It is the mean by which a University/Organization will address the responsibility both to the members of their communities and to the public. It is a new channel for structuring the University contribution to the border world and as such invites policy and cultural reassessment of this relationship.

IMPORTANCE OF INSTITUTIONAL REPOSITORIES

Institutional repositories centralize, preserve and make accessible the knowledge generated by Academic Institution. It also form part of a larger global system of repositories which indexed in standardizes way and searchable using one interface, providing the foundation for a new model of scholarly publishing. Institutional repositories often employ a method of article submission known as author self-archiving and rely on user communities to control the input of content.

These can include academic departments; research centers administrative groups and other sub-group who will determine what content merits inclusion and act as arbiters for their own research communities. Author self-archiving is the broad term often applied to the electronic posting of author-supplied research without publisher mediation. It involves a simple web interface where the depositors types or copy/pastes in the metadata and then attaches the full text documents. Institutional repositories also have roles beyond disseminating and managing the works of individuals scholars that are part of the dialog of scholarly communication and it is also a place where we can put much of the material that research libraries identify as worth collecting and they offer a frame-work for organized stewardship and accessibility of these materials. It can encourage the exploration and adoption of new forms of scholarly communication that exploit the digital medium in fundamental way.

They can support new practices of scholarship that emphasizes data as an Integral part of the record and discourse of scholarship. They can structure and make effective otherwise diffuse efforts to capture and disseminate learning and teaching materials symposia and performances and related documentation of the intellectual life of Universities. Institutional repositories benefit both the Institution and its scholars by raising the Institutional profile while also bringing broader.

Dissemination, increased use and enhanced professional visibility of scholarly research others benefits are:

- Improved visibility and impact-Institutional, National;
- Contribute to institutional knowledge management;
- Improve Research collaboration-interdependent, inter-Institutional, International;
- Enhanced status and reputation;
- Enhanced research capacity.

Realizing the needs of the scholars and the benefits of building an Institutional Repository Centre the INFLIBNET (Information and Library Network Centre) being the nodal point of all the Indian University has started this Institutional Repository Centre called Dspace INFLIBNET using the open source software package dspace developed by MIT and Hewlett-Packard (H P).

DSPACE

Dspace is an open source software platform that enables institution to:

- Capture and describe digital works using a sub-mission workflow module;
- Distribute an institutions digital works over the web through a search and retrieval system;
- Preserve digital works over the long term.
- The mission is to create and establish an electronic system that captures, preserve and communicates the intellectual output.

The vision is a federation of system that makes available the collective intellectual resources of the world leading research Institution. It supports all manner of digital format (*e.g.* Articles, preprint, working paper, technical reports, and conference papers).

- Books
- Thesis
- Datasets

- Computer programmes
- Visualization, simulation and other models
- Multimedia publication
- Learning objects.
- The other facilities which are available in this open source software package are:
- Browse
- Search
- Advance search
- Communities
- Collection
- Sign on to Dspace
- Submit
- File format
- My Dspace
- Edit profile
- Subscribe to e-mail alerts

INSTITUTIONAL REPOSITORIES, OPEN ACCESS MOVEMENT AND OAI-PMH COMPLAINT SOFTWARE

Institutional repositories of scholarly content have been receiving increasing attention recently. The main purposes of institutional repositories are to bring together and preserve the intellectual output of a university. The number of signifi-cant developments, such as the launch of MIT's Dspace, University of California's eScholarship and the growth of repositories based on the University of Southampton's EPrint software, have brought the issue of institutional repositories increasingly to the fore.

Further the open access and open archives movement and the changes in scholarly communication to remove barriers to access have begun driving the establishment of institutional repositories.

Keeping in view the recent changes in scholarly communication, emergence and various standards and protocols, and trend towards open access INFLIBNET being a national Centre for library and information Centre too is exploring the possibility of institutional repository and archiving faculty publication of universities in India.

During the course of development of experts database and research projects database of academic and scientific community in India, it was observed that faculty generates enormous amount of information, which is untapped and not available for access. These content needs to be managed, preserved, and maintained for larger access to the users. Faculty members want additional visibility for their resources. INFLIBNET in future aims to provide a comprehensive system for managing these resources and play a pivotal role of repositories of these valuable resources. In this direction, Centre has opted Dspace open source software for achieving institutional publications including CALIBER and PLANNER proceeding.

WHAT IS INSTITUTIONAL REPOSITORIES

An institutional repository (IR) is a digital collection of a university's intellectual output. Institutional repositories centralize, preserve, and make accessible the knowledge generated by academic institutions. IRs also form part of a larger global system of repositories, which are indexed in a standardized way, and searchable using one interface, providing the foundation for a new model of scholarly publishing.

An institutional repository (IR) is defined to be a web-based database (repository) of scholarly material, which is institutionally defined as opposed to a subject-based repo-sitory; cumulative and perpetual (a collection of record); open and interoperable (*e.g.* using OAI-compliant software); and thus collects, stores and disseminates. In addition, most would include long-term preservation of digital materials as a key function of IRs.

Definition

Despite of the amount of press that the topic of institu-tional repositories has received in the past few years, providing a concrete, precise definition of an institutional repository (IR) is difficult to do. Clifford Lynch (2003), executive director of the Coalition for Networked Information, describes an IR as "a set of services that a university offers to the members of its community for the management and dissemination of digital materials created by the institution and its community members." Other than replacing "a university" with "an organization," this definition reflects how IRs are discussed in this report. Lynch's definition is particularly appropriate because services, and not technologies, are the emphasis. Nevertheless, even with this definition in hand, the question remains: what exactly comprises this "set of services" to which Lynch refers? Unfortunately, this question has no single, correct answer because an institutional repository must be *institutionally defined.*

To be successful an IR must provide the set of services needed by its unique community of users, and these services will and should differ from institution to institution. The SPARC position paper on IRs has been influential in setting the agenda for the IR debate.

Crow argues that there are two key rationales for IRs:

- Reform of scholarly communication, and in particular scholarly publishing;
- To enable the institution to enhance its prestige by making visible the fruits of its faculty's academic and research labours.

CORE FEATURES OF INSTITUTIONAL REPOSITORIES

Despite this ambiguity, all IRs share some common features and functions, and it is this combination of features and functions that distinguishes IRs from other types of services. The first of five common features, and perhaps most obvious, is that an IR contains digital content. The range of different types of digital content can be vast, including text, audio, video, images, learning objects, and datasets. The material may be born digital or of a physical medium that has been digitized, such as scanned images. A second core feature of an IR is that it is community driven and community-focused.

The community of users not only determines what should be deposited into the IR, but they are individually responsible for making the deposits. The members of the community also are the authors and copyright owners of the content. As a result, the IR reflects or showcases the scholarship, research, and interests of an organization. A third core feature is that the IR has institutional support. An institutional repository is not a simple or cheap undertaking.

A successful IR requires collaboration among divisions across an institution, which is accomplished most easily with top-down institutional support. Moreover, an IR necessitates ongoing, long-term financial support to ensure, for instance, the integrity of the content through digital preservation. Without an institutional commitment to the project, the costs and obligation of an IR likely are too great for any one department or unit to bear on its own.

An assumption of durability and permanence is the fourth common feature of an IR. When a digital file is deposited into an institutional repository, the author expects that the document will remain there for the perceivable future. Finally, an IR is not a black archive; the content in an IR is not hidden from the entire world. With some exceptions, the content of an IR can be accessed by more than just the content's owner because the material within an IR is meant to be shared. Access can vary greatly from just a few people within a department to the entire world, but the cost and scale of an IR discourages its use as a person's private, digital dumping ground.

ISSUES FOR INSTITUTIONAL REPOSITORIES

There are various issues which needs to be properly addressed before establishing any Institutional Repositories.

The main issues for establishing are:

- *Cultural Issues Affecting Faculty Take-up:* The biggest problem facing those setting up IRs is persuading faculty to use and contribute the content from them. Outside a few disciplines (*e.g.* physics, computer science and economics) there is little tradition of preprints or working papers and apparently still little interest in self-archiving. There is a great deal of inertia in the current publishing systems. The organisers of IRs need money for advocacy (marketing campaigns, meetings, flyers, websites, e-mails, etc.), for training users and producing guidelines, and for ensuring the interface design does not put off potential users.

- *Intellectual Property Rights/Copyright:* Institutional repositories raise issues of rights-not just copyright but other intellectual property rights such as patent rights. The copyright issues have been extensively reviewed by the RoMEO project, in UK. As RoMEO notes, there are rights associated with metadata as well as with the content itself.
- *Existing Digital Collections:* New IRs at most organisations will have to take account of existing collections. Some of these *viz.* personal self-archiving websites may be best source for the IR
- *Organisation and Administration:* Who will manage the IR? Where will it be located? What will be the rela-tionship between the centre and the departments?
- *Funding/business Model:* How will the IR be funded, and what business model will it adopt?
- *Preservation:* This is very important issue. The long-term preservation of digital objects are very far from solved.
- *Accession Policies:* The IR has to decide:
  - Who is allowed to deposit materials;
  - What types of materials can be deposited (*e.g.* pre-prints, post-prints, working papers, theses, chapters, datasets, etc.);
  - What digital formats will be accepted (and which formats will be migrated);
  - Quality assurance procedures (*e.g.* none, or approval by departmental head, or even peer review);
  - Storage limits etc.
- *Open Access:* Although IRs can be seen as part of the open access movement, this is not necessarily the case. IRs may well want to restrict access to part of their content to their own network only.
- *Central vs. Institutional Repositories:* This argument is somewhat theological. Central, subject-based repositories have been very successful in a few fields (physics, computer science, economics, cognitive science) but have failed so far to migrate to other disciplines. Institutional repositories may offer a new route to reduce the inertia among the non-archiving communities. From the perspective of a web-based searcher (*i.e.* reader), however, there is (in theory) no difference between the two repositories, as articles are discovered on the basis of metadata independent of location (author, title or whatever), collected via the same OAI protocol. The searcher would be using an interface on a third party site, *i.e.* an OAI service provider. In practice, of course, there are significant benefits in centralised systems, for instance in terms of standardisation, single metadata schemes, etc.
- *Metadata:* Without at least some metadata, nothing can be found. But too comprehensive a metadata requirement will inhibit users. Decisions also have to be taken on which metadata schemes to use.

Metadata requirements may vary from field to field. Most of existing repositories are using Dublin core Metadata scheme.

WHAT IS THE BENEFIT OF INSTITUTIONAL REPOSITORIES

Institutional repositories benefit both the institution and its scholars by raising the institutional profile while also bringing broader dissemination, increased use, and enhanced professional visibility of scholarly research. The main reason for universities to have institutional repositories is to impact of the research output of the university, its publishing faculty, and the institution itself.

Few broader aspects of benefits of IRs are listed below:

- Researchers benefit through wider (and more rapid) dissemination of their work, resulting in more "research impact".
- PG and UG students benefit, as university publica-tions are readily accessible via the institution's virtual learning environment, library system and institutional portal.
- The university benefits from a higher profile by making all output publicly (and freely) available.
- The university benefits by having a comprehensive managed and preserved record of its research output.

WHY INSTITUTIONAL REPOSITORIES

There has been a convergence of technology develop-ments and other initiatives that have made IRs possible. Technology costs, especially storage costs, have dropped significantly so that repositories are now affordable. Standards such as the open archives metadata harvesting protocol are in place and work is being done on the metadata itself. Awareness of the needs for, and challenges of, digital preservation has accelerated. Developments in web publishing such as open archives initiatives, open access journals and disciplinary archives are pointing the way to opportunities to enhance scholarly publishing.

The launch of the DSpace IR at MIT in November 2002 and the subsequent release of the DSpace software under an open source license have been seen as a seminal event and a trigger for the development of IRs. However the release of the EPrint software from Southampton University in January 2001 predated this by nearly two years and at present there are more functioning IRs running on EPrints than on the DSpace platform.

THE OPEN-ACCESS MOVEMENT

For some years now there has been a movement towards "open access" to academic publications. This argues that sources of scholarly information, usually in the form of articles, should be freely available to all on the internet. The establish-ment of repositories contributes towards easy open-access publishing online. By ensuring that access to the results of academic research is not confined solely to subscribers to expensive journals, it allows them to reach a much wider audience. There are over 20,000 peer-reviewed scholarly journals in existence; no academic library can come anywhere near stocking even a tiny proportion of titles appropriate to the needs of the research staff in an institution.

This being the case, individual scholars cannot get access to some – perhaps much – of the literature that is pertinent to their work with the result that the efficient exchange of scholarly information is impaired. To exacerbate this problem, over the last two decades the so-called 'serials crisis' has become a more and more acute issue. Journal prices have risen faster than both the rate of inflation and the increases in library budgets, resulting in the cancellation of subscriptions to journals in large numbers.

This has happened all over the world and India universities have been no exception: indeed, it is there that the problem has been seen to be most extreme. Data collected by the Association of Research Libraries show that in the 16 years between 1986 and 2002, inflation rose by 64% (in the US), library materials budgets rose by 184% and serials unit costs rose by 227%.

One way in which publishers have reacted to the seriousness of the serials crisis has been by developing the 'Big Deal' whereby parts or all of a publisher's journal list were offered to a library (or a group of libraries within a consortium) at a price that equated to less per journal than the library had originally been paying but which included journals that had not been required. These practices seem to conflict with the aims of scientists and scholars who, it is argued, primarily publish research papers for research impact, *i.e.* in having their work read, cited and built on in the research of others. This lead to the open access initiative and movement.

Open Access Initiatives

In the last three years there have been several key events that serve as milestones for the movement. In December 2001, the Open Society Institute organised a meeting in Budapest to assess the state of play on open access and to see how the various initiatives up to that point could be progressed. The outcome of this meeting was the Budapest Open Access Initiative (BOAI). This took the form of a public statement in support of open access for scholarly journal articles. In addition, a website was launched in February 2002 where supporters could add their signatures.

The Budapest Initiative formally announced its endorse-ment of two strategies for open access–the establishment of open access journals and self-archiving by scholars of their work. The Budapest Open Access Initiative defines open access as: "free availability on the internet, permitting users to read, download, copy, distribute, print, search, or link to the full texts of these articles, crawl them for indexing, pass them as data to software, or use them for any other lawful purpose, without financial, legal, or technical barriers other than those inseparable from gaining access to the internet itself.

The only constraint on reproduction and distribution, and the only role for copyright in this domain, should be to give authors control over the integrity of their work and the right to be properly acknowledged and cited. Even mainland Europe is getting in on the act. In October 2003, the leading research associations of Germany, France and Switzerland signed what has become known as the "Berlin Declaration"—another call for free access to research findings. One of the groups behind the declaration, Germany's Max Planck Society, is now changing its employment contracts to require staff to return the copyright of their work to the society.

At the moment it gets assigned to the publishers. Although the society's researchers will still be able to publish in journals, their work must eventually be put into an online repository. The Open Society Institute continues to donate resources to the open access movement The Budapest Open Access Initiative and later Berlin Declaration promote the development of open access electronic journals and digital repositories, free to anyone with internet access.

It may be possible in some fields to support open access journals by authors or research funding bodies covering the costs with article fees, following the economic model of BioMed central and the Public Library of Science. For example, BioMed Central currently charge $500 per paper as an 'article processing charge,' while the PLoS initiative has estimated that authors will be asked to pay around $1,500 per paper when their journals become available sometime in 2003.

A US House of Representatives committee has recomm-ended that the National Institutes of Health (NIH) provide free access to all research it funds and asked the NIH to submit a plan by December 1, 2004 for how to implement the new policy in fiscal year 2005. UK parliament Science and Technology Committee recommended Open Access self archiving of funded research. The Australian Government has recently done the same for Australian universities along with numerous other institutions around the world.

SPARC (The Scholarly Publishing and Academic Resources Coalition) has recently proposed a hybrid model, whereby each article in a journal would be made electronically available only to subscribers, unless its author chooses to pay, in which case it would be freely available to all. There are other subject specific model *viz.*, covering physics, mathematics and computer science repository operated by Cornell University.

This was set up at the Los Alamos National Laboratory (LANL) in the early 1990s to facilitate the communication requirements of high-energy physicists. Now based at Cornell University, it remains one of the largest e-print repositories with almost 230,000 papers, growing by more than 30,000 per year. Other subject-based e-print repositories exist, *e.g.* for cognitive sciences (CogPrints) or chemistry (the Elsevier-run Chemistry Preprint Server), but there is now a growing interest in the creation of interoperable repositories based on research or educational institutions.

Today, about 5% of academic publishing follows the open-access model. But the model is quickly gaining ground, including among both for-profit (BioMedCentral-BMC) and not-for-profit (Public Library of Science PloS) publishers. In fact, more than 80% of conventional journals already allow their authors to deposit their postprints in OA repositories. Most OA repositories are interoperable in the sense that users can search them without knowing which repositories exist, where they are located, or what they contain.

TECHNICAL DEVELOPMENTS

The existence of institutional repositories has been made possible by the development of standards and tools that facilitate interoperability between multiple repositories. The most important of these is the Open Archives Initiative Protocol for Metadata Harvesting (OAI-PMH). The OAI-PMH was developed from the 'Santa Fe Convention' agreed at the initial meeting of the Open Archives Initiative (OAI) in 1999. Version 1.0 of the protocol was issued in January 2001; the latest version (Version 2.0) being released in June 2002. The protocol provides an interoperability framework based on the harvesting of metadata.

To that end, it defines a simple set of metadata that can facilitate federated resource discovery. The protocol divides users of the OAI-PMH into two main categories: Version 1.0 of the OAI-PMH was released in January 2001 for experimental use, the latest in June 2002. A growing number of open-source software tools that help support the implementation of the protocol are now becoming available. For data providers, the most important of these are the University of Southampton's EPrints software and MIT Libraries's DSpace system.

WHAT IS OAI-PMH

The OAI-Protocol for Metadata Harvesting (OAI-PMH) defines a mechanism for harvesting records containing metadata from repositories. The OAI-PMH gives a simple technical option for data providers to make their metadata available to services, based on the open standards HTTP (Hypertext Transport Protocol) and XML (Extensible Markup Language). The metadata that is harvested may be in any format that is agreed by a community (or by any discrete set of data and service providers), although unqualified Dublin Core is specified to provide a basic level of interoperability.

Thus, metadata from many sources can be gathered together in one database, and services can be provided based on this centrally harvested, or "aggregated" data. The link between this metadata and the related content is not defined by the OAI protocol. It is important to realise that OAI-PMH does not provide a search across this data, it simply makes it possible to bring the data together in one place.

In order to provide services, the harvesting approach must be combined with other mechanisms. Open Archives Initiative Protocol for Metadata Harvesting is a protocol which facilitates access to heterogenous web-accessible material from various repositories. The Open Archives Initiative develops and promotes interoperability standards that aim to facilitate the efficient dissemination of content. The OAI protocol provides access to metadata from OAI-compliant repositories.

There are two classes of participants in the OAI-PMH framework:

- Data Providers administer systems that support the AI-PMH as a means of exposing metadata; and
- Service Providers use metadata harvested via the OAI-PMH as a basis for building value added services.

"OAI-compliant" means that the archive complies with the metadata harvesting protocol of the Open Archives Initiative (OAI). This makes the archive interoperable with other compliant archives so that the many separate archives behave like one grand, virtual archive for purposes such as searching. This means that users can search across OAI-compliant archives without visiting the separate archives and running separate searches. Hence, it makes your content more visible, even if users don't know that your archive exists or what it contains.

SOFTWARE

There are a handful of open-source packages for creating and maintaining such archives. The four most important are eprints (from Southampton University), DSpace (from MIT), CDSWare (from CERN), and FEDORA (from Cornell and U. of Virginia). In addition to this there are few more software, which is being used for archiving. I have listed them with brief description, these are:

Arno

The ARNO project—Academic Research in the Netherlands Online—has developed software to support the implementation of institutional repositories and link them to distributed repositories worldwide (as well as to the Dutch national information infrastructure). The project is funded by IWI (Dutch acronym for: Innovation in Scientific Information Supply). Project participants are the University of Amsterdam, Tilburg University and the University of Twente. The ARNO system was released for public use in December 2003. It has been in use at the universities of Tilburg, Amsterdam, Rotterdam, Twente and Maastricht.

CERN Document Server Software (CDSware)

The CERN Document Server Software (CDSware) was developed to support the CERN Document Server. The software is maintained and made publicly available by CERN and supports electronic preprint servers, online library catalogues, and other web-based document depository systems. CERN uses CDSware to manage over 450 collections of data, comprising over 620,000 bibliographic records and 250,000 full-text documents, including preprints, journal articles, books, and photographs. CDSware was built to handle very large repositories holding disparate types of materials, including multimedia content catalogues, museum object descriptions, confidential and public sets of documents, etc. Each release is tested live under the rigors of the CERN environment before being publicly released.

DSpace

The DSpace software has been purpose built in collaboration between Hewlett Packard and MIT to offer IR services. It is specifically designed to manage diverse heterogeneous types of digital content. It offers interoperability via OAI-MHP (Open Archive Initiative–Metadata Harvesting Protocol–a software standard that allows specialised search engines to gather article metadata from compliant websites) and built-in support for Dublin Core metadata (Dublin Core is an agreed metadata standard used in library cataloguing and elsewhere, though other metadata schemes are possible). It uses persistent identifiers (which are like URLs but have the benefit that unlike ordinary URLs they do not change when the linked document's physical location is changed) via the CNRI Handle system.

Eprints

The Eprints software has the largest and most broadly distributed installed base of any of the repository software systems described here. Developed at the University of South-ampton, the first version of the system was publicly released in late 2000. The project was originally sponsored by CogPrints, but is now supported by JISC as part of the Open Citation Project and by NSF. Eprints worldwide installed base affords an extensive support network for new implemen-tations. The size of the installed base for Eprints suggests that an institution can get it up and running relatively quickly and with a minimum of technical expertise. The number of Eprints installations that have augmented the system's baseline capabilities—for example, by integrating advanced search, extended metadata, and other features—indicates that the system can be readily modified to meet local requirements.

Fedora

The Fedora digital object repository management system is based on the Flexible Extensible Digital Object and Repository Architecture (Fedora). The system is designed to be a foundation upon which fullfeatured institutional repositories and other interoperable web-based digital libraries can be built. Jointly developed by the University of Virginia and Cornell University, the system implements the Fedora architecture, adding utilities that facilitate repository manage-ment. The current version of the software provides a repository that can handle one million objects efficiently. Subsequent versions of the software will add functionality important for institutional repository implementations, such as policy enforcement, versioning of objects, and performance enhancement to support very large repositories.

i-TOR

i-Tor — Tools and technologies for Open Repositories—was developed by the Innovative Technology-*Applied* (IT-*A*) section of Netherlands Institute for Scientific Information Services (Dutch acronym: NIWI). NIWI calls i-TOR "a web technology by which various types of information can be presented through a web interface," irrespective of where the data is stored or the format in which it is stored. i-Tor aims to implement a "data independent" repository, where the content and the user-interface function as two independent parts of the system.

In essence, i-Tor acts as both an OAI service provider, able to harvest OAI compatible repositories and other databases, and an OAI data provider. Because i-Tor is able to publish data from a variety of relational databases, file systems, and websites, the system allows an institution considerable latitude in the way it organizes its repository. It can create new databases for the repository, but it can also use already existing relational databases. Further, i-Tor supports harvesting of data directly from a researcher's personal home page Because of this design, i-Tor does not enforce a specific workflow on a group or subgroup. Rather, i-Tor gives an institution tools (for example, fine grained security, notification, etc.) to set up any required workflow required by the organization, without integrating this workflow into the i-Tor system itself. i-Tor's design might make it an appropriate choice for an institution that wishes to impose a repository on top of an existing set of disparate digital repositories.

MyCoRe

MyCoRe grew out of the MILESS Project of the University of Essen. The MyCoRe system is now being developed by a consortium of universities to provide a core bundle of software tools to support digital libraries and archiving solutions (or Content Repositories, thus "CoRe"). The bundle is designed to be configurable and adaptable to local requirements (hence, the "My"), without the need for local programming efforts.

In contrast to MILESS, which provides a hard-coded Qualified Dublin Core data model, the MyCoRe data model is completely configurable. Further, MyCoRe provides a sample application, based upon a "core" of functionality, that shows users how to build their own applications using metadata configuration files. The core contains all the functionality that would be required in a repository implementation, including distributed search over geographically dispersed repositories, OAI functionality, audio/video streaming support, file management, online metadata editors etc.

INSTITUTIONAL REPOSITORY AND ROLE OF INFLIBNET

In India most of the research is being funded and supported by the Government. The software for implemen-tation of IR is available free of cost and has been used to establish an e-print archive at very few institutions. The prominent among are the Indian Institute of Science and DRTC. The US and UK openaccess proposals are inspiring and encouraging steps for other countries. In UK, JISC has funded number of e-print repositories.

A US House of Representatives committee has recomm-ended that the National Institutes of Health (NIH) provide free access to all research it funds and asked the NIH to submit a plan by December 1, 2004 for how to implement the new policy in fiscal year 2005. In our country, we too need such initiative and we should move towards open access. In last one decade INFLIBNET has published reasonable amount of content in the form of database on it's central server. The foundation of repositories has already been established at the Centre, it further aims to provide many more potential services to support academics. On experimental basis, INFLIBNET has configured DSpace software and content is being archived. Establishing IR though seems very simple but while implementing it has been observed that collection of content and faculty participation and pursuing them to submit the content are major issues. Thus success and failure of IR is reply upon these two factors. In order to implement IR successfully, we need to study the existing model of IR and adopt best model for universities in India. It is need of ours to develop a series of national, discipline-focused services through which the higher education community can access the collective output of e-print papers available from compliant Open Archive reposi-tories, particularly those provided by universities. A policy and strategy in collaboration with UGC and universities has to be framed and faculties need to take the lead in ensuring that their papers are suitably archived. INFLIBNET can play major role by establishing central/discipline based repositories and fecilitate to create and maintain these archieve. UGC and other funding agencies should put a condition on research grants to submit the finding of research in to central repositories. When a grant recipient publishes the results of funded research in a journal, pre-print of the article should be submitted to INFLIBNET central repository.

Similarly, faculty courseware and submission of full text of Phd Theses in digital form from universities at central repository should also be made available from INFLIBNET. Long-term preservation of these content has to be addressed by framing a policy with proper guidelines, involving UGC, INFLIBNET and universities so that repository can offer digital hosting, preservation and more effective web dissemination to the users.

8

Implementation of Automated Library Management System

AN INTRODUCTION

Since, the 1960s, libraries have used technology in general, and computers in particular, to automate a wide range of administrative, public, and technical services tasks. Designed as an overview of major facets of automation activity, this chapter surveys the current state of computer applications in six areas of library work: circulation control, descriptive cataloguing, catalogue maintenance and production, reference service, acquisitions, and serials control. For each area, the discussion briefly indicates the motives for automation and describes current dominant approaches, citing examples of representative products and services.

CIRCULATION CONTROL

Library interest in automated circulation control is, in large part, based on a long-standing awareness of the problems inherent in manual circulation systems. These problems include labour-intensive and time-consuming record keeping work routines, inaccuracy, high personnel turnover, an inability to generate statistics about circulation activity, and the lack of an interface between circulation files and other library files which contain much the same bibliographic data. Circulation control is one of the most widely automated library operations, and it is often the first and simplest activity to be automated in a given library, possibly because circulation control systems bear an obvious resemblance to inventory management, retail charge card operations, and other transaction processing activities which have been successfully automated in general business applications.

While specific circulation policies and procedures may be subject to considerable local variation, the major component of circulation control-the check-out/check-in procedure—is typically performed in a straight forward manner that is easily understood by computer application developers and systems analysts lacking formal library training. As library users, many data processing professionals have experienced the circulation activity firsthand and are at least broadly familiar with its purpose and nature. Because the bibliographic data required for automated circulation control are often less extensive and complex than those required to computerise such activities as cataloguing and acquisitions, data conversion costs, software development time, and storage requirements may be substantially reduced. Perhaps more than any other library activity, the historical development of automated circulation control has reflected changes in state- of-the-art data processing technology.

Through the mid-1970s, most automated circulation control systems were custom-developed for a single library or library system. As early as the 1930s and extending into the 1960s, a number of libraries used keypunched cards in combination with sorters, collators, and other unit record equipment as an alternative to manual record keeping. Tabulating keypunched cards with information about books, borrowers, and due dates could be sorted to select overdue items or to identify all books on loan to a given person. Such 'precomputer' data processing systems, several of which were developed for academic libraries by methods and procedures analysts and operations research specialists, were typically based on inventory control models used in business.

With the introduction of computers for business applications in the mid-1960s, a number of libraries developed computerised circulation control systems based on batch processing techniques. Such systems were usually implemented on a computer located in a data processing centre operated by a university, municipality, corporation, or government agency with which the library was affiliated. In the typical installation, keypunch or key-to-tape devices were used to convert information about individual circulation transactions to computer-processible form.

The resulting data were then hatched for processing at predetermined intervals, a computer writing individual borrower numbers into item records contained in a master circulation file maintained on magnetic tape and printing a list of all items in circulation for library reference. While some of these batch-processing circulation control systems remain in use, they are now mainly of interest for their limitations and impact on the design of subsequent systems. As a particular disadvantage, the printed lists produced by batch-processing systems necessarily reflect the status of a library's circulating collection at the time when the last batch of transaction records was processed. Part of the information contained in such lists is necessarily invalidated by circulation transactions occurring after that time. By the mid-l970s, library automation specialists had begun to concentrate on the development of online, real-time circulation control systems which process circulation transactions as they occur. Because pertinent data files are updated immediately, such real-time systems accurately reflect the status of a library's circulating collection. Printed lists are replaced by online terminal enquiries to determine the circulation status of specific items.

While real-time circulation control systems have been custom- developed for individual libraries, a number of vendors offer generalised, preformulated approaches to the computerisation of circulation control that eliminate the need for customised system development and speed the implementation process.

Such preformulated approaches, currently the dominant method of automating circulation control, can be divided into two related groups:

- Prewritten circulation control software intended for execution on a computer system operated by or for a given library; and
- Turnkey systems, consisting of preconfigured combinations of hardware and software marketed as self-contained products.

Introduced in the early 1970s, the earliest prewritten circulation control software packages and turnkey circulation systems were single-purpose products designed specifically and exclusively for library circulation activities. While such single-purpose systems remain available, library administrators, systems analysts, automation planners, and pro- duct developers are increasingly emphasising integrated, multifunctional turnkey systems and software packages which combine circulation control with other capabilities.

In addition to circulation control, the most complete integrated system implementations include interrelated application modules for cataloguing, online catalogue access by library users and/or staff, acquisitions, and serials control, a community bulletin board system, and electronic message transmission. In some cases, circulation is a standard integrated system component which may be implemented alone or in conjunction with other functions; in others, circulation control is an optional application module which must be purchased separately. Whether designed as single-purpose products or as integrated system components, prewritten circulation software packages and turnkey systems can be implemented far more quickly than customised circulation control systems which may require months or perhaps years to develop. Speed of implementation is an especially important consideration in applications where automation of the circulation activity will result in a cost reduction.

Similarly, prewritten software packages and turnkey systems minimize or eliminate requirements for local software expertise. Libraries acquiring such products usually do not need to hire programmers. In fact, customer programming is specifically prohibited by most vendors. Because the system design is predetermined, user training is limited to operational considerations. As a distinctive advantage of turnkey implementations, procurement-related tasks are greatly simplified by the availability of a preconfigured combination of hardware and software components that are specifically designed to work together. With a single source for central processing equipment and peripheral devices, the necessity of dealing with multiple hardware vendors is eliminated, as are potential problems of equipment compatibility.

While prewritten circulation control software packages are available for computers of all types and sizes, medium-sized and larger public and academic libraries have typically relied on mainframe—and minicomputer-based products. Examples for IBM mainframes include the NOTIS software package, originally developed by Northwestern University for its own use; IBM's own DOBIULIBIS programme; and the TECHLIB/STATS implementation of the BASIS software package which is marketed by the Information Dimensions subsidiary of Battelle.

Originally developed by libraries in the Minnesota State University system, the PALS software package is marketed by Unisys for use with its own mainframe computers, while the LIAS system, developed by Pennsylvania State University, operates on Honeywell computers. Examples of circulation software packages for popular minicomputer systems include Comstow's Bibliotech system for Digital Equipment's VAX product line; the Georgetown Library Information System (LIS) for Digital's PDP-11 Series models; the Washington University BACS system for Data General and other minicomputers which run under the MIIS operating environment; and the VTLS and Index systems for the Hewlett-Packard HP-3000 product line. Minicomputer- based turnkey circulation control systems are available from CLSI, Geac, Data Research Associates (DRA), Dynix, OCLC, Universal Library Systems, and other vendors. Reasonably priced and designed for readily available hardware configurations, microcomputer-based circulation control programmes have proven particularly popular with small public, school, and special libraries. Vendors include Follett, Gaylord, Easy Data, Data Trek, Aball Software, Nichols Advanced Technologies, Scribe Software, Winnebago Software, and Richmond Software. While the earliest circulation control programmes and turnkey systems forced libraries to accept predetermined loan periods, borrower categories, and other operating parameters, most newer products flexibly support a varied range of library requirements.

Unlike earlier systems which contained rigidly coded procedures to control charging, discharging, and related activities, all newer products are parameterised, *i.e.*, they allow libraries to specify the conditions under which items will be circulated, file enquiries made, and printed output produced. Rather than being written into programmes, particular operating parameters are selected by libraries from a range of possibilities. The resulting flexibility broadens the range of applications which a given system can address and is particularly important in installations where a single prewritten software package or turnkey system will be shared by many libraries.

AUTOMATED CATALOGUING

Descriptive cataloguing is an intellectual activity requiring considerable decision-making and one that is time-consuming. As a result, many libraries experience cataloguing backlogs which impede the flow of materials into circulating and reference collections thereby preventing library catalogues from representing those collections fully and accurately. Recognising that the cost of descriptive cataloguing can approach or even exceed the value of certain materials, many libraries do not catalogue paperbound books, low-cost government publications, or other relatively inexpensive items.

In some research libraries, materials of presumably limited interest may be placed in off-site storage facilities with only an abbreviated catalogue record created. In most libraries, conventional descriptive cataloguing is not even considered for individual titles in large microform sets, even though such materials may significantly augment a library's resources in particular subject areas, and the failure to catalogue them impairs their utility. To simplify decision-making, to save time, and to reduce costs associated with descriptive cataloguing, libraries have historically relied on cataloguing copy, *i.e.*, descriptive cataloguing information prepared by other libraries, especially the Library of Congress.

The automation of descriptive cataloguing depends on the availability of such cataloguing copy in computer-processible form. In the late 1960s, the Library of Congress developed the MARC format for the communication of bibliographic data on magnetic tape and began distributing machine- readable cataloguing copy through its MARC Distribution Service. Since, the late 1960s, MARC formats have been developed for various types of library materials, and the scope of the MARC programme-once limited to English-language monographs—has broadened steadily and significantly. The LC MARC database-the accumulation of Library of Congress cataloguing data in machine-readable form-now contains more than 2.5 million records, most of them catalogued since, the inception of the MARC programme.

Although MARC tapes can be purchased from the Library of Congress for input to local computer systems, most libraries obtain access to MARC data through products and services developed by publishers, computer system developers, time-sharing services, and other intermediaries. Among the earliest of these MARC-derivative products were computer-generated micro publications such as MARCFICHE, produced by MARC Applied Research, and Books in English produced by the British Library. Created by Computer-output Microfilm (COM) technology, both products provided more timely and varied access to LC cataloguing data than could be obtained through the conventionally printed National Union Catalogue, which was itself discontinued in favour of a COM implementation in the early 1980s.As an equally timely and flexible alternative, several search services, including DIALOG and WILSONLINE, offer online access to the LCMARC database.

A growing number of vendors supply the MARC database on CD-ROM disks or digital optical videodiscs accompanied by software which supports the retrieval of specific cataloguing records and the printing of card sets. Examples include the BIBLIOFILE system from the Library Corporation in Washington, D.C., the LASERSEARCH system from General Pesearch Corporation, and the MINI MARC II system from Library Systems and Services Incorporated. Although these products and services are important, most libraries obtain access to machine-readable cataloguing records through one of the bibliographic utilities-organisations which maintain large databases of cataloguing records and offer online access and other services to subscribing libraries.

Examples include the Online Union Catalogue implemented by the Online Computer Library Centre (OCLC), the Research Libraries Information Network (RLIN) operated by the Research Libraries Group, the cataloguing support service operated by the Western Library Network (WLN), the Cataloguing Support System (CATSS) offered by Utlas International, the LIONS system operated by the New York Public Library, the AGILE II service offered by Auto- Graphics Incorporated, and Brodart's Interactive Access System (IAS).

While they differ in database size and composition, the number and nature of their subscribers, and the specific capabilities they support, these bibliographic utilities each maintain a database of MARC records obtained from the Library of Congress and other sources, supplemented by original MARC-format cataloguing contributed by subscribing libraries. Working at local terminals, participating libraries can retrieve cataloguing copy, modify it to meet local requirements, and order printed card sets, machine-readable cataloguing records on magnetic tape, and other bibliographic products.

Local workstations are also used to input original cataloguing records for use by other subscribers. Supporting thousands of online terminals accessing millions of machine-readable records, the bibliographic utilities are among the world's largest and most intensively utilised computer-based information services.

COMPUTER-PRODUCED CATALOGUES

The automation of descriptive cataloguing addresses only one part of the cataloguing activity. In addition to using computers to facilitate access to cataloguing copy, libraries are interested in computer-based solutions to the much discussed problems of card catalogues. The most frequently cited of such problems include substantial space consumption; the purchase of expensive cabinets and supporting furniture; labour-intensive and time-consuming catalogue maintenance routines which are intensified by changes in cataloguing rules affecting the choice and form of entries; and limited convenience and retrieval capabilities.

These problems can be minimized or eliminated by the replacement of card catalogues with computer-based book-form or online catalogues. Broadly defined, a book-form catalogue contains successive bibliographic records listed in a page format on paper or microforms. Among the earliest applications of library automation, computer preparation of book-form catalogues can lower production time and costs while eliminating the labour-intensive file maintenance routines associated with card catalogues.

As an alternative to computer printed or typeset catalogues, computer-output microfilm catalogues have been widely implemented by libraries and library systems since, the early 1970s. A number of service bureaus, book jobbers, bibliographic utilities, and other vendors have developed software to produce COM catalogues from library-supplied data, thereby eliminating the need for in-house COM recorders and customised programming catalogues. Broadly defined, an online catalogue is an organised, machine-readable accumulation of bibliographic records which are maintained on disks or other direct-access computer storage media for retrieval by library users and staff members working at inter- active terminals or appropriately configured microcomputer workstations. In addition to saving space and automating file maintenance, online catalogues permit remote access by authorised persons equipped with compatible terminals, and they can support information retrieval operations—such as keyword searching of titles and series names—which are not conveniently possible with card or book-form catalogues.

Online catalogues may be custom-developed for specific library installations or purchased as prewritten software packages or turnkey systems. Examples of custom-developed online catalogues include the Library of Congress Computerised Catalogue, the MELVYL system at the University of California, the LIAS system at Pennsylvania State University, the Library Computer System (LCS) at Ohio State University, and the Dartmouth College Online Catalogue. Prewritten software packages suitable for online catalogue implementations include BRS/SEARCH from BRS Information Technologies, a powerful information retrieval programme that is available in mainframe, minicomputer, and microcomputer versions; INMAGIC, a versatile data management programme for dominated by integrated library systems which combine database management and catalogue access capabilities with circulation control, acquisitions, serials control, and other operations.

Such systems may be implemented as complete turnkey configurations of hardware and software or as prewritten software packages designed to operate on a library owned mainframe, minicomputer, or microcomputer. Vendors include CLSI, Geac, Notis, Dynix, OCLC, Virginia Tech, Data Research Associates, Carlyle, Comstow Information Systems, Universal Library Systems, Sobeco, Sigma Data/Centel, George- town Medical Library, Washington University, IBM, Inlex, Sirsi, Utlas, Innovative Interfaces, Eyring Research Institute, Easy Data, Data Trek, and Unisys. Among the newest and most widely publicised approaches to online catalogue implementation, a growing number of vendors offer public access catalogue systems which employ CD-ROM storage technology. Examples include the IMPACT system from Auto-Graphics, LASERGUIDE from General Research, THE INTELLIGENT CATALOGUE from the Library Corporation, and the LEPAC system from Brodart.

In such implementations, the library provides a machine- readable version of its catalogue, typically consisting of MARC format records on magnetic tapes obtained from bibliographic utilities or other sources, to a CD-ROM system vendor who indexes and otherwise prepares it for conversion to one or more CD-ROM disks. The disks themselves are created by a mastering process in special manufacturing facilities, and the library receives a specified number of disk copies plus menu-driven software designed for public catalogue access at microcomputer-based workstations. Updated by periodic replacement in the manner of book-form catalogues, such CD-ROM catalogues are increasingly mentioned as an alternative to computer output microfilm for union catalogues and similar implementations.

AUTOMATED REFERENCE SERVICE

Since, the late 1960s, many publishers of printed bibliographies, indexing and abstracting journals, and other reference works have offered machine-readable versions of their products for use in computer assisted reference applications. Initially intended for government, corporate, and academic libraries supporting research in scientific and technical disciplines, such machine-readable reference sources have become widely available in business, the social sciences, and the humanities. In addition to databases which correspond to printed publications, a growing number of reference sources have been developed specifically for use in computer-based systems and have no printed counterparts. While the earliest machine-readable databases were bibliographic in character, non-bibliographic numeric and directory-type databases are increasingly commonplace. During the late 1960s and early 1970s, a number of libraries purchased machine-readable bibliographic and non-bibliographic data- bases for processing on in-house computers using custom-developed information retrieval software. Most libraries, however, lacked access to the hardware and software resources required to implement such systems.

Through the early 1970s,the needs of such libraries were addressed by fee-based search services operated by the producers of machine-readable databases or other organisations such as large research libraries. Such services, which operated in the offline, batch processing mode, were replaced in the mid- 1970s by services offering online database searching on a time sharing basis to libraries equipped with conventional terminals.

Now widely utilised by libraries of all types and sizes, online search services can be divided into two broad groups:

- Multidisciplinary services—including DIALOG, BRS, ORBIT,

WILSONLINE, DATA- STAR, and ESA-IRS-that provide database coverage of a varied range of subjects for a broad clientele; and

- Specialised services-such as the NLM SEARCH SERVICE, STN INTERNATIONAL, LEXIS, and WESTLAW-that provide online access to one or more databases relevant to a single subject discipline, profession, or activity, such as medicine, law, or engineering.

Various types of specialised search services provide online access to databases containing a specific type of information such as news. Examples include the NEXIS, VUITEXT, DATA TIMES, and NEWSNET search services. While they differ in the number and type of databases offered and in the specific retrieval capabilities supported, multidisciplinary and specialised search services share a common operating methodology: they purchase or otherwise obtain bibliographic and non-bibliographic data-bases in machine-readable form from their producers, convert the dataases to a form required for storage on their computers, and allow libraries or other subscribers to perform various retrieval operations on such data using prewritten data-base management software. The software features a non-procedural query language which permits a user at an online terminal to initiate litreature searches or other information retrieval operations by entering specified commands.

While their query languages are relatively easy to learn, online search services are more often providing menu-driven interfaces for novice users. Some services also offer private file capabilities which allow libraries to establish their own databases. As a recently implemented supplement or alternative to online search services, an increasing number of bibliographic and non-bibliographic databases are available on CD-ROM disks. Accompanied by information retrieval software, such CD-ROM reference products permit database searching at local microcomputer workstations (over 100 titles were available at the time of this writing). Offered on a subscription basis, they can prove less expensive than online searching for databases that are accessed frequently, although infrequent updating, slow response time for complex searches, and other performance limitations may make them unsuitable for some applications.

As a hybrid implementation with potentially attractive cost/performance characteristics, several vendors combine CD-ROM searching of back file data with online access to the most current information.

ACQUISITIONS

More informed decision-making through improved statistical analysis and reporting of procurement activity is the most frequently cited motive for automating acquisitions operations. Since, the 1960s, automated acquisitions systems have been implemented in at least four different ways: as a custom-developed programme designed to operate on a computer owned by a library or its parent organisation; as an acquisitions-specific prewritten software package or turnkey system; as an application module supported by a multifunctional integrated library system; or as a time-sharing service offered by a bibliographic utility or a book jobber.

Each method has advantages and limitations. Customised acquisitions systems, an implementation option in any automated application, can be developed to a particular library's specifications but are expensive and time-consuming to create. Prewritten acquisitions-specific software, and the acquisitions application modules supported by integrated library systems, can minimize the worst implementation problems associated with customised software development, but a library must have access to required hardware and system software components. Turnkey systems, consisting of preconfigured combinations of hardware and software, are available as both acquisitions—specific products and as integrated systems.

In the latter group, the integration of acquisitions with cataloguing and circulation in a single system offers several advantages, including the ability to establish a preliminary bibliographic record at the time an item is ordered. All of the foregoing approaches require a substantial capital investment which can be minimized if automated acquisitions capabilities are obtained on a time-sharing basis through a bibliographic utility or bookseller. Because charges are incurred as the acquisitions facility is used, this approach is especially attractive to libraries with modest annual volumes of acquisitions activity.

Use of a bibliographic utility for acquisitions offers other advantages as well. Its database can be used for bibliographic verification, and data can be transferred from cataloguing records to facilitate order preparation. In addition, the use of a single system for acquisitions and cataloguing simplifies staff training requirements, while the immediate online availability of information about the holdings of other libraries supports cooperative collection development. Acquisitions systems offered by booksellers typically feature online access to inventory data with electronic ordering capabilities.

SERIALSCONTROL

Current serials automation activities are directed towards two types of tasks-the bibliographic control of serial publications and the management of serials collections in individual libraries. The task of bibliographic control is the establishment of definitive bibliographic information about serial publications. Among automated approaches to this task, R.R. Bowker offers machine-readable versions of its various printed guides to serial publications including Ulrich's International Periodicals Directory.

The International Serials Data System (ISDS) and the International Centre for the Registration of Serials are charged with responsibility for the establishment and maintenance of a comprehensive machine-readable registry of bibliographic information about serials published through out the world.

In the United States, the Library of Congress has developed a MARC format for serial publications and participates in the CONSER programme which creates and maintains a high-quality machine-readable database of cataloguing records. The CONSER data-base is maintained by OCLC, and CONSER records are disseminated through the MARC distribution service.

To manage local collections, a number of libraries and several vendors have developed systems which automate one or more aspects of serials processing, including union list production, ordering, check-in, claiming, and the routing of received issues to designated persons. Computer-based production of union lists of serials is routinely sup- ported by data management software or word processing systems. Such lists may be printed on paper or microfiche. The last option is especially useful for very long lists that will be mailed or otherwise distributed to multiple locations. As an example, microfiche is the output medium for the California Union List of Periodicals (CULP) which contains information for over 63,000 periodicals held by 700 California libraries.

The CULP database is also accessible online through BRS. As with conventional book acquisitions, computers can be used to minimize the labour-intensive sorting, filing, and other paper-handling work routines associated with manual serials processing. A number of libraries developed customised serials control systems during the 1960s and 1970s. The PHILSOM system, developed by the Washington University School of Medicine Library, is perhaps the most famous example. As an alternative to the time and expense associated with customised system development, libraries can obtain access to serials control capabilities on a time-sharing basis through subscription service companies. Examples of such time-shared serials control services include F.W. Faxon's LYNX system and the EBSCONET system offered by EBSCO Subscription Services.

Several companies and other organisations have developed pre- written software and turnkey systems designed specifically for serials control. The INNOVACQ Acquisitions and Serials Control System, for example, offers a comprehensive range of serials ordering, check-in, and claiming capabilities. It can download records from bibliographic utilities and transfer serials records to a local circulation control or public access catalogue system. Among microcomputer-based products, OCLC's SC350 Serials Control System can retrieve bibliographic information, local data, and publishers' addresses from the OCLC online union catalogue.

It facilitates the check-in of received issues, produces claims and claim cancellations, maintains binding instructions, and prints bindery slips. It can also transmit serials records to OCLC's union list component. As an alternative to single-purpose implementations, several integrated library systems support serials control modules, and others have announced such capabilities for future implementation.

PLANNING FOR LIBRARY AUTOMATION ACADEMIC LIBRARIES

Library Automation refers to the use of computers to serve the needs of library users. The operations of a library get a quantum jump with the introductions of computers. The computers help to provide fast and reliable access to the resources available in the library as well as elsewhere. The application of computers in the library operations avoids repetitive jobs and saves lot of labour, time, speeds up operations, increases use of library resources.

Computers are not only used as a tool for processing the data, but also for data storage and accessing. Planning for an automated system, no matter how big or small, should be part of an overall long-range plan for the library. Automation should always be used as a means to achieve overall better patron service.

Careful planning for technology will assure that your automation project is 'sustainable', *i.e.*, enhances the organisation's ability to meet its service mission without disrupting the organisational stability of the institution.

The present scenario of library worldwide is:

- Vastly expanded storage of indexes, statistical data bases, and document databases within the library.
- Full-text storage of documents, complete with full-text keyword searching and on-demand printing.
- Access by users to library databases from home or office, with direct downloading of information and text on demand.
- The ability to access remote databases across the country and the world, and to download information and text on demand.
- Storage of pictorial and graphic material.
- Availability of 'intelligent systems' providing transparent, one-step searching and access to various library in-house and remote databases.

These capabilities and far more have become reality. Accordingly, today's integrated system must not only provide access to the traditional cataloguing, circulation, public catalogue (OPAC) and acquisitions modules, but must be capable of connecting through the local system into the systems of other vendors, remote bibliographic databases, CD-ROM drives on a local area network (LAN), and the Internet.

Users are expecting that their library systems be capable of, among other things:

- Providing seamless integration between system gateway and OPAC modules.
- Providing access for external users on the Internet to the library's OPAC.

- Monitoring the usage of remote databases that have been accessed through the gateway.
- Accessing the Internet using a variety of graphical interfaces.

Essentially, what this means is that libraries must plan to use a local library system as a vehicle for achieving access to resources outside that system. Stimulated by the Internet, which has created universal connectivity to information resources heretofore unknown and/or inaccessible, and by Z39.50 interoperability standards and 'gateways,' users of individual local systems are expecting to access the resources of other systems—anywhere and anytime. Moreover, the traditional definition of 'publishing' has been stretched by the creation and instant availability of informational home pages and Web sites worldwide.

Given such increased complexities and heightened levels of expectation, libraries must learn all the more how to plan for the introduction of automation in an organised and systematic fashion. There is little mystery involved here: It is entirely a matter of building upon what you already know about your library, using tools that are readily at hand and, most importantly of all, involving the people—staff and users—who must live with the consequences of any automation decisions.

WHAT IS LIBRARY AUTOMATION

Traditional library work consisting of acquisitions, technical processing, serials control, circulation and reference services all entail time consuming manual work. Though these activities are essential to proper functioning of a library, they consume professional staff time that might otherwise go towards user services and library development. Library computerisation is now gaining importance necessitating the establishment of profession-wide standards. Comprehensive studies of library computer systems world over include discussions of machine-managed acquisitions, cataloguing, serials control, circulation and bibliographic service modules. The litreature in this area highlights major aspects of computer's role in the library environment. Similar to several aspects of library management, the demand for more and faster information services and the decline in library resources are compelling librarians to appreciate the role of computers within their operations.

In general, librarians are looking to maximize the benefits of automation by spreading computer use to as many aspects of library activities as possible by taking advantage of developments in computer hardware and software and telecommunications.

NEED FOR LIBRARY AUTOMATION

Even though this question seems to be very fundamental it is essential to emphasise this aspect, as the library automation is yet to take off in majority of the Indian libraries. Secondly, while justifying need for library automation more than cost-effectiveness the benefits derived by the library users become the major consideration. To appreciate the advantages it becomes necessary to highlight the different levels of library automation.

Following are considered as important factors for Library Automation:

- Information explosion.
- Increase in the collection of libraries.
- Inability of users to explore the unlimited litreature and information of their interest.
- Advances in the computer and communication technology.
- Wastage of user/ staff time in locating the information.
- Provide wide access to resources within the libraries and elsewhere.
- Better access.
- Quality in service.
- Cooperative efforts (Resource Sharing).

Out of all libraries an academic library has a difficult task of defining its mission and operating objectives. The automation programme will have to mange a wide range of litreature associated with numerous departments and educational programmes of the academic institution. Furthermore, in an academic library the collections will be diverse unlike a special research library where the collection is relatively homogeneous.

The user group will also range widely, including faculty, staff, students, scholars, administrators and the general public. The position of an academic library funded largely by the government further complicates the process of identifying and prioritising objectives. As difficult as the task might at first appear, it is nevertheless essential to the process of establishing automated systems of any type. In addition the overall health of ones library operation will benefit from a modicum of intellectual rigour in this area.

AREAS OF LIBRARY AUTOMATION

As a first step in a planning process, it is desirable to formulate a model for computerisation listing all itemised and prioritised information systems being maintained on a manual basis by the library. For this exercise it is necessary to break down these procedures into their constituent parts. When further subdividing these activities, each item is to be considered of its functional elements. The systems and subsystems listed below are only indicative and may vary with differing library system environments.

These are:

- Acquisitions:
  - Selection
  - Ordering
  - Claiming/cancellation
  - Receiving/invoice processing
  - Extended procurements

  - Gift tracking
  - Fund Control
  - Maintains information about all library related funds
  - Ability to group funds (nesting)
  - Track fund allocations and adjustments
  - Fund encumbrance
  - Fund expenditure
  - Cash Balance
  - Free Balance
  - Automatic updating of fiscal information through recording of specific transactions
  - Track year-to-date expenditures
  - Create Purchase Orders
- Technical Services:
  - Books
  - Serials
  - Special Collections
- Cataloguing:
  - Books
  - Serials
  - Special Collections
- Circulation:
  - Charge/Renewal
  - Discharge
  - Loan Periods
  - Processing schedules
  - Holds
  - Messages
  - Blocks
  - Notices
  - Transaction Recording Devices for off-line processing
  - Member control
  - Inventory control
- Serials Control:
  - Receipt (check-in)
  - Claiming
  - Bindery control
  - Replacements
  - Monographic serials
  - Invoice processing
- Reference Services:
  - Desk services
- User tools

- Bibliographic utilisation
- Reprography
- Inter-library communications
- General Administration
- Grants Administratiuon
- Library Publications
- Bindery
- Periodical Citation Searching
- OPAC
- Bibliographic Database

PLANNING OF LIBRARY AUTOMATION

Planning for library automation has been defined as planning for 'integrated systems' that computerise an array of traditional library functions using a common database. While this is still generally true, rapid technological change is forcing a re-examination of what it means to 'automate the library.' As physical, spatial and temporal barriers to acquiring information are crumbling, libraries must plan for a broader and more comprehensive approach to providing automated services.

DEVELOPING A LIBRARY 'PROFILE'

One of the most important planning tools involves collecting basic statistical information on the library and its operations. You will find that the same basic data will be needed again and again—whether for vendors from whom you are requesting cost estimates, or for other libraries with whom you may be seeking to cooperate in implementing automation.

The following are examples of commonly needed data:

- Number of titles and volumes in the collection, current and projected.
- Number of borrowers, current and projected.
- Number of materials circulated, current and projected.
- Number of new materials acquired, current and projected.
- Interlibrary loans, lent to and borrowed from other libraries.
- Description of any cooperative arrangements involving the library.
- Library address and hours of operation.

In addition, it is important to take stock of any existing automation in the library by compiling the following data:

- Percentage of collection that has catalogue records in machine-readable form.
- Description of collection without machine-readable records, by category, (, monographs, audiovisuals).
- Description of currently-automated library functions (if any).
- Estimates of the location and number of workstations (to show where you intend to have equipment in any future system).

- Specifications for any existing equipment to be re-used with any future system (if any).

At the same time that this data is being assembled, it is important to assess user needs and set service priorities. This can be accomplished by undertaking a focused, strategic planning process designed to involve the library's 'stakeholders.'

DEVELOPING A STRATEGIC PLAN

A library planning to automate should undertake a process by which representative staff and users can identify service needs and objectives. The purpose of such an effort is to allow participants to articulate their interests and concerns, share perspectives and learn about possibilities in a collaborative setting. Group interaction is an important contributing factor in the success of the goal, which is to develop and sustain library automation in the years ahead.

Here are the basic steps involved in this process:

- Plan on a two-day, intensive planning effort.
- Ask participants to identify strengths, weaknesses, opportunities and threats in the library's environment (known as 'SWOT' factors in strategic planning) that are characteristic of or that confront the library.
- Group these factors into critical issue areas that are likely to have an impact on the libraries' future in developing and sustaining automation.
- *Ask participants to identify ideas and perceptions in relation to the question*: "How do you see the library providing user-friendly, cost-effective automated services in five years?
- Through a method of your own devising, ask participants to prioritise all of the ideas that come out of the above two 'brainstorming' exercises.
- Ask participants to shape these priorities into the draft of a strategic 'vision' for automation development consisting of a statement of purpose, goals and objectives for the library.

SETTING SERVICE PRIORITIES

Your strategic vision must now provide the framework or context for the next step in the automation process, which is to determine which library functions should be automated and in what order of priority. For example, processes that are repetitive, occupy large amounts of staff time, require retrieving information from large, unwieldy files, or are high-profile functions of the library (such as the public catalogue) are prime candidates for automation.

Determining the functions that you wish to automate and their priorities relative to each other is important for all sorts of reasons.

If needs and priorities are clear, functions can be automated in phases, allowing for more effective use of frequently scarce funding. Moreover, it is a way to develop credibility with funding agencies and be able to take advantage of 'sudden' funding opportunities. Finally, evaluations of systems and options will be easier and more productive if you are able to match your highest functional priorities against the corresponding modules available in the marketplace.

A WORD ABOUT COSTS

Speaking of funding, planners need to be aware that there are certain cost elements involved in the installation and operation of any automated system.

These may be summarised as follows:

- Planning and consulting costs include direct, out-of-pocket costs, (*e.g.*, hiring a consultant) and indirect costs, (*e.g.*, training staff) associated with getting started.
- Purchase of the system includes the cost of acquiring the initial system hardware and software, as well as the cost of preparing a site for the computer system.
- Telecommunication costs are those fees paid to telephone companies for connecting remote terminals or workstations to a central computer system.
- Conversion costs are those associated with the creation of machine-readable bibliographic and, for circulation systems, patron, records.
- On-Going Operating costs include:
  - Maintenance fees
  - Utility costs
  - Bar code labels
  - Miscellaneous supply costs
  - Telecommunications costs
  - Salaries and benefits (if extra staff are hired).
- Additions to the existing system may be required to maintain performance specifications, to accommodate new users, or to allow for additional automated functions.

SYSTEM SPECIFICATIONS

At some point, you will need to re-formulate your functional priorities into 'functional specifications,' which may be defined as what you want an automated system to do for you, including things that your current manual system cannot do. 'Technical specifications' must also be established. These include standards that must be adhered to, system performance, operation, and maintenance, as well as infrastructure requirements, such as stable sources of electricity and telecommunications, and sufficient bandwidth. Developing clear and accurate functional and technical specifications that are specific to your library is one of the most important, if not THE most important, activity that you will engage in as you plan for your automated system.

These specifications will carry you through the entire procurement process, and will ensure that the system which most closely matches them will be the most useful and the most responsive to your needs.

DEVELOPING A FORMAL SPECIFICATIONS DOCUMENT

It is very difficult to compare systems sensibly and pragmatically solely by randomly looking at systems, talking to sales representatives, reading litreature or comparing broad cost quotations. For this reason, libraries use a formal document—often known as a 'Request for Proposal,' or RFP—that organises and standardises the information provided to and requested from the various system vendors. Utilising an RFP to solicit written responses from vendors makes it possible for you to systematically compare functionality, cost, maintenance, support, and all the other issues that are involved in system procurements. The process can save you money and will result in a wiser decision.

An RFP document should include these essential elements, among others:

- Background information on the library.
- A description of how the proposals should be arranged and submitted.
- Instructions on receiving vendor business and financial information.
- Criteria the library will use to evaluate vendor proposals.
- Questions regarding vendor training and documentation.
- Your functional and technical specifications.

Also, vendors should be asked to describe:

- How they will create bibliographic, item and borrower databases.
- Their system maintenance programmes and services.
- Their site preparation requirements.
- Their delivery and installation methodologies.
- Their system performance guarantees.
- Their pricing and cost strategies, in detail.

EVALUATING VENDOR PROPOSALS

Upon the receipt of vendor proposals, it will be time to begin the process of system evaluation and selection.

This process involves a number of key steps:

- If possible, form a project team of persons to assist with the evaluations and the selection who have some knowledge of automation or who work in the area(s) being automated. People involved in the strategic planning process would be a good choice.

- Try to weed out proposals that are 'fatally flawed,' *e.g.*, where the vendor fails to reply to any of the functional specifications or the system is missing a module for a high-priority function.
- Begin in-depth reading of the 'surviving' proposals, carefully noting both deviations from the requirements as defined by the RFP and any aspect that is handled unusually well. Make a list of any parts of the response that are not clear and require further clarification.
- Schedule system demonstrations. They are an important component of the evaluation process. Allow the vendors to show off the vendor's system in the most attractive light; however, be prepared with a list of what you want to see along with questions you would like answered. Use the same list with each vendor. This permits more effective cross-comparisons.
- Consider using computerised spreadsheet software in order to compare and evaluate vendor cost proposals. Costs may not be what they seem at first glance.
- Contact some of each vendor's current clients—sites of the same library type, and of similar size, where the hardware and software modules that have been proposed to you are currently in use.
- Assign point values to the criteria listed in the RFP and assign scores to the different proposals. The system with the highest score becomes the number one finalist, the system with the second highest score number two and so on. To maintain a negotiating edge, it is better to cut to two vendors rather than one. If that is impossible, maintain the illusion anyway. Remember: The selection process is not over until the contract is signed. Until that point, never let any vendors know that they have been eliminated, including those with fatal flaws.

PUTTING SYSTEMS INTO PLACE

After the system selection process is complete, there are several important steps which must occur. You and your vendor will have to negotiate and sign a contract. You will want to test the system and make sure it suits your needs. You will want to make provisions for system maintenance. Finally, you will want to train both your staff and your users as much as possible to prepare them for when the system is up and running.

With regard to training, the following must be considered: In thinking of automation planning, there is often a tendency to focus on the hardware and software aspects of planning, and to ignore the human aspects of automation—training and public relations. Without these, however, even the most carefully designed system may not be accepted by library staff or library users. To assure the success of your hard planning work, a training and public relations plan should be part of any automation project.

Fortunately, training can begin long before the system is installed. By involving staff at all levels in the analysis of operations, the identification of needs, the setting of priorities, the development of specifications, and the evaluation of systems, staff will gain much of the knowledge they need as the planning progresses. User acceptance and enthusiasm for your new automated system is certainly an important ingredient in a successful planning effort. If you are implementing a public access catalogue, it is probably the most important measure of success.

Public relations can allow you to accomplish three things:

- Make users aware of your new system and services;
- Motivate them to use the system; and
- Train them in using the new system and services effectively.

RETROSPECTIVE CONVERSION

In the rush to acquire hardware and software, librarians often forget that their most valuable product is the library's database. The creation of a high-quality machine-readable database provides the cornerstone upon which all present and future automation efforts rest. Vendors will come and go, hardware will become obsolete, software will be replaced, but a well-constructed, well-maintained database, with its accompanying local holdings, will be the library's transportable and viable link from system to system. Moreover, as library users begin to access not only their local system but systems in other libraries as well, the quality of respective databases will influence both the outcome of search strategies and the availability of materials.

Database readiness has several important facets:

- Catalogue records must be carefully converted from manual to machine-readable formats.
- Collections must be prepared for conversion through effective and ongoing weeding and inventory programmes.
- Once converted, collections must be properly maintained as titles are added, withdrawn, transferred and recataloged.
- Standards—for bibliographic, item and patron records as well—must be adhered to. In particular, adherence to well-established and accepted standards of description for bibliographic information in a machine-readable database is critical because: without standards, files cannot easily be transferred from one automated system to another.
- It is essential for libraries wishing to participate in resource sharing arrangements with other libraries, who will require such adherence as a condition of participation.

LIBRARY AUTOMATION IN DEVELOPING COUNTRIES THE LAST 25 YEARS

When Information Development was launched in 1984, library

automation was, looked at from today's perspective, very much in its infancy. The largest libraries in the world such as the Library of Congress and the British Library had sizeable databases of catalogue records. University library catalogues were available on-line within their institutional four walls and library circulation was also automated, but data was generally confined to the institution that held it since, there was no network resembling the internet. In 1983 the JANET network had begun to connect the universities in the United Kingdom, and some catalogues were beginning to be available online from other institutions.

The most common way of accessing remote data if there was a possibility at all was by dial-up modem using ordinary phone lines and a modem or an acoustic coupler in which the phone handset was pushed into a rubber holder to ensure no extraneous noise seeped into the phone line when it was transferring electronic signals between computers. Businesses including libraries were also connected by dedicated phone lines to locations where their computers were located when they were remote. But most automation was firmly confined to the institution where it was based. Twenty five years ago was also the beginning of the period when computers were being introduced as desk top computers, with IBM PCs and subsequently IBM PC lookalikes. Personal computers were about to make a huge impact on automation in libraries as no longer was it necessary to have a dedicated air-conditioned room to house computers.

In the early days cataloguers had to have terminals on their desks to enable access to the catalogue but eventually all staff had PCs for general administration so no longer was it was the responsibility of the library budget to purchase desk-top computers. Modems were in fact used to access remotely catalogues for bibliographical purposes, to search databases like Medline. It was already possible to dial up databases such as the British Library's BLAISE database or the US National Library of Medicine's Medline. But these facilities required good phone lines and were not available outside Western Europe and the United States.

There was no such thing as 'full text' then. Computers did not have the capacity to store so much data and data stored was often coded to ensure that it did not take up more space than was necessary. 25 years ago, while most libraries in industrialised countries had not only computerised their catalogues but also computerised their circulation, in developing countries there was very little library automation outside that organised by the United Nations agencies such as FAO's AGRIS and IAEA's INIS and these were very much in their infancy or in their planning stages.

To return to the situation in industrialised countries. In the early 1990's catalogues began to be accessible on the internet but were not web-based and required the catalogue software to be run interactively across the Internet using various different protocols. By the end of the decade, true web-based catalogues using the power of hypertext were available. Libraries began to include in their catalogues digital resources internally held and externally held (predominantly external). MARC formats thenceforward incorporated a field 856 used to link to an external resource by means of a URL (the internet address).

Users of the catalogue could click on a link and go straight to a digital resource that could be anywhere in the world. Subscriptions were possible to electronic journals but they were often not available in developing countries or if they were available the bandwidth of tehinternet in those countries was not enough to enable the materials to be read. Digital library software became available and UNESCO encouraged its implementation in developing countries by making Greenstone available free-of-charge, a digital library software package developed at Waikatu in New Zealand. Links could be made from a library catalogue to material in such a digital library. Material available on the internet which might not be easily accessible in institutions in developing countries with low bandwidth could be downloaded or sent on CD-ROM to the digital libraries and hosted locally.

The Soros Foundation set up eIFL (Electronic Information for Libraries) with the aim of creating national purchasing consortia. They have since, become involved in supporting other activities such as promoting library automation systems, mindful of the fact that without a catalogue of print and digital materials the library user cannot easily find out what is accessible. eIFL supported the European Union funded project to implement NewGenLib, a system under development in India, in Aleppo and Al Baath university libraries in Syria alongside providing them with licences at a reasonable price to access electronic resources.

INASP, the International Network for the Availability of Scientific Publications, was set up by the International Council of Scientific Unions (ICSU) in 1992. Aware of the need to establish good catalogues in order to access scientific litreature, they have also participated in some library automation projects.

The Andrew W. Mellon Foundation, well known for philanthropic projects in developing countries, is also supporting the development of a new library automation system at Duke University, the Open Library Environment (OLE). Although there is no participation from developing countries at this stage it is likely that any open source package developed would be supported with necessary tailoring in line with the needs of developing countries wherever they might be different.

The main feature in the last 25 years then has been in the expansion of computers into every aspect of libraries. Possibly the biggest change has been the development of digital libraries, acquiring, transforming or accessing data in digital format. In developing countries this methods of digitisation has taken place to a certain extent.

TRENDS IN THE INDUSTRIALISED WORLD

Library systems in developing countries have obviously developed alongside systems in the industrialised world. First we should look at systems for large institutions. The majority of library systems have been developed in the United States. Many commercially available integrated library systems were developed by universities for their own use and later made available to a wider audience. Dynix was one such, developed for a university library and later sold around the world to universities, public libraries and special libraries. Other systems were based from the outset on cooperatives, such as TALIS which originated as BLS, the system of BLCMP (Birmingham Libraries Cooperative Management Project) which was a cooperative set up with government funding in the 1960s.

This project was one of two established from the beginning by OSTI, the UK Office of Scientific and Technological Information, to support cooperative cataloguing. They had less incentive to expand outside their country of origin as it was their aim to serve a cooperative all of whose members were equal. In 1967, the Ohio Colleges Library Centre was established to bring library automation to Ohio academic institutions by sharing costs. OCLC as it is now has developed from being a cooperative between libraries in Ohio to being an international cooperative, and at one time promoted a library management system.

Then they ceased to support it returning eventually to the market by acquiring OLIB, an Oracle based library system. Its vision is to connect libraries of the world. Originally, as with BLCMP, it was a shared cataloguing system receiving records from participating libraries and adding them to a database which in turn could be used by member libraries to populate their own catalogues. Records were transferred between computers initially by sending large magnetic tapes, a thing of the past, from the Centre to the remote libraries. Later they were transferred by telephone lines and subsequently the transfer was done by a client computer, a PC in a remote institution, accessing the Centre's servers by the Internet. Jumping to the present, OCLC have established Worldcat which could act as a large union catalogue for the world if every library in the world added its holdings.

This concept is called Cloud Computing, on the basis that the computer is somewhere remote and no one knows or cares where exactly it is! To return to library systems established in individual institutions, VTLS (Virginia Tech Library System), another large library automation system, always had an interest in working with developing countries and have a large number of installations in the Third World after having expanded into Eastern Europe as well.

Another popular system, Aleph, is based in Jerusalem surrounded by a number of developing countries some of which have considered installation though by far the largest share of the market is in Europe.

As for cooperatives like OCLC, there has existed for many years in former Yugoslavia a miniature version of OCLC, COBISS (Co-operative Online Bibliographic System and Service), which since, the break-up of Yugoslavia has expanded to include Albania and Bulgaria on the same basis as other ex-Yugoslav states. They act as a cooperative cataloguing agency but they also keep data on research projects. This institution would be a good model for other regions to adopt. Now and again a commercial library system has been licenced to a developing country institution which has subsequently found it difficult to pay the maintenance fees. Maintenance in any case is often more expensive in a developing country because of economies of scale and distance from the supplier. Additionally there may be problems caused by shortages of foreign exchange.

Now the internet reaches much of the world, distance is not so important. But there have been many instances of institutions retaining a package but not paying maintenance fees and therefore not updating it. Marshall Breeding keeps records of as many library automation packages and the sites where they are used as he can find the information. He publishes the results each year in Library Journal. The latest was published on the web in January 2009. He reviews the market as well as providing statistics about library automation suppliers.

This is a useful guide to make comparisons with developing countries. Unfortunately in his tables he makes only the distinction between the US and the rest of the world. However he also includes a general review and this year he reported that the use of Open Source packages is increasing mainly bring provided by third parties. For example, a company called Equinox provides support for the Open Source package Evergreen.

PACKAGES WHICH HAVE HAD AN IMPACT IN DEVELOPING COUNTRIES

Large libraries in developing countries had always had a certain amount of access to library automation systems. For example, the National Library of Venezuela had a system found in many US academic libraries called NOTIS. However this library's catalogue is still not available on the web. A number of countries in the former Soviet Union use IRBIS, the CDS/ISIS clone developed by the Russian National Library for Science and Technology. But ordinary libraries, public and academic, in developing countries have always lacked a wealth of possibilities for library automation.

Hardware used to be expensive, and relatively speaking is still expensive for developing countries. Other problems raised by writers on the subject range from the power supply to the problems of training staff. Another issue not often raised is the need for collaboration both within and between institutions to get library automation project off the ground and then maintain it.

This is a much more complex activity than a pre-automation situation where there is a library card catalogue maintained by cataloguers and used manually by staff and library patrons. Smaller systems than the ones developed for universities or networks have been developed which could be regarded as being similar sized to CDS/ISIS, for instance Inmagic and Tinlib. Some of these were not very easy to use and were not well maintained. Others were adopted by consortia or organisations in the industrialised world with branches in developing countries such as the British Council.

The main problem in developing countries has been support because of their remoteness and so those packages offering less support would be more attractive as they would be less expensive overall. This may well change in the future with the increase in the power of the internet and the next 25 years will surely see a difference in the availability of and the charges for support.

CDS/ISIS

CDS/ISIS has undoubtedly had a huge influence on library automation in developing countries. This author reviewed the package onits twentieth anniversary. Time and again, libraries have begun automation. There is even a reference to a library which began with Tinlib and has migrated to CDS/ ISIS. Since, CDS/ISIS is well mentioned in the litreature, concerning library automation in developing countries, it will not be covered here.

However the most interesting feature which has become available over the last five years in CDS/ISIS is a Z39.50 import facility which is available as part of IsisMARC, and which enables MARC records from external sources to be downloaded into a CDS/ISIS database compatible with the version of MARC of the records. CDS/ISIS is not essentially a library management system, rather a database management system aimed at bibliographic records which by their very nature are variable length (with for example book titles being of indeterminate length) rather than fixed length which is the case for most data processing systems. Because it is attractive to small institutions with little funding and because of its parentage (UNESCO), it has attracted a certain kind of institution, for example those in the development community. UNESCO developed a DOS version in 1985 and a Windows version which was available for many years as a beta test version but was eventually released around 1998.

However libraries were already requiring to place their catalogues on the web and a number of organisations began to develop compatible web-based systems which could be used by institutions which were developing databases for in-house use on Windows or DOS versions of CDS/ISIS. The main developer of the official version was BIREME with WWWISIS but already others were available such as Webisis. CDS/ISIS is no longer being developed by UNESCO but BIREME in cooperation with UNESCO is leading the development of ABCD on an Open Source basis.

Tinlib

Tinlib was a package which was used extensively in British Council libraries. In Ilorin Nigeria it was used from 1996 as reported by Adewoye. The library had by 2001 almost replaced its card catalogue by the OPAC. The chapter was optimistic about the future and reporting on the use of other electronic resources. However e-mail and the internet were not then available. However, TINLIB had its problems. It was not an easy system to use and contracts for it dwindled outside developing countries and it ceased to be supported. Adeyoyin describes in 2004 how the Development Policy Centre Library in Ibadan migrated their catalogue from Tinlib to CDS/ISIS.

DEVELOPING COUNTRY SCENARIOS

It is of course a fallacy to make assumptions that all developing countries will have approached and will approach library automation in the same way. The wealth of the country the distribution of that wealth and the culture of the residents will make a difference.

Nigeria and other African Countries

Nigeria has oil money and had automation early, being one of the first users of CDS/ISIS for mainframe computers. Already in1989 Eyitayo could write a paper on the attitude of automated library system vendors to investing in Nigeria. Many respondents hoped to open an office and increase their marketing. Enakrire describes a few instances in Africa where automation has been implemented, indicating that, except for branches of international organisations, it depends on the generosity of donors. In Makerere University in Uganda, the library has benefited from donor funding through the African Virtual University Library Initiative of the World Bank to equip the library with computers and installed Internet connectivity. Other university libraries are developing their information service as they are also benefiting from the Programme for the Enhancement of Research of (PERI) under the sponsorship of the International Network for the Availability of Scientific Publications (INASP).

Through PERI, donors have paid subscriptions on behalf of libraries in Africa to access web-based journals. The University of Ibadan had a long history of automation, having begun in 1979. Georgina D. Ekpenyong wrote in 1997 about the history so far. The University of Ibadan Library was already seen as a leader in Nigeria. At that time they used CD-Rom extensively to provide bibliographic data. They took training seriously but did not yet have an OPAC. In 2008, the John D. and Catherine T. MacArthur Foundation in Chicago awarded grants totalling US $7.1 million to expand academic and research programme and strengthen staff development at two Nigerian universities as part of the Foundation's efforts to improve higher education in Africa. The result is that they signed up to VTLS, Virginia Tech Library

System, a commercially available package developed originally as Virginia Tech's own system.

Thailand

In Thailand there were efforts in the 1990s to computerise the libraries with foreign-based systems being purchased. Thammasat University library had Dynix, supported from Ameritech's Australia office, and planned to move to Ameritech's new system Horizon. In 1997 the university library sent three cataloguers to Middlesex University to learn to use Horizon. Since, then they have implemented Horizon and exchange of experience took place between Middlesex University and Thammasat University until the Systems librarian at Thammasat moved to a different post around 2006. Many universities in Thailand are able to purchase these systems often through local distributors of international or American packages. Early on though, CDS/ISIS was used and at Thammasat University they used it for databases of journal articles.

OPTIONS FOR DEVELOPING COUNTRIES

Developing countries depend on developments in the industrialised world but they do not necessarily benefit from the same options as the industrialised world can use. Moreover, some of the options may be much more attractive in developing countries or at least may seem to be so.

Developing a Library System

One solution for organisations in developing countries which might have problems with paying organisations in foreign currency but which have good local technical staff is to develop their own software system. One interesting example of this is the University of Colombo in Sri Lanka. They had begun to automate in 1991 by using CDS/ISIS and then later adopted CDS/ISIS for Windows when it became available. In 2002, Seneviratne and Amaraweera reported in Information Development that in Sri Lanka there was discussion on developing a library automation system to bridge the gap between CDS/ISIS and what commercial software was able to provide, such as Alice for Windows (UK commercial) and LibSys (Indian).

In 1997 the National Agency for Research Energy, Science and Agriculture (NARESA) now the National Science Foundation, used the CDS/ISIS DOS version to handler acquisitions, cataloguing, serials management, Current Awareness Services as well as cataloguing and indexing; this package called PURNA was then used in 34 special and academic libraries. AGRIS using CDS/ISIS was widely influencing libraries in the agricultural sector and the Windows version was then used in the National Library of Sri Lanka for its union catalogue.

Now they are using Genisis, a package to make it easy to implement BIREME's WWWISIS on the web, development of which was undertaken in

France by Pierre Chabet but for which a manual was written in Sri Lanka (partially a translation from the documentation in French) by Ms. Deepali Talagala Director/Information of the Sri Lanka Scientific and Technical Information Centre based at the National Science Foundation in Colombo Seneviratne and Amaraweera discussed in their paper the features a system would need and the platforms, hardware and operating system, most used and as a result decided to make a prototype using MS Access on Windows. Development took two phases.

Firstly a web-based interface to physically dispersed databases with a user-friendly front-end reported by Kumara et al in 1998, and a library automation system described in a BSc dissertation by DMS Dilrukshi, 1999 NetLib—a library management system through the Internet. In 2002 a prototype had been developed and the system was due to be maintained by the Computing Service Centre of the University of Colombo. Unfortunately there is a high overhead in developing and maintaining systems especially for a small client base.

In the UK all university libraries have commercial systems. Newcastle, used to have their own system in the 1980s but only Lancaster remained, eventually contracting with Ex Libris to take Aleph in 2001. By 2008 both the University of Colombo and the National Library of Sri Lanka had signed up to Softlink Europe's Alice system, a system used by the British Council worldwide (for example in Oman, Jordan and Sudan: the catalogue of the British Council in Sudan is available on the internet) and so has proven maintenance in developing countries. So developing one's own system is not to be recommended: Eyitayo noted that despite the availability of numerous off-the-shelf systems, most libraries in Nigeria that have attempted automation have chosen to commission expensive and time-consuming in-house projects, most of which have suffered severe set-backs and in most cases are not adequate for library work and often lack the capability for sharing information and interconnection with other systems.

Open Source

In the context of moving towards commercially supported systems, it is interesting to see that CDS/ISIS was attractive to libraries in developing countries. It was available without charge and so there was no danger of not being able to pay for it. Of course it was supported by an organisation with as much prestige though not so much turnover as many industrial companies. It also operated on a legal footing. Institutions had to sign a licence agreement to use the software. No doubt many institutions obtained the software illegally but the software was protected in law by the licence agreement. UNESCO were more concerned with illegal copies being made and sold for illegal profit than with institutions using the software without being officially licenced since, the spirit of the software following the ethos of the developer Giampaolo

Delbigio was that it should enable institutions to participate in worldwide record sharing at many different levels.

Nevertheless there was established a network of distributors which is still in place. Some acted merely as local distributors sending out the software on diskettes by post and thereby easing the burden of the hard-pressed office in UNESCO dealing with this. Other distributors were able to provide support usually of a limited nature though sometimes of a more extensive nature akin to the commercial support that is found in the large-scale library automation systems. The shareware movement was in place when CDS/ISIS was released in 1985.

In 1984, Andrew Fluegleman programmed a communications software package, PC-Talk and Jim Knopf a file management application called PC-File a year before the IBM PC was released and called it Freeware. The developers wanted to avoid commercial distribution networks and distribute the software over the now seemingly primitive and slow dial up systems whereby PC users could transfer programmes by dialling up a central computer using a modem and phone lines. The idea was that users would download the software, test it and if they liked it make a small contribution to the developer to support further development. Knopf established the term freeware as his own and no one else could use it.

There were other microcomputers around at the time, most notably the Apple Macintosh and others which are only part of history such as the BBC Microcomputer, though none ever reached the level of popularity that the IBM PC with the Microsoft Windows operating system has now reached. Incidentally Fluegleman distributed his software with the source code which led to many other developers producing their own versions and PC-Talk was improved and sold on by other developers such that Fluegleman lost control of it. Knopf however established a multi-million dollar company on the basis of PC-File.

In 1983 Bob Wallace created PC-Write which became a well used word processor and was used extensively in developing countries. Because the word freeware was reserved he called it shareware. The concept was pretty much the same. Over the years, freeware and shareware became less used as concepts probably because the most used programmes for business purposes were monopolised by Microsoft with the operating system and Microsoft Office applications. Shareware was in a sense reborn with the open source movement. It is difficult to see any difference between Open Source and shareware but the Open Source Movement has been supported from the outset by large foundations such as the Soros Foundation which founded the Open Society Initiative.

In English 'Open Source' means freely available source software which developers can use to advance the software in question. In all these cases, software developed is free though usually developers ask for a voluntary contribution. They cannot be sold on. Open Source does not necessarily mean free-of-charge but there is an implication that the availability of the source code will enable organisations to acquire and develop it for free. CDS/ISIS was no shareware or open source but many of the features of open source and shareware were responsible for the popularity of CDS/ISIS.

For example, Open Source has the possibility for users with access to programming skills to make their own developments. CDS/ISIS has a feature of being able to write programme exits which enable further development. Unlike open source the source code was not made widely available but UNESCO did make it available to BIREME in Brazil where further developments have taken place. Moreover, in the Soviet Union the Russian National Library for Science and Technology developed with permission from UNESCO IRBIS, a functionally equivalent package copied from the DOS version of ISIS.

The Open Source movement gained much greater political credibility than the earlier movements did and UNESCO came under pressure to support the movement. They now have on their web site a Free and Open Source software portal. Because of UNESCO's lead in this concept, CDS/ISIS came under pressure to be declared open source in the early 2000s. But the source code is still not available.

This author believes it would lead to many different versions of the software that could generate records in databases that were no longer compatible with each other. Moreover, Open Source is seen by some as the solution to some of the problems facing the library software industry. Is Open Source all it promises to be? Over the last few years there has been a spate of mergers in the library systems industry led by the equity market resulting in a trend to discontinue the development if not the support of library systems when a company has acquired more than one such package. This severely inconveniences the using institutions which have to migrate from one system to another. Would open source be a protection against this? Open Source has become so much a fashionable option for library software that the International Federation of Library Associations and Institutions held a meeting in Senegal prior to the annual conference's meeting in Durban South Africa.

The proceedings are illustrative of the views on Open Source. The argument in Savard's introduction goes that Open Source may help to smooth out the inequalities between industrialised and developing countries. The connection with commerce is weaker than with commercial software but it is not non-existent. In industrialised countries libraries often use third-party services to support Open Source. This means the connection with the commercial world strengthens. There is no way put from paying for support. The question is who pays and there is not much difference between paying a developer or a third party.

In the conclusion of these proceedings, Diop feels there are clearly economic advantages to adopting an open source software solution but agrees that mastering open source software can take a lot of time and effort because library and information professionals are often isolated. User communities need to be built up to provide mutual help. However it remains to be seen what will be the impact of open source on library automation, particularly integrated library systems in the industrialised world. A pessimistic outcome might be that the institutions using such software feel no differently being supported by the commercial open source support companies than by the current range of commercial companies who promote systems they themselves own.

THE CURRENT SITUATION AND FUTURE PROSPECTS

Making predictions is a very hazardous occupation in anything to do with computers since, the future only tends to bring surprises. Developments in many developing countries are not as advanced as might be expected and in some places there is still a problem with electric supply: Adebibo reporting on usage of catalogues by students at the University of Ilorin in Nigeria stated: "Most respondents claimed to know how to use the card catalogues and OPAC but only a few use them. The possible reason for this low level use of the OPAC is power outages, which have become the rule in Nigeria rather than an exception. Overall, as the power of the internet increases, particularly its bandwidth and its reliability, library automation in developing countries will have the same capabilities as the industrialised world, but not the finance to support it.

In developed countries it is felt by some that the future of library automation lies in open source (outside the control of commercial suppliers) or 'Cloud Computing' (very much controlled by commercial suppliers who provide software on their own hardware and the clients access the data via the Internet). However if solutions to library automation are hosted services in the industrialised world, the suppliers of the service would be able to charge developing countries as little as they wish on the basis that every amount, however little, is profit. This has happened with hosted electronic journals where deals have been made by publishers to cover entire countries which are less than the licence fee required for a university in the west. As suggested, see if this happens. As with e-journals, it needs a champion like eIFL to promote to the suppliers the benefits of their working with developing institutions in what may be perceived as an altruistic way.

LIBRARY AUTOMATION IN ACADEMIC LIBRARIES IN INDIA PROBLEMS AND PROSPECTS

The history of library automation is sufficiently old now. It started in early fifties in the Untied States of America. The landmark was the initiation of MARC project by the Library of Congress. During 1960s some experiments were carried out in India in this field but very sparingly. During late seventies there were some achievements like production of National Union Catalogue of Scientific Serials by INSDOC, production of Union Catalogue of DRDO libraries of Western Region by the Institute of Armament Technology at Pune. Then came eighties and the whole focus of the librarians shifted towards library automation. A number of seminars were organised on the library automation and still being done so. We graduated from simple library operations to specialised functions including networking. Now we talk about digital libraries and e-journals. We have come a long way. But we are a country where bullock cart and cars are seen on the same road so blocking the fast moving traffic and those bullock carts restrict the speed of the cars to its own speed. To overcome this problem there are only two ways. First, replace the bullock cart with a car, and second, bypass the bullock cart and leave it behind. The state of library automation in our university libraries is more or less the same. We have the libraries like IIT libraries which are highly automated and also totally manual libraries which are really restricting the speed of academic and research in the country.

FACTORS RESPONSIBLE FOR AUTOMATION IN ACADEMIC LIBRARIES

There are several reasons which can be cited for this difference. *Some of them are*:

- Attitude and awareness of the management
- Attitude and awareness of the Users specially faculty
- Resources available
- Non-availability of suitable software
- Level and skill of staff
- Geographical locations.

Attitude and Initiative of the Management

Attitude and initiative on the part of the management has played major role in library automation in Indian University Libraries. The management here includes both the university management and the librarian as a secretary of the management whose task is to carry out the decisions taken by the executive bodies of the university, such as Syndicate, Executive Council, etc. If the Librarian had the initiative then he was able to convince the authorities about this emergent need. In some of the cases, the initiative also came from top and the Librarian was forced (or bypassed) to do it. But the best blend was when the initiative of both the Librarian and University Authorities was synergised. If there was no initiative on both the ends than there was no progress.

Attitude and Initiative of the Uses

A library may be as smart as its readers. If the readers are smart and well aware they may force the authorities to work towards library automation. If the readers are knowledgeable about the development being taking place in the information technology, they have influenced the use of computers in library to a great extent. This is more true about faculty as they are the people who participate in decision making process. The good examples are the libraries of IITs and other higher engineering educational institutions.

Resources Available

The third important factor is the resources available with the university libraries. The resources include both financial as well as human resources. In most of the universities, the librarians are given funds only for books and journals. Some libraries do not want to or are not allowed the funds received for books and journals to be used for any other purpose, even though the University Grants Commission (UGC) guidelines permit the use of a certain percentage towards such activities (In VIII Plan it was 15 per cent and in IX plan 10 per cent).

Most of the libraries depend on the funds provided by the UGC under Inflibnet project. The distribution of the money under this project was not done logically. Big and small libraries were equated at par and as a result while some libraries remained fund starved some were not able to use the funds. Before distributing funds to libraries there should have been a survey of the requirement and certain guidelines laid down. Besides this there are no other financial resources available with the university libraries.

In order to save the university libraries from going further down UGC must do something in this direction. Another very serious problem, may be more serious than the financial one, is the lack of trained manpower.

Many of our library science schools have not based their curricula on the automation requirement of the university libraries. Some of them are even teaching today what was designed thirty or forty years back although that has become totally outdated. Not many library schools produce a candidate who can straight away go the Automation Department of a University Library and can independently work without any further training. The bifurcation of the library science schools from libraries are perhaps the one of the main important reasons for that.

As a result our profession became the only profession where practice went far ahead of the teaching. In the country people are talking about digital libraries and web-OPACs and we are teaching fundamental of computers in our library schools. This is the only profession where getting a professional degree does not require any professional training. Can you imagine a doctor without hospital training or an engineer without a training in Industry.

Non-availability of Suitable Software

Non-availability of suitable software has also played an important role. Though there are a number of software available for library management but most of them are non- standard. The main reason behind is that most of the software have been developed without the help of a qualified librarian. As a result there were a stream of non-standard software. Some of these softwares have been developed by big corporations like CMC but have not been proved very successful. The software developed by institutions (for example DESIDOC, INSDOC, etc.,) could not be successful as they were lacking in marketing and after sales service. The librarian is confused as he is not in a position to decide what to select.

Level of Skill of Library Staff

The level of skill of library staff also played a very important role. In our country there are no standard for level of subordinate staff to be recruited in academic libraries. There educational and professional qualification vary from state to state. In some of the cases the library assistants are recruited with 12th pass and a six months certificate in library science while in Central institutions like IITs and Central Universities it is minimum graduation and degree in library science. The institutions having better stuff went far ahead (though there are exceptions to that). The better qualified staff was better oriented towards progressive thinking which could move the things fast. This point emphasises the requirement of a uniform qualification policy for the recruitment of staff in academic institutions.

Geographical Location

Geographical location of an institution also played a very important role. The institutions near to a metro city were benefited by the availability of the resources. They were having better approach to hardware and software market and also the manpower for data entry. They were having approach to better training facilities. Hyderabad is a good example which can be cited.

PRESENT STATUS OF LIBRARY AUTOMATION IN UNIVERSITY LIBRARIES

The real boost in library automation came from the establishment of the INFLIBNET Centre. Before Inflibnet scattered efforts were being made in academic libraries specially in the institutions of special characters like IITs, IIMs, etc. INFLIBNET proved a real catalyst. Inflibnet started with scratch. At that time there were no financial assistance available to the University Libraries for automation. For the first time it was established that automation was the need of hour. The finances were allocated for the first time. The standards were established about the data capturing. The format was finalised and the Karvan started. As one estimate at present about 120 university libraries have been using computers in their activities. Some of the University libraries are even establishing digital libraries not only of already available digital resources but are digitising their own litreature. About 50 university libraries have their web pages.

AREAS WHERE COMPUTERS ARE BEING USED

The following are the areas where computer are being used at present:

- Online public access catalogue
- Circulation
- Acquisition
- Serial control
- Intranet
- Internet
- CD-ROM services

Online Public Access Catalogue (OPACs)

The problem being faced by the users in locating the document was the first to be targeted in the library automation. As a result the work first started in this direction. There was one more reason for this and that was the availability of CDS/ ISIS software which had the facility of catalogue only. It was in contrast of the special libraries where the work first started on providing information services like CD-ROM search. Even today this area of automation has more activity than any other area. It has now graduated to Web-OPAC (web based online public access catalogues) where university libraries have made their databases available on their web sites. This has eliminated the need of installation of search software on the user's terminal. One potential which remains unutilised is the use of search data for research purpose as the search history can provide very useful tools for the librarians to formulate their collection development plans.

Circulation

Circulation is one of the main activities of a university library or any library per say. In university libraries, however, the number of books issued and retuned are more than in special libraries. Therefore, the next area which was taken up was the circulation. In some of the libraries the number of books issued/returned may be more than one thousand per day. We at IIT Roorkee (formerly University of Roorkee) has experience of issuing 1500 books in six working hours. Sometimes there used to be a queue of more than 100 students, since, the free hours for all students used to be the same, before automated circulation started.

Use of barcodes had made the life very simple due to added accuracy and speed. Besides speeding up the issue/return, printing reports, sending reminders also become very easy. Circulation data also provides a very important insight into the book use pattern. Librarians should try to use this data for research and development purpose.

Acquisition

Use of computers in acquisition remains a low priority area. Not many libraries are using computers in acquisition. On reason may be the continuously reducing budget for purchase of books. But this area needs to be strengthened. Computerisation at the stage can help not only in order processing but also can be a very effective tool in budget control. You can allocate funds to different departments based on a set formula, can send department heads about non- availability of funds, can control over ordering and also utilise the data entered at this stage for technical processing and OPAC.

Serial Control

Idiosyncracies involved in serial control affects the use of computers in serial control and hence, the area is not very well represented at automation scenario. One more reason is the unsuitability of serial control modules available in most of the library Management Softwares. The procedures developed by these softwares are so cumbersome that sometimes it looks easier to use normal method rather than automation. However, this area provides very good stage for use of computers as it can help tracking the missing issues very efficiently and provide the current awareness services and even the SDI services besides budget control.

Intranet

Making the information available on intranet is also growing popularity as it eliminates the need of installing the software on the users' terminals. Users can access the catalogue through intranet or they can find the status of the books issued to them through web access. CD-ROM resources and other digital resources can be accessed on intranet. The beauty is that one need not be conversant with the software as the web links are available through the web page. Growing installation of campus wide networks is also playing a positive role in this direction.

Internet

Use of Internet for academic purposes is also increasing day by day. More and more libraries are putting their resources on Internet. Internet is the medium both to access and disseminate information. Internet has emerged as a very big virtual library which has information on practically every subject and in every media may it be text, audio or video. Libraries should use this facility to the best of their capability. They should provide links to similar type of libraries through web pages. One very good use can be designing of e-gates where user can have access to the electronic resources through a common user interface.

Digital Libraries

Digital library has recently become the buzzword for librarians. In the last year most of the seminars and the conferences had 'digital libraries' as their theme. Digital libraries can be of two types, *i.e.,* digital libraries of the digital text available in the market such as e-journals, CD-ROM databases, e-books, software, etc., or it can be developed from the printed text available in the library. If a library takes a decision to develop a digital library of its collection specially theses, dissertations and old journals, it can solve the problem of space and preservation both. But the decision about creating such decision is taken to be very carefully as it will prove a very costly venture both in terms of money and manpower.

PROSPECTS

Having talked about the problems and areas of applications let us talk about future prospects. I can definitely say that the things are changing for the good. Now University authorities are realising that there is no way to escape library automation. They are finding various ways to finance their library automation projects. Librarians are also realising that they can not remain indifferent to the change, otherwise they will be labelled outdated. One area of concern is the library science graduates being produced by our library schools It is surprising that UGC is giving responsibility of refresher courses of library science to the library science school and not to the libraries who are established themselves as advanced libraries and uses the technology far ahead than the library science schools. Existing staff is getting rid of the fear of computerisation. They are coming forward to learn and make themselves suitable to face the challenges of the new millennium. Standardisation is increasing and the better softwares are available.

9

Digital Library as a Tool of Library Networking

A digital library is a library in which collections are stored in digital formats (as opposed to print, microform, or other media) and accessible by computers. The digital content may be stored locally, or accessed remotely via computer networks. A digital library is a type of information retrieval system.

The DELOS Digital Library Reference Model defines a digital library as:

An organization, which might be virtual, that comprehensively collects, manages and preserves for the long term rich digital content, and offers to its user communities specialized functionality on that content, of measurable quality and according to codified policies.

The first use of the term digital library in print may have been in a 1988 report to the Corporation for National Research Initiatives The term digital libraries was first popularized by the NSF/DARPA/NASA Digital Libraries Initiative in 1994.

These draw heavily on As We May Think by Vannevar Bush in 1945, which set out a vision not in terms of technology, but user experience. The term virtual library was initially used interchangeably with digital library, but is now primarily used for libraries that are virtual in other senses (such as libraries which aggregate distributed content).

TYPES OF DIGITAL LIBRARIES

The term digital library is diffuse enough to be applied to a wide range of collections and organizations, but, to be considered a digital library, an online collection of information must be managed by and made accessible to a community of users. Thus, some web sites can be considered digital libraries, but far from all. Many of the best known digital libraries are older than the web including Project Perseus, Project Gutenberg, and ibiblio.

Nevertheless, as a result of the development of the internet and its search potential, digital libraries such as the European Library and the Library of Congress are now developing in a Web-based environment. Public, school and college libraries are also able to develop digital download websites, featuring eBooks, audiobooks, music and video.

A distinction is often made between content that was created in a digital format, known as born-digital, and information that has been converted from a physical medium, e.g., paper, by digitizing. The term hybrid library is sometimes used for libraries that have both physical collections and digital collections. For example, American Memory is a digital library within the Library of Congress. Some important digital libraries also serve as long term archives, for example, the ePrint arXiv, and the Internet Archive.

Academic Repositories

Many academic libraries are actively involved in building institutional repositories of the institution's books, papers, theses, and other works which can be digitized or were 'born digital'. Many of these repositories are made available to the general public with few restrictions, in accordance with the goals of open access, in contrast to the publication of research in commercial journals, where the publishers often limit access rights. Institutional, truly free, and corporate repositories are sometimes referred to as digital libraries.

Digital Archives

Physical archives differ from physical libraries in several ways. Traditionally, archives were defined as:

- Containing primary sources of information (typically letters and papers directly produced by an individual or organization) rather than the secondary sources found in a library (books, periodicals, etc);
- Having their contents organized in groups rather than individual items;
- Having unique contents.

The technology used to create digital libraries has been even more revolutionary for archives since it breaks down the second and third of these general rules. In other words, "digital archives" or "online archives" will still generally contain primary sources, but they are likely to be described individually rather than (or in addition to) in groups or collections, and because they are digital their contents are easily reproducible and may indeed have been reproduced from elsewhere. The Oxford Text Archive is generally considered to be the oldest digital archive of academic physical primary source materials.

Leaders in the Field

Project Gutenberg, Google Book Search, Windows Live Search Books(shutdown), Internet Archive, Cornell University, The Library of Congress World Digital Library, The Digital Library at the University of

Michigan, and Carnegie Mellon University's Million Book Project are considered leaders in the field of digital library creation and management.

The Future

Large scale digitization projects are underway at Google, the Million Book Project, and Internet Archive. With continued improvements in book handling and presentation technologies such as optical character recognition and ebooks, and development of alternative depositories and business models, digital libraries are rapidly growing in popularity as demonstrated by Google, Yahoo!, and MSN's efforts. Just as libraries have ventured into audio and video collections, so have digital libraries such as the Internet Archive.

Searching

Most digital libraries provide a search interface which allows resources to be found. These resources are typically deep web (or invisible web) resources since they frequently cannot be located by search engine crawlers. Some digital libraries create special pages or sitemaps to allow search engines to find all their resources.

Digital libraries frequently use the Open Archives Initiative Protocol for Metadata Harvesting (OAI-PMH) to expose their metadata to other digital libraries, and search engines like Google Scholar, Yahoo! and Scirus can also use OAI-PMH to find these deep web resources.

There are two general strategies for searching a federation of digital libraries:

- Distributed searching, and
- Searching previously harvested metadata.

Distributed searching typically involves a client sending multiple search requests in parallel to a number of servers in the federation. The results are gathered, duplicates are eliminated or clustered, and the remaining items are sorted and presented back to the client. Protocols like Z39.50 are frequently used in distributed searching.

A benefit to this approach is that the resource-intensive tasks of indexing and storage are left to the respective servers in the federation. A drawback to this approach is that the search mechanism is limited by the different indexing and ranking capabilities of each database, making it difficult to assemble a combined result consisting of the most relevant found items.

Searching over previously harvested metadata involves searching a locally stored index of information that has previously been collected from the libraries in the federation. When a search is performed, the search mechanism does not need to make connections with the digital libraries it is searching - it already has a local representation of the information.

This approach requires the creation of an indexing and harvesting mechanism which operates regularly, connecting to all the digital libraries and querying the whole collection in order to discover new and updated resources. OAI-PMH is frequently used by digital libraries for allowing metadata to be harvested. A benefit to this approach is that the search mechanism has full control over indexing and ranking algorithms, possibly allowing more consistent results. A drawback is that harvesting and indexing systems are more resource-intensive and therefore expensive.

CONSTRUCTION AND ORGANIZATION

Frameworks

A digital library can be built around specific repository software. The best known examples of this are DSpace, Eprints, Fedora, dLibra(Poland), and Greenstone Digital Library Software. In 2009, Fedora Commons and the DSpace Foundation merged to create a new organization, DuraSpace

The Reference Model for an Open Archival Information System (OAIS) provides a framework to address digital preservation.

Other formal frameworks include the DELOS Reference Model(Agosti, et al., 2006) and the Streams, Structures, Spaces, Scenarios, Societies (5S) formal framework.

Digitization

In the past few years, procedures for digitizing books at high speed and comparatively low cost have improved considerably with the result that it is now possible to plan the digitization of millions of books per year for creating digital libraries.

ADVANTAGES

The advantages of digital libraries as a means of easily and rapidly accessing books, archives and images of various types are now widely recognized by commercial interests and public bodies alike.

Traditional libraries are limited by storage space; digital libraries have the potential to store much more information, simply because digital information requires very little physical space to contain it. As such, the cost of maintaining a digital library is much lower than that of a traditional library.

A traditional library must spend large sums of money paying for staff, book maintenance, rent, and additional books. Digital libraries do away with these fees. Both types of library require cataloguing input to allow users to locate and retrieve material.

Digital libraries may be more willing to adopt innovations in technology providing users with improvements in electronic and audio book technology as well as presenting new forms of communication such as wikis and blogs; conventional libraries may consider that providing online access to their OPAC catalogue is sufficient.

An important advantage to digital conversion is increased accessibility to users. There in also availability to individuals who may not be traditional patrons of a library, due to geographic location or organizational affiliation.

- *No physical boundary*: The user of a digital library need not to go to the library physically; people from all over the world can gain access to the same information, as long as an Internet connection is available.
- *Round the clock availability*: A major advantage of digital libraries is that people can gain access to the information at any time, night or day.
- *Multiple access*: The same resources can be used simultaneously by a number of institutions and patrons. This may not be the case for copyrighted material: a library may have a license for "lending out" only one copy at a time; this is achieved with a system of digital rights management where a resource can become inaccessible after expiration of the lending period or after the lender chooses to make it inaccessible (equivalent to returning the resource).
- *Information retrieval*: The user is able to use any search term (word, phrase, title, name, subject) to search the entire collection. Digital libraries can provide very user-friendly interfaces, giving clickable access to its resources.
- *Preservation and conservation*: Digitization is not a long-term preservation solution for physical collections, but does succeed in providing access copies for materials that would otherwise fall to degradation from repeated use. Digitized collections and born-digital objects pose many preservation and conservation concerns that analog materials do not.
- *Space*: Whereas traditional libraries are limited by storage space, digital libraries have the potential to store much more information, simply because digital information requires very little physical space to contain them and media storage technologies are more affordable than ever before.
- *Added value*: Certain characteristics of objects, primarily the quality of images, may be improved. Digitization can enhance legibility and remove visible flaws such as stains and discoloration.

PROBLEMS

Digital Preservation

The work needed to ensure that digital content is maintained and accessible into the future is beginning to be addressed.

Technological standards change over time and forward migration must be a constant consideration of every library. Migration is a means of transferring an unstable digital object to another more stable format, operating system, or programming language. Migration allows the ability to retrieve and display digital objects that are in danger of becoming extinct.

This is a rather successful short-term solution for the problem of aging and obsolete digital formats, but with the ever-changing nature of computer technologies, migration becomes this never-ending race to transfer digital objects to new and more stable formats. Migration is also flawed in the sense that when the digital files are being transferred, the new platform may not be able to capture the full integrity of the original object.

There are countless artifacts sitting in libraries all over the world that are essentially useless because the technology required to access the source is obsolete. In addition to obsolescence, there are rising costs that result from continually replacing the older technologies. This issue can dominate preservation policy and may put more focus on instant user access in place of physical preservation.

Copyright and Licensing

Some people have criticized that digital libraries are hampered by copyright law, because works cannot be shared over different periods of time in the manner of a traditional library. The republication of material on the Web by libraries may require permission from rights holders, and there is a conflict of interest between them and publishers who may wish to create Web versions of their content for commercial purposes. There is a dilution of responsibility that occurs as a result of the spread-out nature of digital resources. Complex intellectual property matters may become involved since digital material isn't always owned by a library.

The content is, in many cases, public domain or self-generated content only. Some digital libraries, such as Project Gutenberg, work to digitize out-of-copyright works and make them freely available to the public. An estimate of the number of distinct books still existent in library catalogues from 2000BC to 1960, has been made. The Fair Use Provisions (17 USC § 107) under copyright law provide specific guidelines under which circumstances libraries are allowed to copy digital resources. Four factors that constitute fair use are purpose of use, nature of the work, market impact, and amount or substantiality used. Some digital libraries acquire a license to "lend out" its resources. This may involve the restriction of lending out only one copy at a time for each license, and applying a system of digital rights management for this purpose.

Metadata Creation

The ability to find works of interest in large libraries is directly related to how well they are catalogued. While cataloguing electronic works digitised from a libraries' existing holding may be as simple as copying moving a record for the print to the electronic item, with complex and born-digital works require substantially more effort. While full text search can be used for some searches, there are many common catalog searches which can't be performed using full text, including:

- Finding texts which are the translation of other texts
- Linking texts published under pseudonyms to the real author (Samuel Clemens and Mark Twain, for example)
- Differentiating non-fiction from parody (The Onion from The New York Times, for example)

FRAMEWORK FOR BUILDING DIGITAL LIBRARY

The Greenstone digital library software provides a wide range of tools for building digital library collections. Based on our own extensive and varied experience, and that of others, we have designed a new framework for building digital library collections. We call it "Greenstone 3" to distinguish it from the earlier system, "Greenstone 2". The new framework is supported by a fresh implementation that is completely independent of the existing one.

It capitalizes on the best ideas from the existing system, which we have further refined and developed to open new avenues through which users can tailor their digital library collections.

Several pertinent new open standards have emerged since the original design many years ago, and a key objective is to incorporate them into the new design. The trend towards increasingly open, flexible architectures can be traced in the development of digital library protocols.

The Open Archives Protocol for Metadata Harvesting has provided a simple base-line for metadata access, and subsequent work strives to base component-based, modular protocols upon it. The METS document framework provides an open, extensible system for representing documents in digital repositories. Greenstone 3 adopts the same approach for a range of digital library functions, as this paper demonstrates.

Set against the move towards standard protocols, today's digital library systems must confront an increasing range of document formats and media, architectural designs for browsing and classification, indexing requirements, and user interface techniques.

This drives the demand for open architectures, but makes it hard to provide well-formed and supportive infrastructures that maximise reuse of individual components and the reliability of the system as a whole. This paper proceeds as follows.

First we introduce and describe the configuration structure and document representation used through our new building architecture. The second section describes the building process itself.

This is followed by the model that we have adopted to ensure that the new architecture is extensible. Fourth, we compare this with the previous Greenstone 2 design and present an example use-case scenario, identifying the key advantages of the new open collection-building architecture. We conclude by relating the new architecture to existing collection-building systems.

COLLECTION CONFIGURATION AND DOCUMENT REPRESENTATION

Before describing the process by which collections are built, we will show how the collection-building process is configured, and how documents are represented internally within the system. In we described our "plugin" mechanism and showed how it provides great flexibility for such varied tasks as ingesting both document files and metadata files, extracting text and metadata from different file formats, and expanding compressed files.

It has proved so successful that we have adopted it in the new framework. However, we depart radically from our earlier system by using the METS framework (which postdates that system) throughout for internal document representation.

Configuration

Collections are designed individually, and the structure of a collection is encapsulated in an XML file called the "collection configuration file." Its contents include build-time configuration options such as:

- The document types that the collection should recognise
- The metadata access structures or "classifiers" that are to be provided for users to browse the collection, such as by Titles A–Z
- The full-text indexes to build for searching the collection. The configuration file also contains run-time information about the collections, for example display options.

All that is omitted is the part concerning the purely runtime configuration. It defines a simple collection of HTML pages and plain text files, along with XML files that define metadata that is to be associated with these documents.

A document may consist of several separate files—for example, in this collection any images associated with the HTML pages will be contained within the HTML document rather than being identified as documents in their own right. Or a document may comprise complementary pairs of files—like a Word file and matching PDF version.

A collection configuration file

```
<documenttypes>
<document type="HTML">
<document type="Text">
<document type="MetadataXML">
</doctypes>
<search type="mg">
<index name="dtx" level="document" field="text">
```

```
<displayItem name="name" lang="en">entire documents</
displayItem>
<displayItem name="name" lang="fr">documents entiers</
displayItem>
<displayItem name="name" lang="es">documentos enteros</
displayItem>
</index>
<index name="stx" level="section" field="text">
<displayItem name="name" lang="en">chapters</displayItem>
<displayItem name="name" lang="fr">chapitres</displayItem>
<displayItem name="name" lang="es">cap?tulos</displayItem>
</index>
<index name="stt" level="section" field="title">
<displayItem name="name" lang="en">section titles</displayItem>
<displayItem name="name" lang="fr">titres des sections</displayItem>
<displayItem name="name" lang="es">t?tulos de las secciones</
displayItem>
</index>
<format>
<gsf:template match="documentNode"><td
valign="top"><gsf:link><gsf:icon/></gsf:link>
</td><td><gsf:metadata name="Title"/></td></gsf:template>
</format>
</search>
<browse>
<classifier name="CLSubject" type="Hierarchy" file="subject.xml"
field="Subject"/>
<classifier name="CLTitle" type="AZList"/>
<classifier name="CLOrganization" type="Hierarchy"
file="organization.xml"
field="Organization"/>
<classifier name="CLKeyword" type="List" file="howto.xml"
field="HowTo">
<displayItem name="name" lang="en">HowTo</displayItem>
</classifier>
</browse>
```

In this case the MG indexer will be used to build document-level and section-level indexes of the main text, and a section-level index of Title metadata. The browse block defines the metadata-based browsing mechanisms through which users can access the collection.

This configuration file specifies a hierarchical subject browser by defining a Hierarchy-type classifier of each document's Subject metadata, and the file that defines that hierarchy is named.

Other browsing classifiers are also defined. Run-time configuration items can be seen in both the classification and indexation parts of the file. For example. the "displayItem" nodes give names for the indexes (in English, French and Spanish) and for one of the browsers.

The Greenstone 3 building programme reads this file and configures the components to be used by the collection-building process. Many default options are implied. For instance, this collection would automatically expand Zip files— because the Zip expansion plugin is enabled by default. The process followed during building will be described later.

METS and Document Representation

We were eager to adopt an open, standard form for modelling the content and metadata of a document. The METS framework supports a free selection of metadata formats and avoids duplicating data that is already stored in constituent files. Using this standard, open framework should facilitate interoperation with other digital library systems. These are the METS Header, Administrative Metadata, Descriptive Metadata, File lists and Structural lists.

The structural content is the only required section, and the content of the remaining sections is mapped onto the encoded structure. For the sake of clarity, this example shows only the connections between sections and the descriptive metadata and files.

A document is encoded into METS form by a plugin that corresponds to the type of the document. Each such plugin extracts any appropriate metadata from the document files (e.g. title), catalogues the files that comprise the document, and extracts the document text in subsequent phases.

In other words, it encapsulates the document content and acts as a standard gateway to its METS representation. This means that other phases of the building process are able to access data without having to understand the particulars of each file format—even if the data is stored as a binary object.

Document text can be provided in one of three ways, as the processing component requires. Plain Unicode is a simple baseline recognized throughout the system. At a higher level of sophistication, an XML representation is supported.

Finally, indexers can use the underlying binary files if they so desire. A complete document plugin provides all these formats, though the XML representation is optional. In any case, a document may have no textual content whatsoever (in which case all forms are empty).

For example, a PostScript file can be translated into an XML format. The PostScript plugin allows a plain-text reduction of this, but if an indexer wishes to treat PostScript files in a special way, it can access the original files directly. METS documents are partitioned into several components, the most common elements being structure, files, administrative metadata and descriptive metadata.

A given document may form part of a single file, or be an agglomeration of individual files and parts of files. Metadata can be associated with a document as a whole or with any part of its structure. A document may also have more than one structural form.

For instance, it may have both a page based structure and a logical chapter-and-section based structure. Metadata may be provided in several different formats and standards, and this allows for the native coding of metadata on the document in different formats—for instance RFC1807 and Dublin Core. When a document first enters the library, it is given a unique identifier. That identifier will remain with the document throughout any subsequent revisions, and is recorded within the METS framework. Having described the configuration controls and document representation that underpin the new collection-building architecture, we now describe the building process itself.

Building Digital Library Collections

In our new architecture, collections are built in several distinct phases, which occur in sequence.

- *Expansion*: Compressed files such as Zip archives are expanded, and links to web sites are expanded into lists of constituent web pages.
- *Recognition*: All files are sent to the Recognition Manager, which identifies groups of files as documents.
- *Encoding*: All the recognised documents are catalogued for the subsequent phases of building.
- *Extraction*: Every document is passed through extractors, which use special processing algorithms to extract information from the document (e.g. title, keyphrases) or add metadata stored in special files.
- *Classification*: Documents are assigned to classifiers (e.g. topical classifiers, ordered list classifiers) depending on their inherent and extracted metadata.
- *Indexation*: Documents are sent to indexers to build indexes that support later searching.
- *Validation*: Post-building checks are carried out on the collection as a whole, and on its constituent documents.

Expansion

Before any individual documents are identified, any files that are compressed, or refer to external sources, are expanded. The case of a Zip archive has already been mentioned; other cases include OAI repositories, and links to web sites via a file of URLs.

The purpose of this phase is to create a complete list of all files that are available for building the collection. These raw files are then passed to the next phase for grouping into documents.

Recognition

The relationship between files and documents is complex. A file of emails may be seen as one file that contains many documents. Conversely, a JPEG image and a plain text file that describes it may constitute a two-file document. Our architecture uses special "recogniser" plugins to address the problem of distinguishing documents from files.

When the building process is initialised, all plugins listed in the collection configuration file are registered by a "Recogniser Manager." When the Expansion phase terminates, this Manager is handed each file in the collection in turn. It sends these files to each plugin.

For some simple cases—like a plain text document comprising a single file—the plugins are trivial. However, in other circumstances conflicts can emerge, and the Recogniser Manager includes a scheme for resolving these. For example, suppose a collection includes both web pages and digital photographs. A single JPEG file may be a document in its own right, or form part of a web page. By default, JPEG files that are referred to by web pages, being constituent parts of a larger whole, are not treated as documents in their own right, while JPEGs that do not appear in the web pages are identified as separate, discrete documents. This default behaviour can be adjusted, if desired, to allow all JPEG files to be treated as documents, even ones that also appear in a web document.

The same issue arises with any image file on a web page. Furthermore, such a file (for instance a logo) could well be part of more than one document. In this case it is treated as a subcomponent of all the documents in which it appears. A web page and associated files cannot form a strict subset of another web page, because the.html files must necessarily differ. The same strategy is used in other cases.

Once the Recogniser Manager has taken a pass through the entire inventory of files and identified the documents, it resolves any conflicts that occur and hands the output on to the Encoding phase.

At this stage all that is known of a document is the list of files that constitute its content. No metadata has yet been assigned—even that found within the document itself. The content and representation of any metadata internal to the document is identified in the next phase.

Encoding

Documents appear in a wide variety of forms, textual encodings and file formats. The Encoding phase creates the document framework that is used throughout the remainder of the building process.

This framework supports the retrieval of the full text of the document. It contains metadata defined within the document, and will also contain any metadata added to it. Finally, it binds the document, with its representation, into the classification and indexation structures.

The METS document framework is used to encapsulate the files, metadata and structure of each document. At the end of the Encoding phase, documents are ready to be processed by extracting further metadata, indexation and storage.

Extraction

The Extraction phase is controlled by the Extraction Manager, which filters the documents through a series of extraction plugins. These can have one of two origins:

- Metadata-only files identified in the recognition phase above
- Explicit mention in the collection configuration file

The former method is typically used for files of descriptive metadata that are provided with the documents. The latter is used to invoke automatic extraction tools such as the KEA Keyphrase Extractor.

At the conclusion of the Extraction phase, all metadata has been collected and stored in the METS document representation. The next two phases place the documents into the context of the collection as a whole.

Classification

The Classification phase uses each document's metadata to site it within the browsing structures, or "classifiers," that are supplied by the collection to access the documents it contains. Each classification is represented by a plugin specified in the collection configuration file.

There may be more than one instance of any given classification type, achieved by initiating a separate copy of the plugin for each classification. Classifications are stored in a database, and when a document is matched to a node in a classification, this fact is recorded in both the document and the classification node.

Indexation

Indexing follows classification. To support the widest range of indexing systems, indexers are also treated as plugins. Again, the indexer—or indexers—used when building a collection are determined by the collection configuration file. For each indexer, parameters can be supplied that control its behaviour.

Indexers can build several different indexes, each with its own parameters. In the case of MG, for example, the structure level (e.g. document, section) and field (full text, title, etc.) can be controlled.

Validation

Validation plugins are used to control the quality of the collection by checking the final form of each document, and the collection as a whole. For example, a collection may insist on a complete metadata set—that is, all compulsory fields must be present. Or the databases may be checked for empty classification nodes, which may be suppressed. Validation could be done in earlier phases, but we separate it into a final phase for architectural clarity.

Summary

Greenstone 3 uses a seven-phase build architecture. The first three phases identify and store each document. The next three phases enrich and index those documents. The final phase provides for quality control. The phases support different behaviours and activities that are required by different types of software, and a set of distinct functions that should assist programmers in extending any given implementation of the architecture.

Individual documents are recorded in the METS framework, which provides a standard form that gives access to different metadata formats, file formats and document structures. The document plugins give the indexation and classification components access to content without having to decode or transcribe documents.

EXTENDIBILITY: MANAGERS AND PLUGINS

The central role of plugins in each phase should now be apparent. However, we have made little mention of the structure of plugins themselves, or how they connect to the core system. The architecture achieves extensibility through Plugins and Managers. Each phase of the building process is controlled by a Manager— e.g. the Recogniser Manager, the Indexer Manager.

Managers are configured through the collection configuration file when the building process starts; and in some cases further configuration occurs when special files—like metadata-only files—are found when building.

Each manager coordinates the plugins for its phase of the build cycle. Each manager works in the same way. It initialises and configures its plugins. Then, when its phase runs, it takes each plugin in turn and tells it to do any necessary preparatory work. Next it passes each document or file in turn to that plugin. Finally it sends the plugin a termination message. Document plugins are unique in that they apply to several different phases of the building operation, whereas other plugins appear only within one phase. Managers accept a list of plugins from the configuration file.

New plugins are readily installed into the system by placing them into the plugin directory corresponding to their type, and adding them to the configuration file of one or more collections.

There is a standardised interface for all extraction, indexation and classification plugins.

This includes:

- GetNumberOfPasses Return the number of passes required by the plugin
- StartPass(int) Begin a pass for this plugin

- ProcessDocument(Document) Process the given document
- EndPass(int) Terminate a given pass
- Tidyup Close the plugin
- Configure(Node)

Pass configuration information to the plugin. The configuration information mentioned in the last method is taken from the collection configuration file, where it is specified as an XML node. It is particular to each plugin. The get Number Of Passes method allows plugins to request multiple passes over the documents. The MG indexation plugin, for example, requires a minimum of two passes plus a further two passes for each index it builds. Running each plugin separately and serially keeps memory overheads down.

ADVANCE OVER EARLIER WORK

The architecture that we have described capitalizes on lessons learned from the existing Greenstone digital library system, and incorporates some very significant improvements. At the time the earlier system was designed several important open standards did not exist, or were available only in draft form.

For example, the METS Document Framework, a key component of the new architecture, was unborn. The original Greenstone design adopted ad hoc file formats that became inconsistent with emerging norms.

Collection configuration was viewed as a compilation process directed by a configuration file whose format was similar to the Makefile format rather than by directives couched in a structured markup language. It used an HTML-like structure, the Greenstone Archive format, to store documents and metadata, which is less structured than modern XML.

The internal formats were also inconsistent with each other—configuration files being flat files whereas document files were derived from HTML. These simple and apparently cosmetic differences magnified into large-scale divergence.

Architecture

In Greenstone 2, collections are constructed in two phases: importing and building. The first parallels the Expansion, Recognition and Encoding phases of Greenstone 3, while the second mirrors the Extraction, Classification and Indexation phases. Both phases use the same set of plugins, which are listed in the collection's configuration file and loaded separately in each phase—despite the fact that some plugins only pertain to one phase.

Document plugins, like HTMLPlug, played a rather different role from that described above. Documents were identified by a single key file—e.g. an HTML file—and complex document structures were poorly supported.

A special generic plugin was later developed that recognized multi-component documents such as a Word file and its corresponding PDF version. However, the plugins had to be carefully ordered in the configuration file to recognize this compound document. Once a file was captured by a plugin, subsequent plugins could not see it. The Recognition phase described above facilitates complex document forms and arbitrates competing claims for a file by different document types.

Plugin Details

Document plugins handle Encoding very differently in the new design. Originally, all documents were encoded into the standard Greenstone Archive Format as soon as they were encountered. This duplicated content, and could lose, or render inaccessible, some information in the original file.

The benefit was that all documents were presented to subsequent phases in a standardised format. In the new architecture, plugins convert document content to either plain text or well-formed XML, which allows formats such as TEI to be retained verbatim.

The METS Framework provides a standard container for metadata and structural information. This open public standard retains the benefits of the original Greenstone Archive Format, and goes further by allowing multiple structures within the same document. Plugins in Greenstone 2 could be of three types—Expansion (then called "structural"), Document, and Extraction (called "metadata").

All were placed in the same pipeline. The new architecture makes a clearer distinction between phases and allows a richer variety of documents. For most tasks, it supports clearer, more compact, interfaces. In addition, monolithic parts of the old design, such as indexation, are now readily adjusted and extended in the flexible manner exhibited by other phases (such as Expansion).

Example: The Kids Digital Library

We briefly present an actual digital libraries that was difficult to accommodate within the earlier design, and show how it benefits from the new architecture. In the Kids Digital Library each document can belong to several collections. Some collections are private (e.g. a child's own documents), others public. Some documents are unchanging (accepted final essays); others are under continually revision by a restricted group of users.

Students can annotate the work of others, and teachers provide feedback too. All collections support full-text searching and metadata-based browsing; some have additional browsing facilities. Collections sometimes change rapidly over a short period—e.g. during a scheduled class. Using the new architecture, many of these requirements can be delivered far more easily.

Consistent document identifiers and explicit change history allows revisions of a document, and comments made between changes, to be tracked. Incremental indexing is supported by recording accession and revision data as METS administrative metadata. The METS framework allows files to be duplicated between collections yet reside in only one location. The Kids Digital Library featured some unusual browsing classifiers such as the "Top ten" and

"Latest ten" stories. These require simple support for feature extraction. In the earlier design, this could only be done by altering the building scripts—which caused portability problems, and made it difficult to install new versions of the software. The new architecture circumvents the problem by modularizing feature extraction.

Comparison with other Digital Library Systems

Cheshire II emphasises the construction of digital libraries from original scanned documents. The process described for collection building reveals a system of fixed metadata fields and a strict control of the format in which documents are presented to the system.

Nowhere is support for feature extraction, expansion of compressed files, or novel indexes described. The CORR 2 is built on the NCSTRL software. The CORR documentation reports that the system requires documents to be submitted in a standard source format. No documentation on CORR or NCSTRL describes the parameters for collection configuration.

Conclusion

In the new collection building architecture we have described, the building process is segmented into a number of distinct phases. Once documents are identified, they are encoded into a flexible, open framework (METS) and are passed in that form to the succeeding phases of the build process. Within each phase, the elements are componentised to support greater portability and simpler development.

The build process is configured through a simple XML format file which is readily extensible for future components. We have implemented this architecture in a practical digital library system.

The use of a document framework rather than standardised document encoding has not created any obstacle to providing existing features. Rather, it supports our move to more complex document file structures and permits any processing of the document (e.g. by an indexer) to either refer to the original binary or to extracted content as it chooses.

We believe that the challenge of providing effective, portable solutions to building digital library collections is an important one. As file formats diversify, the issue of digital preservation grows. Similarly, if extraction and indexation technologies are not made more portable their adoption will slow. Our new architecture provides a step forward in meeting these challenges.

CONSTRUCTION OF DYNAMIC DIGITAL LIBRARY

This paper describes a digital library architecture and implementation that is configurable, extensible and dynamic in the way it presents content and in the services it provides. The design manifests itself as a network of modules that communicate in terms of XML messages.

All modules characterize the functionality they implement in response to a "describe yourself" message, and can transform messages using XSLT to support different levels of configurability.

Traditional library values such as backwards compatibility and multiplatform operation are combined with the ability to add new collections and services adaptively. The paper describes the new design and shows how it can be used to build four different digital library systems.

We conclude by showing how the design fits existing interoperability frameworks. This paper describes a digital library design that improves upon the Greenstone toolkit. First, it provides more flexible ways of dynamically configuring the run-time system and adding new services to it. Second, it lowers the overhead incurred by collection developers when accessing this flexibility to organize and present their content. Third, it modularizes the internal structure and simplifies the addition of new modules.

The design is based on widely-accepted standards such as XML, current software practices such as simple protocols (like SOAP), cross-platform development strategies (Java), and contemporary schemes for software modularization and dynamic updates. Most important of all, it is informed by our experience with the current Greenstone system and the problems and challenges faced by real users, international collection developers, and practicing librarians.

The structure of the paper is as follows. First we give some background out of which the requirements for the digital library software arose. Next we describe the new design, called Greenstone, and discuss how it meets the identified needs. Fundamental to the approach is the use of XML throughout for data representation, combined with XSL Transforms to provide a flexible mechanism for adjusting the functionality of the runtime system without having to modify and recompile the source code.

To promote cross-platform independence (which has consumed inordinate human resources in the present Greenstone system) and facilitate the dynamic loading of services and other modules, the implementation uses Java. Following this we describe four very different examples built using the new design. The first demonstrates backwards compatibility, and, in addition, operates within a distributed environment. The second augments text at display time, using an established software tool for text mining developed elsewhere, to show how functionality can be enriched through the introduction of a new service.

The third is a map-based digital library that introduces two new services to support geographic functionality and, while still accessed through a web-based interface, is highly tailored to the specific domain of its source documents. The fourth is a radically different interface for the interactive viewing of search results as a hierarchically organized cluster of documents, and illustrates the versatility of the design in coping with fine-grained interaction. We conclude with a commentary on how the design fits existing interoperability frameworks, from which many valuable lessons have been learned.

Background

Over the years the Greenstone digital library software has been employed by many users internationally to develop a wide variety of digital libraries. In addition to operation over the Web, an early application, and still a major one, is collections of humanitarian information in the form of CD-ROMs that run on any Windows computer (including Windows 3.1).

There are now over two dozen of these collections, and they have been distributed widely by the United Nations and other non government agencies. Many other styles of collection have been developed under Greenstone. They range from numerous personal collections based around common document formats such as E-mail, photographs, Word, and PDF documents through to largescale bibliographic catalogs such as the BBC radio and TV archives.

There are mixed media collections involving text, images and audio drawn from data such as historic newspapers and oral history. Several demonstration music collections support direct content-based retrieval through "query by humming." Many customized and branded user interfaces exist, such as the New York Botanical Gardens, and many international collections in local languages created by institutions in China, India, Croatia, Russia and Israel. The software is distributed in source form, and for convenience binaries are available for Windows, Linux and MacOS X. The user interface is available in 30 languages. A recent addition is a graphical interface for collection design and construction which is also multilingual.

A portfolio of demonstration collections is available at www.nzdl.org, and selected example collections built internationally can be found at www.greenstone.org.

Weaknesses

Many experimental interfaces have been built for Greenstone, some of which make use of a CORBA-based protocol to support distributed client-server interaction. These include a Venn diagram tool for formulating Boolean queries graphically, and a bibliographic visualization tool that plots matching citations on an x-y grid based on publication year and ranked relevance score to the query terms.

However, while perfectly functional, some of these variants are implemented inelegantly, exposing limitations caused by certain aspects of the design. For instance, the immutable nature of the index files generated during the building process makes incremental adjustments to a collection expensive. Another hindrance is the low level of functional customization supported by the runtime system. Although minor presentation tweaks are easy, more extensive changes involve modifying and recompiling the source code. The strongly typed nature of the CORBA protocol was also found to be overly restrictive in many practical situations.

Requirements

From these and other considerations arose the following requirements for an improved design.

- *Backwards compatibility:* Naturally we wish to retain the existing system's strengths. This is accomplished by ensuring that the new design is backward compatible, which has the added benefit of providing existing developers and users with an easy migration path.
- *Levels of customization:* To match the different categories of people involved in constructing digital libraries, different levels of customization are required. For instance, a content developer may wish to include source documents in a new format; a collection editor may seek influence over diverse issues of presentation.
- *Software modularity:* To facilitate development and long-term management of the software, code modularization—a mantra of any software engineering approach—is essential. This is promoted by adopting off-the-shelf technology such as a database system, indexing tools, and page rendering software; and by the use of standards.
- *Service based:* Basing a digital library around a set of services is another way to accomplish modularity—in this case, modularity of function.
- *Distributed architecture:* A rich digital library infrastructure can only be supported by a distributed architecture, and the addition of an open protocol helps to foster interoperability.
- *Future compatibility*: Libraries are long-term institutions with a mandate for preservation, and it is essential that old collections can be presented by future versions of the system. This is a more ambitious requirement than mere extensibility which, although an admirable quality in any design, does not necessarily ensure that future versions can safely interact with current ones.
- *Dynamic:* Many aspects of the library should be dynamic, for example content, whereby documents and metadata can be added, revised and removed while a repository remains on-line, and configuration, where presentational issues can be adjusted and services added at runtime.
- *Integrated documentation:* Large-scale software systems such as digital libraries benefit immensely from the use of an integrated documentation system.
- *Self-describing modules:* This goes a stage further than the previous

item: modules describe themselves in a machine-readable format so that other modules can interact with them without the need for explicit control. Computer environment integration. A digital library should mesh well into a user's existing computer environment. Full integration makes a digital library become a seamless component of each user's work environment.

SOFTWARE DESIGN

The new software design has evolved from the requirements articulated above, our own experience of developing digital library systems, and studies of other open source software and research projects. This section provides an overview of modularity and inter-module communication, and then works through a simple, stand-alone example. The next section describes four very different examples built using the new design, to illustrate the general applicability of the approach.

Modularity

We decided that the best way to meet the challenges posed by the list of requirements was to reimplement Greenstone using a modular topology. In the design, a digital library manifests itself as a network of modules, and communication between them is expressed through an instantiation of XML.

A mandatory requirement for a module—enforced through its base class definition—is that it handles "describe yourself" messages. What kinds of messages follow typically depend on the outcome of an initial "describe yourself". Modules have the ability to transform messages by applying an XSL Transform. This is a particularly useful mechanism for dynamically controlling levels of configurability—one of our requirements. Within the network of modules comprising a digital library, a set of services are defined that prescribe the functionality supported by that particular digital library configuration.

Communication

Modules communicate using synchronous request-response pairs. It does this, providing information about the structure of the service as well as fragments of text to be used for display. These are returned in the language specified in the request. While the language used is structured and typed, it has been crafted in such a way that the information it contains can be open-ended. For example the paramList structure allows other items to be included, such as whether stemming is on or off. In addition to supporting optional parameters, extensions can be introduced without having to update the protocol's API, thereby avoiding the need to propagate code changes to the entire distributed network (which may require taking it off-line while the changes are made).

Programming for a sample XML exchange as a request/response pair.

```
<request to='demo/TextQuery' lang='en' type='describe' uid='21'/>
<response from='demo/TextQuery' lang='en' type='describe'>
<service name='TextQuery' type='query'>
<displayItem name='name'>Search</displayItem>
<displayItem name='description'>Full text search</displayItem>
<displayItem name='submit'>Search</displayItem>
<paramList>
<param name='index' type='enum_single' default='stx'>
<displayItem name="name">Index to search in</displayItem>
<option name="dtx">
<displayItem name="name">entire documents</displayItem>
</option>
<option name="stx">
<displayItem name="name">chapters</displayItem>
</option>
</param>
<param name='maxDocs' type='integer' default='10'>
<displayItem name="name">Maximum hits to return</displayItem>
</param>
<param name="query" type="string">
<displayItem name="name">Query string</displayItem>
</param>
</paramList>
</service>
</response>
```

A Simple Stand-alone Example

It comprises a "back end" server, termed a digital library site in our design, coupled to a "front end" that provides the user interface. The modules' names were chosen to emphasize the roles they play.

The Receptionist's point of contact with the server is the Message Router (MR) module—all communication with the site occurs through this module. The configuration is designed to generalize to a distributed environment.

Add Document is a service that adds a document to a collection. Import Collection imports into the system all documents associated with a collection, converting them where necessary from their original form. Build Collection builds all indexes and browsing structures that are associated with a collection. Activate Collection makes a newly-built collection active, so that it can be seen by digital library users.

These services are all concerned with creating a digital library collection. Being related, they are grouped together into a "service cluster." As far as the digital library user is concerned, a "collection" is a focused group of documents with a uniform means of access. For the system, it is a service cluster that groups a set of services that are related by the data they work on.

Cluster Visualizations

To function it needs the addition of a new build-time service, Vis Construct, which is responsible for computing additional statistics about the collection necessary to perform subsequent document clustering operations, and a sub-classing of the Applet service, tailored for the HTML necessary to embed the visualization applet within a web page.

Besides this, the visualization can interact with any text-based Greenstone collection that defines keyword metadata. The distinctly different interface behaviour is achieved through fine-grained interaction with the existing Text Query and Metadata Retrieve services using SOAP. Derived from the query term entered, there are four views in the visualization. The first is the standard result list format; the other three are based around a shared model of hierarchically clustered documents. The user has entered the query term "recession" to a collection based on the Wall Street Journal and is viewing the result as a Dendro map—the circular arranged tree displayed in the main panel—which contains words like slowing, slowdown and inflationary around the circumference. The size of nodes in the tree represents the number of documents clustered at that point in the hierarchy, and for reasons of space only 5 levels of the tree are shown at a time. Clicking on a node shows a popup menu with the precise number of documents in the cluster and the option of "drilling down".

The consequence of choosing this option is for the tree to be redrawn with the selected node at the centre of the map, thereby exposing more of the detail in that part of the hierarchy.

While all this is going on, the left-panel displays the keywords relevant to the selected cluster, and the bottom panel lists the documents involved. Within the left panel, keywords can be activated or deactivated and the bottom panel dynamically filtered to reflect the changes.

INTEROPERABILITY FRAMEWORKS

This modular, service-based and dynamically configurable approach to digital library architecture can be found in other designs and systems. Two key examples are the Extended Open Archives Initiative protocol (XOAI) proposed by Suleman and Fox and the Open DLib system of Castelli and Pagano. The XOAI protocol, based upon XML and related technologies, builds upon the basic OAI Protocol for Metadata Harvesting. It is a modular protocol which represents each service as a different type of OAI request. This service-based approach is readily seen in Greenstone's protocol, where each service has its own request and response format.

Like OAI and XOAI, Greenstone uses XML for representing requests and responses; providing a gateway between Greenstone and XOAI servers and clients should be readily achievable. The Open DLib system also takes a modular approach to service communication and library construction.

Many of its features are similar to those of XOAI and Greenstone, and the handling of requests to the library map as readily as for XOAI. However, Open DLib is centered upon a "manager" service that coordinates services, responding to the introduction of new services and alterations to existing ones.

Coordination is achieved through a communication protocol between the manager and each service. Individual services, including each library in a federation, acquire data from the manager. The manager does not itself control or direct requests for searches, documents, and so on but instead coordinates between services to ensure consistency. Greenstone provides many of these features—for instance, service description requests—without requiring a centralized manager.

The similarity of protocols between Greenstone, XOAI and OpenDLib echoes experience with the previous generation of DL protocols and augers well for interoperability. Greenstone's widespread adoption and free availability allows others to adopt it as a platform for experimenting with the service-centered design approach.

It facilitates the addition of new digital library features which would have been hampered by the less open structures of Greenstone and its contemporaries. Greenstone retains and extends the lightweight configurability of its predecessor without requiring centralized management processes. This paper has presented a new digital library design which is significantly different from the present Greenstone, but strongly rooted in past success. To meet a broad range of requirements a modular based topology is utilized to provide a flexible infrastructure.

Written in Java to promote portability, dynamic loading of objects and internationalization, modules communicate by streaming XML messages between each other. Using SOAP this communication can be distributed across a network. All modules have the ability to describe themselves in a machine readable form, and to apply an XSLT to transform messages.

The latter is instrumental in providing different levels of configurability, an important ability given the different types of people involved in the life-cycle of a digital library. Several working examples have been given to convey the general applicability of the design.

The first example demonstrated backwards compatibility to collections built with Greenstone, and satisfies another of the identified requirements: to help minimize the migration path of existing developers and users. It also demonstrated the design functioning in a distributed environment. The second example augmented an existing DL site with text mining capabilities with the introduction of a new service. The third and fourth examples illustrated substantially different user interfaces: one specialized for maps that required two extra services to provide the necessary geographical functionality; the other provided an interactive visualization to search results through a Java applet that was applicable to a wider realm of text-based collections.

Numerous aspects of the design contribute to its dynamic configurability. The "describe yourself" feature allows receptionists to adapt to the facilities that a server presents. Through XSLT a corpus editor can exert significant control over the function and appearance of a digital library such as modifying the structure of a generated page, for example adding a transform that sorts the query results alphabetically by title rather than ranked score. Alternatively they may reformat the results according to OAI syntax in preparation for exporting. Previously such changes required editing the source code and restarting the digital library software after recompilation. Implementing the design in Java has promoted dynamic attributes in the system, particularly through the ease in which modules can be loaded at runtime.

The re-reading of configuration files is also straightforward to arrange and adds dynamic abilities that a digital library administrator can take advantage of. In addition to integrating the documentation with the software using JavaDoc and other techniques, usability of the software also benefits from the development of self-documenting collections that both demonstrate and describe particular aspects of design.

The list of requirements is ambitious, however, and not all of them have been proven yet. For example, while none of the sample implementations demonstrate computer environment integration, the design is capable of supporting the idea through specialized receptionists. For future compatibility, more time is needed to establish if the design successfully meets such a criteria.

DIGITAL LIBRARY EVALUATION

When an animal bred in captivity runs, flaps or slithers into the wilderness for the first time, scientists do not simply wave goodbye, wish it well and move on to the next project. Usually the animal is tracked and observed for a long time thereafter—the point of release is where the research really begins.

However, this has been less true for grant-funded digital library projects. Administrative and institutional barriers tend to confine evaluation to the funding period when the system is being designed, and when its uses and effects can only be guessed at.

In this short paper I will discuss a digital library project in environmental science where some of these evaluation issues arose, the value of eliciting narrative data from users, and some ways to take better advantage of existing but underused mechanisms for long-term evaluation of digital libraries. Viewing information technologies and society as inextricably co-determined makes it necessary to gather data both on the design process and on how the finished systems are used by people—often in quite unexpected ways.

Iterative design and formative evaluation are ways to introduce user feedback into ongoing design, but while these strategies can serve as an effective translation layer between users, designers and builders, the focus is on how an evolving system *might* be used.

How it is *actually* used can be more accurately determined when the system is in the wild, when the designers and their formal evaluation instruments have gone away. Digital libraries are social entities. They tell stories about a culture, a science, a place or a time, through the items represented and organized in the collection, and in use, they help generate new stories as well. Manovich has advanced the idea of database and narrative as two ends of same continuum; both structure information, but where a database aims for access, a narrative aims for psychological immersion in the story. From an institutional standpoint, digital libraries are rarely ends in themselves.

The social missions of the funding organizations—the stories they wish to tell— often drive the creation of digital libraries, but how well a finished system supports the mission can't be fully evaluated until the digital library has had some time to develop a user base.

This line of research began with a participant observation of the design of a digital library of environmental science collections. Funded by an Library Services and Technology Act (LSTA) grant, the project involved diverse designers, content, metadata and institutional participants. As one of the participants in the environmental science digital library noted, "Part of the art of grant writing is interpreting vague language in a way that lets you do what you want to do," or in other words, making project proposals and achievements dovetail with the mission and goals of the funding agency.

These goals included outreach and evaluation, so a usability component was included in the grant proposal. My initial role in the project was to develop the instruments and conduct the evaluation. Understandably, digital library designers tend to create evaluation instruments that demonstrate in a measurable way the work they've done, a tacit statement of the value produced for the grant funds received. For example, the design of the interface, the appropriateness of descriptive metadata, and user success at canned search tasks are classic evaluative measures.

However, in an analysis of the Perseus Digital Library (PDL), Marchionini writes: "Operational data are powerful components in a chain of inferences that address impact but the PDL evaluation illustrates the value of anecdotes and "stories" that illustrate new effects, i.e., how DLs augment existing capabilities with new ones. These augmentations garner public support for a DL and should not be underestimated in assessing impact.

Integrating multiple views is more naturally done with narratives than summary statistics and integrating these forms of evidence can aid in assessing complex change." In the evaluation, statistical and demographic data were not hard to come by. Observation, interviews, document analysis, narrative analysis and social network analysis were effective ways to construct as complete a picture as possible about the interactions of the designers.

But the usability component needed to be completed at the same time as the digital library, in time for the results to be included in the final LSTA grant report (though the exact LSTA grant regulations vary by state, most LSTA grantees must submit a final grant report within 15-30 days of project completion).

Participants in the usability study were evaluating a still evolving system, and had to project potential uses into their responses to open-ended interview questions. By the time they might integrate the collections into their professional lives, and perhaps surprise themselves with unexpected dimensions of usefulness, the evaluation would be long over. This is certainly not to say that there is no such thing as continuing evaluation of grant-funded digital libraries.

But the mechanisms for long-term evaluation are usually little more than Web forms or e-mail links, not organic components of the digital library. In practice, designers are more concerned with present and future digital library projects than with continuing evaluation of those of the past.

Digital library researchers have an opportunity to conduct this longer-term research, to question and reveal the impacts of digital libraries as social entities, and to apply the resulting knowledge to future projects.

The good news is that in some situations, a mechanism for longer term evaluation already exists. For example, the State Library of Ohio's LSTA grant process makes use of a "year-after" evaluation form (http://winslo.state.oh.us/publib/lstayraft.html), which includes questions such as "Did the project produce any unexpected results?" and encourages narrative ("Please provide a success story of how your project has impacted someone's life or had a positive impact on the community.").

This is precisely the sort of openended data collection instrument that can reveal how a digital library is actually being used—but even this document is only the length of a one-page questionnaire. Subsequent research will attempt to evaluate the usefulness of this and other longer-term evaluation instruments, and how they might be expanded.

While longer-term evaluation should include quantitative data such as transaction logs and perhaps a list of external sites that link to collection content, evaluation instruments should also be open-ended, designed to encourage narrative expressions of unexpected use, the kind of data that reveal to funding agencies the real impact of their grants.

Iterative digital library design philosophies have always had at their core the sense that user input should feed back into ongoing system design. I propose here simply a wider iterative design circle, one that allows for more naturalistic data about longer-term use to be fed back into future systems. In sum, lessons learned that will be explored in future research include an increased emphasis on:

- Long-term evaluation of digital libraries
- Narrative data; allowing users to tell stories
- Unexpected uses
- Evaluating social outcomes, not just the design process or product
- Linking findings more directly to the higherlevel goals of funding agencies

DIGITAL LIBRARY INFORMATION APPLIANCES

Although digital libraries are intended to support education and knowledge work, current digital library interfaces are narrowly focused on retrieval. Furthermore, they are designed for desktop computers with keyboards, mice, and high-speed network connections. Desktop computers fail to support many key aspects of knowledge work, including active reading, free form ink annotation, fluid movement among document activities, and physical mobility. This paper proposes portable computers specialized for knowledge work, or *digital library information appliances*, as a new platform for accessing digital libraries. We present a number of ways that knowledge work can be augmented and transformed by the use of such appliances.

These insights are based on our implementation of two research prototype systems: XLibris, an "active reading machine," and Tele- Web, a mobile World Wide Web browser. The standard platform for accessing today's digital libraries is a desktop computer with a keyboard, a mouse, information retrieval software, and a network connection. Unfortunately, desktop computers are not suitable for many types of knowledge work.

Studies of people using electronic and paper documents show that desktop systems fail to support four important activities:

- Active reading
- Free form ink annotation
- Fluid movement among document activities
- Physical mobility

As a result of focusing on the desktop, today's interfaces for accessing digital libraries support retrieval in isolation, without addressing these broader work practices. We propose a new platform for accessing digital libraries: specialized portable computers designed for knowledge work, or *digital library information appliances.* In this paper, we draw on our experience designing and building two research prototype information appliances— the XLibris "active reading machine" and the TeleWeb mobile Web browser— to show how these devices can support a broad range of activities in the digital library.

READING AND DIGITAL LIBRARIES

The first and most fundamental document activity is reading. "Reading" encompasses a broad range of complex and poorly understood practices involving documents, including skimming, searching, browsing, speed-reading, surfing, reviewing, and rereading. Although we often take it for granted, reading can be hard work. We use the term *active reading* to distinguish this rich collection of activities from simply looking at words on a page.

Desktop computers do not support active reading. Once expected to create a paperless office, computers have instead produced ever-increasing quantities of paper documents. Dataquest predicts printers and copiers will generate over 1012 pages in the U.S. in 1997.

This statistic suggests that people do not use computers to read. The reason for this is obvious: paper supports extended, focused, deep reading practices better. Current research on digital libraries does not address a broad range of reading activities. Instead, as David Levy points out, digital libraries support shallower, more fragmented, and less concentrated reading.

The research focus in this field is on tools for search, selection, and distillation, tools that promote identification and extraction of information fragments. Because digital library interfaces do not support active reading, people search online and then print documents to read them. This "search and print" reality contrasts with the "search and read" ideal held by researchers.

Although a dual online/paper system is not *a priori* undesirable, we will show the many advantages of an online system that enables a variety of reading practices. The XLibris active reading machine supports a broad class of reading activities by employing a "paper document metaphor" (as opposed to the desktop metaphor) that imitates the physical experience of reading and marking on paper.

The paper document metaphor follows lessons learned from a number of studies comparing reading online to reading on paper, summarized below.

TANGIBILITY

Readers often move paper documents to avoid glare, to speed up handwriting, or to adjust their perspective of a text. In contrast, most computer displays are stationary while in use, so that readers must move themselves—their heads, their bodies, and their arms— rather than their display. XLibris supports paper document-like tangibility by running on tablet displays. Although XLibris has not been deployed for real use, people say that holding a page-sized display in their lap and being able to easily reposition it changes their online reading experience. The tangibility of paper documents also supports navigation. Turning paper pages seems easy and natural, and the weight and thickness of a paper document convey length and location.

In XLibris, pressure strips on the case of the device provide a tangible interface for page turning: pressing on one side of a sensor moves to the next or previous page, and holding down initiates riffling through pages. The harder you press, the faster you move. A quick animated transition indicates the direction of turning. Finally, "location guides" of varying thickness drawn in the top cor- ners of each page provide feedback about the length of the document and the reader's current location.

Page Orientation & Fixed Layout

Paper documents are laid out on fixed-size pages. The page layout often communicates the type of the document (e.g., business letter versus technical article) and where to find important information (e.g., a return address). The fixed layout also supports spatial memory and helps readers find old information.

In these and other ways, paper pages give readers an excellent "sense of the document." This sense of the document is often lost online.

Most CRT monitors cannot display a full page of text legibly, leading to awkward scrolling and zooming. Word processors and Web browsers commonly re-flow the text on a "page." And hypertext versions of paper documents can lead to disorientation and a sense of being lost. XLibris respects pages by displaying the image of a single page at a time.

Because the LCD panels we use are designed for landscape viewing, XLibris rotates the image 90º to approximate the portrait orientation of a typical printed page. XLibris stores the image of each page and the underlying text; this "image + text" file format is compatible with printed and with scanned documents.

Multiple Displays

People often work with multiple pieces of paper simultaneously, either with several pages from one document or with several documents. Most of today's computers provide multiple virtual displays through use of a windowing system. Unfortunately, the effort of managing window layout and switching among windows can interfere with reading.

Therefore XLibris displays a single page image and does not support windows. Since limiting the digital library information appliance to a single page image is problematic, we have considered a number of ways to address the need for collateral displays.

Presenting two full-page images side by side, as in Book Emulator, makes text unreadable on current tablet displays, but may be feasible as LCD technology evolves. A form factor with multiple physical displays is another approach.

(Bush's vision of a Memex desk included multiple displays). In our case, to maintain mobility, a book (instead of a tablet or desk) with two opposable LCD panels may be appropriate. Weiser presents an enticing vision of ubiquitous computing with devices so cheap they can be scattered and used as paper.

In the near term, however, a small number of pen computers in conjunction with nearby desktop displays or even paper may provide the most practical solution to the problem of collateral document work. In summary, XLibris employs tangibility, page orientation, and fixed layout to provide an online reading experience comparable, in many ways, to reading from paper.

FREE FORM INK ANNOTATION

"Until we provide support for smooth integration of annotation with reading, it is likely that people will continue to annotate paper materials, even as they read materials in a digital library." – Cathy Marshall The second key document activity is annotation. Knowledge work involves reading combined with categorizing, speculating, remembering, judging, or, more broadly, critical thinking.

This active reading process is facilitated by underlining, highlighting and making notes on the text or in a separate notebook. Marking on paper helps readers "make the text their own" and is a common practice associated with deep understanding of written information. In a nutshell, readers write.

Unfortunately, annotation online is quite different from its paper-based cousin. Interfaces for annotating often involve selecting a command, pointing with a mouse, and typing on a keyboard. They generally require much more effort than scribbling with a pen. Text annotations are not as visually distinct as ink marks, and online annotations often cause changes in the layout of the document. We believe that the ability to make unstructured, free-form, idiosyncratic ink marks is a crucial feature of any interface to digital libraries.

Although such marks may not have explicit meaning to the computer, they have rich semantic meaning, supporting visual and episodic memory. An essential aspect of ink on paper is its lack of modality: users can write anything they want, anywhere on the page. In XLibris, we followed this principle by letting users scribble notes, draw figures, highlight, or annotate text, all without switching modes or applications. Readers highlight and mark-up document page images as they read or flip to a blank page in a lined notebook for more space. XLibris provides several colors of ink, several highlighter pens, and a stroke-based eraser.

FLUID MOVEMENT AMONG DOCUMENT ACTIVITIES

The third key aspect of knowledge work is fluid movement among different styles of reading and different document activities. As an example, consider the process of "information triage" where an analyst skims through a pile of search results and reduces them to a manageable set.

The current practice is to fire off a query to a search engine, retrieve the 100 top-ranked documents, print them out, mark them up with highlighters, and put them into piles. Analysts then read the most relevant passages to answer the original question. Consider an alternative scenario where the analyst owns a digital library information appliance. After conducting a search, the analyst skims the documents online. The appliance enhances skimming by emphasizing important material. As on paper, the analyst marks up important information as it is found. Instead of reviewing the collected information by thumbing through piles of paper, the analyst views a concise collection of his or her text annotations.

If any of the annotated material is worth reading in greater depth, the analyst can do so comfortably online. If the analyst needs more information, the text that has already been highlighted can be used to generate the next query. At a high level, this scenario demonstrates fluid movement among document activities. The analyst quickly moves among searching, skimming, annotating, reviewing, and deep reading.

There is no waiting for a printer. Because skimming and deep reading are tightly integrated with retrieval, analysts can determine if the information they are collecting is useful before they invest much effort. This scenario also demonstrates how computation can enhance skimming, reviewing, and searching. Because the interface is based on a paper document metaphor, the reading and annotation activities remain much the same as on paper. In our design, the "computer" remains in the background and, when requested, rises to the surface to assist the reader with the tasks of skimming, reviewing, and searching. Below we describe how XLibris supports and augments these three activities.

Skimming Mode

Skimming is one way readers gain a quick impression of a text. When skimming, the reader's eyes typically search for and alight on key words or sentences and take in short passages before moving on. Sometimes the reader becomes engaged and shifts into deep reading, or is distracted and moves into quicker skimming or into riffling.

XLibris' "skimming mode" highlights phrases and sentences that are characteristic of the document being skimmed. We call out key phrases because they can be read at a glance and tend to reflect the topic of the nearby text. This assists with the activity of scanning the text for relevant portions to read. The *Wall Street Journal* and *People Magazine* use a similar technique of boldfacing company names and Hollywood celebrities' name to help readers find information. We also highlight summary sentences to support a speedreading– like activity. Skimming mode uses a commercial text summarizer to identify summary sentences that are emphasized. Skimming through a document of highlighted summary sentences provides a narrative overview that is not available by just reading key phrases.

Both of these highlighting techniques permit a smooth transition from skimming to deep reading: key terms and sentences can help readers decide whether a passage is worth reading and are likely to be appropriate places to transition to deep reading. Skimming mode uses shades from gray to black to indicate term importance. Meaningful terms are identified by heuristics that select noun phrases.

The shade for each term is then based on a statistical information retrieval measure: terms that occur frequently in the document but occur rarely in other documents are colored black, while terms common to many documents are colored light gray. For example, the term "digital library information appliance" would be colored black when it appears in this document. Skimming is a common practice: a study of college students' reading habits reported that skimming occupied 32% of their reading time, and that "86% of the descriptions of skimming strategies mentioned a selection process based on key words and/or particular sentences and paragraphs in certain text locations". Although our design requires empirical evaluation to confirm its utility, from our experiences thus far, we are optimistic that computers can improve the skimming activity and that augmented skimming is a useful function for a digital library information appliance.

Reviewing the Reader's Notebook

Reviewing paper documents is facilitated by the marks made during reading: marks not only record information but are also used to organize it for later review. There are three common venues for marking: annotating on the page, taking notes in a notebook, and writing on loose-leaf paper. Annotations on the page highlight key information but tend to be lost in piles of paper. Notebooks are compact and can be reviewed quickly, but taking notes can be tedious and error-prone.

Unbound notes can be reorganized flexibly, but require even more effort by the note taker. XLibris' Reader's Notebook combines the best features of annotating directly on the page, of taking notes in a separate notebook, and of organizing index cards. As with paper documents, readers mark on the page in the context of the document, yet without the laborious and imprecise step of copying.

As with a bound notebook, readers can review concise annotations by time. Finally, as with note cards, flexible filtering and sorting of the view allow readers to reorganize their information as needs change. The Reader's Notebook extracts "clippings" of annotated text and lays them end to end in a separate, multipage view.

Each clipping is linked to the corresponding annotated page, so readers can move fluidly between notes and documents. Each clipping includes some surrounding text, and is labeled with document title and page number to help readers understand the meaning of the marks. In designing clippings, we had to decide how much of the document should be shown for each annotation.

Starting with the bounding rectangle of each ink stroke, we expand it horizontally to the width of the page and vertically to include complete words.

Snippets that overlap are merged together resulting in reasonably sized clippings of annotated text. The Reader's Notebook can display, sort, and filter clippings from one document or from all documents. By default, clippings are sorted by document page number, which is analogous to rummaging through a pile of paper, but should be faster because readers do not see the less important (i.e., un-annotated) information. Clippings can also be sorted by time so that new information appears at the end, as in a paper notebook.

Finally, readers can filter the clippings by ink colour to search for different kinds of marks or to group related items together. Many readers already use different pens to mark different types of information. For example, some lawyers highlight "pro" information in green and "con" information in red.

Finding Information Related to Readers' Annotations

Readers often search for related material and move from one text to another. For example, an ecology student studying the effects of acid rain in the Appalachian Mountains decides to search the Internet for information on the economy of West Virginia. A doctor reading up on a drug she has never prescribed decides to follow a reference to a study of its side effects.

Unfortunately, in both online and offline situations, finding related materials and reading are not well integrated. Typical information retrieval interfaces force users to stop reading, to identify related documents, and then to print them. References found in paper documents are even more timeconsuming to track down. Although hypertext was designed to address some of these problems, authors cannot anticipate the information needs of all readers. Ironically, despite the fact that readers' interests may change rapidly, interfaces for moving from reading to finding and back to reading again are time consuming and disruptive.

Clearly this is another example where fluid movement across document activities is desirable. XLibris facilitates fluid transitions among reading, searching and browsing by creating a dynamic hypertext from readers' marks.

The system observes readers' annotations and the text of the underlying document and generates hypertext links (margin links) to related documents: no additional effort from readers or authors is required. Because XLibris suggests links of interest to particular readers at particular times— based on the passages they are marking— people can discover useful information *serendipitously*. This type of serendipitous retrieval is a benefit of paper libraries: as people walk to the shelf for a particular book, walls of related books surround them, making it possible to find interesting material accidentally.

Although serendipity in the library is often a rewarding experience, it is generally lacking in online systems. XLibris provides two user interfaces that integrate reading, searching, browsing, and serendipity. These are described below.

MARGIN LINKS

Margin links provide serendipitous access to related documents *during* the active reading process. As readers mark up passages, the system finds related documents and presents links unobtrusively in the margin; our intent is to provide a modeless link suggestion mechanism. Because margin links persist, readers can follow links at their leisure.

We use thumbnail images of the target page as anchors. The reader taps on an anchor to move to that page. For the most part, link creation does not disrupt the reading process since the reader is free to disregard the suggestion and to continue reading. In the current design, however, margin links intrude on the reading process more than we would like.

One problem is that XLibris computes a separate query for each stroke (although strokes often do not result in margin links because of a similarity threshold). We have begun to address this by adding a button to turn links off and by designing ways to manage the frequency with which margin links appear.

FURTHER READING LISTS

When readers reach the end of a document, they often want to know more. The document may not emphasize the topic they are most interested in, or it may spark an interest in a new topic without providing enough depth or detail. Sometimes this need is addressed.

The *Scientific American* example illustrates the limitations of authored reading lists. The article describes a technological vision for protecting digital copyrights. Consider a reader with a narrower interest, such as "how digital copyright affects librarians." The reference to a six-page article on digital copyright law may help track down this information, but the reference is unlikely to answer the question directly. Furthermore, by the time the reader scans the further reading list, more appropriate articles may have been written. XLibris augments this traditional editorial practice by automatically generating further reading lists for each document.

Unlike static references, these lists reflect the interests of a specific reader at a specific point in time. As with margin links, the reader's interests are inferred from annotations, and no additional intervention from the reader is required.

Further reading lists are presented as a separate set of pages, or *view*, associated with each document. Readers can access this view at any time, whether or not they have annotated the current document.

Of course, the more annotations the user has made, the more focused the resulting list is on the reader's interest as opposed to the document as a whole. Visually, the further reading list looks like a Reader's Notebook of annotations except that each clipping is a segment of a related document obtained from a search engine.

These clippings, with matching terms underlined, help readers understand the destination of the link and also make the target passage more recognizable if they choose to follow the link.

Query-mediated Links

Both margin links and further reading lists use a technique called *query-mediated links*. Query-mediated links derive a query from a user's interaction with a document and use that query to identify related documents. Golovchinsky has shown that query-mediated links based on explicitly selected words and passages are effective in supporting information exploration tasks.

XLibris computes margin links from the words, phrases and passages that are implicitly selected by the reader's marks. (We do not expect readers to make marks for querying explicitly, but rather as part of their existing annotation practice.)

Marks are converted into text selections, which are then expressed as full-text queries that yield a best-matching passage. The system adds a margin link to the best match if its similarity value (or belief score) is above a threshold. For further reading lists, each annotation is interpreted as a text selection and is transformed into a list of word scores.

The scores for each word are then summed across all annotations. If several annotations select the same instance of a word, then the maximum score for that instance is used.

The words along with their scores are used to generate a query. If not many words have been included, then terms that are most characteristic of the document can be added. This padding reduces the chance that a query based on a small number of annotations will return documents that are entirely unrelated.

Ink Annotations as Queries

XLibris recognizes several distinct ink patterns from which queries are computed. These include underlined words, highlighted words, circled words, circled passages, and margin annotations. We emphasize that there is no "vocabulary of marks" that readers must learn; rather, our heuristics are based on general annotation practices. Each type of annotation results in a slightly different query for the search engine. Marks that select specific words translate into queries that retrieve other instances of the same term. Marks that select longer passages generate queries that search for similar passages.

PHYSICAL MOBILITY

The fourth and final document activity supported by digital library information appliances is mobility. Until now we have discussed reading in XLibris; in this section we describe mobile information access in TeleWeb.

Desktop access to digital libraries is not adequate for mobile workers. A doctor making hospital rounds has no desktop with her to access a digital library. This could have grim repercussions: a recent study concluded that patients for whom prompt MEDLINE searches were conducted have significantly lower costs and shorter hospital stays. Mobile work is not limited to physicians and traveling salespeople; even office workers often work with documents away from their desks. For these people, portable information appliances can provide access to digital libraries anywhere, anytime. Unfortunately, it is not possible to give mobile people the same network access that they would have in their office. Compared to wired desktop networks, wireless networks are slow, expensive (with different billing schemes), and only intermittently available. As workers move from place to place, they are likely to experience three levels of connectivity: high quality connectivity from an office network, lower quality connectivity from a wireless network, and no connectivity at all when disconnected. How can people use digital library appliances to access distributed information sources across this range of operating conditions? Aside from the variable networking conditions, there are two other issues that affect mobile access to digital libraries.

First, downloading a document over a wireless network can be very expensive, and current interfaces for search engines and Web browsers do not help people manage these costs. Second, user interaction is punctuated by surprises: an information request may return right away (when data is locally stored), take a while (when data is remote), or take forever (when the network is down). The TeleWeb mobile Web browser was designed and built to explore these three issues.

TeleWeb runs on a laptop computer with multiple communication channels: it may be docked to an office Ethernet, used from home over a telephone line, used while traveling over a wireless network such as a cell phone, or operated while not connected to a network. The lessons learned from TeleWeb apply not only to the Web but also to digital libraries.

In the design of TeleWeb, we assumed that at least some of the time users would be disconnected but would still want to browse the Web. Some mobile networks are so limited in bandwidth compared to office networks that users may feel like they are disconnected. How can people browse the Web when disconnected? TeleWeb uses "caching for availability," the standard solution for this problem. This means that the system loads documents into a local cache when fully connected.

Later, if the user needs the document while the network is not available, the locally cached copy is returned. Caching for availability only works if the system knows the user's information needs ahead of time. The system can use past history to predict future needs. In addition, the user can tell the system what documents belong in the cache; unfortunately, in practice people find it difficult to articulate which documents they need.

Furthermore, both techniques share the drawback that information needs often change in unpredictable ways. Overall, caching for availability often works, but is frustrating when it does not.

An alternative solution is to replace synchronous interaction (a user request followed immediately by a response from the network) with asynchronous interaction. For example, when the user requests a document not in the cache, TeleWeb asks the user if the system should download it later.

If so, Tele- Web downloads the information the next time the user connects and adds the document to a "to read" list that the user can browse. This interaction style is analogous to sending a request for a book from an out of state library, and eventually receiving it in the mail.

There are other reasons to postpone downloading a document. For example, if a user is connected over a cellular telephone, downloading a large document is going to be expensive, and can tie up the network connection for hours. Given the choice, the user might be happy to download this document overnight or upon returning to the office. There is a tradeoff here between how urgently people need information and how much they are willing to pay for it in time and money.

With a mobile information appliance, users should be able to decide how much they are willing to pay for each document and how quickly they need that document. With this principle in mind, TeleWeb includes a budget monitor that sits between the user and the network. If a request is made for a document that is not in the cache and downloading the document will break the user's budget, then TeleWeb presents a "conditional download" form instead of the document. Users can override their budget to fetch the document immediately, or they can request that the document be fetched at a later time.

Unpredictable Systems are Frustrating

The third problem of mobile appliances is unpredictable behaviour. Those using computer networks already know this problem: sometimes they hit a key and nothing happens. In wireless computing, this experience is magnified many-fold. TeleWeb's solution is to show the user what is going on inside the cache and network manager. Specifically, Tele- Web labels links that will be slow to download with a "road work" icon. If there is no road sign, then either the link destination is cached, or a high-speed connection to the information superhighway is available. This simple change— essentially exposing the state of the system— makes mobile Web browsing much more predictable. This contrasts with the traditional approach of trying to simplify the user's view of the system by concealing the state of the network.

THE FUTURE

The development of tomorrow's digital library information appliances is an iterative process. Our current cycle, however, is not complete until we evaluate the ideas presented in this paper. Towards this end, we have begun a series of laboratory user interface experiments and are in the planning stage for a real-world deployment. One experiment suggests that free-form ink marks made while reading are better for query formulation than traditional relevance feedback.

People who have tried XLibris agree that our approach of taking a work practice and augmenting it— rather than redefining it— makes the system immediately accessible. Information *appliances* must be accessible. The digital library community must decide whether digital libraries should, as we propose, support users throughout the process of turning information into knowledge.

If so, there are many issues that must be addressed.

One reviewer of this paper asked: "Where is the digital library?" We purposely avoided describing protocols, services, and architectures because we believe infrastructure should *support* the vision of working with a digital library information appliance, not *define* it.

The next step is to understand how users of digital library information appliances should interact with external repositories. For example, should users pay authors to cache documents on their devices, even when they do not read them? How should users search repositories that are not always accessible? How should searches be distributed between local and remote databases? These and other issues require further investigation. We have shown how information appliances based on the paper document metaphor can support active reading. Because these systems allow people to work on digital documents much as they would on paper, this provides an alternative to the standard "search and print" model of digital libraries.

Furthermore, by integrating a wide variety of document activities, and by allowing fluid movement among them, disruptive transitions between paper and digital media can be eliminated.

The combination of the paper-like and the digital allows us to augment these activities without redefining them. Finally, the mobility of a digital library information appliance supports work away from the desk. With all these benefits, digital library information appliances can create a rich, universally accessible, digital library experience that improves the way we work. Clearly there is an exciting future for digital library information appliances in the digital library.

ECONOMIC MODELS OF THE DIGITAL LIBRARY

The starting point for a study of economic models of the digital library such as this must be an understanding of the meaning of the term 'digital library'. Numerous definitions of the term have been proposed. They vary considerably with regard to their proximity to the concept of a traditional library. The latter classifies, catalogues, and provides access to quality-controlled information resources. It also offers related services and tends to restrict access to a well-defined user group.

The term digital library is used less precisely and may refer to anything from a limited list of hotlinks to the entire content of the Internet. The only common factor in these definitions is the idea of digitisation.

A study of economic models of the digital library requires a definition. Although the UK Electronic Libraries Programme (eLib) and the US Digital Libraries Programme have done a great deal to progress the concept of digital library and, latterly, the hybrid library, a clear and universal concept is still lacking. Before an economic model of a digital library could be tested, not only would a clear definition be required but considerable progress should have been made towards development and implementation. Such progress has been made with regard to specific digital library resources and services.

Thus, with a view to exploring economic models of the digital library in a systematic and useful manner this study focuses on models of specific digital library resources and services. It takes as a starting point the different areas of the eLib programme. This chapter will review and compare economic models of the academic digital library. Until now, empirical testing of economic models of digital libraries has been limited. Economic issues tend to be tested after solutions have been found to the more pressing technical, cultural and legal issues because no library manager or user would consider paying for a service that had not been shown to be technically sound, legal and useful to its target audience. The pace of development of different elements of the digital library has varied over the last two decades.

This document will include models of aspects of the academic digital library that are sufficiently developed to be modelled. As electronic alternatives to traditional library services are developed, shifts occur in the roles and activities undertaken by different stakeholder in the academic information delivery chain.

Consequently, there have been sometimes unanticipated changes in the apportionment of costs and benefits to those stakeholders. Many roles are still fluid and change will continue until effective models are established.

There will be no attempt here to predict the future. This report evaluates and compares only models that have been proposed or tested. A useful economic model of the digital library must accurately represent all stakeholders in the academic information delivery chain, their relationships to the supply and delivery of digital resources, and the associated costs and benefits. The principal stakeholders involved in digital libraries are:

- Academics as authors; · academics as editors and referees;
- End users (inc. academics as researchers, students, and clinical, professional and industrial users of electronic academic information);

- Academics as teachers and recommenders of texts;
- HE librarians;
- HE computing support departments;
- Publishers of both primary and secondary literature (commercial, not for profit, University presses, etc.) and other electronic content suppliers (such as museums);
- Booksellers;
- Funding bodies;
- Subscription agents;
- National libraries;
- Document suppliers such as the British Library Document Supply Centre (BLDSC);
- Reproduction rights organisations;
- Intermediaries such as the National Electronic Site Licence Initiative (NESLI) and Higher Education Resources ONdemand (HERON);
- Internet service providers and other aggregators and distributors (including companies such as CatchWord and Ingenta which provide Internet publishing for publishers);
- The Higher Education Digitisation Service (HEDS).

These stakeholders are both individuals and organisations of both present and future generations. Some groups have a more direct stake than others.

Arguably, the most important are academics as authors; academics as users of scholarly information; academics as teachers; HE libraries and librarians; publishers; and information brokers (including subscription agents and document supply agencies).

Economics of Digital Library Services

When considering the economics of digital libraries it can be tempting to focus on financial factors that are directly related to digital library services, for example the price of resources and infrastructure. It is important, however, to be aware of other economic factors. These include the cost of downloading bandwidth-hungry images and time spent filtering information in an environment where the signal-to-noise ratio is minuscule. While the authors acknowledge the importance of these factors it was beyond the scope of this project to determine their economic impact.

Electronic Journals and Electronic Individual Article Supply

The Serials Crisis

Much of the incentive for the development of electronic journals and electronic individual article supply (eIAS) services has arisen from the financial pressure on libraries caused by:

- Budget restrictions;

- An explosion in scholarly information;
- The fact that, over the last two decades, journal prices have consistently increased well above the general rate of inflation.

Librarians have become increasingly critical of publishers, focusing on journal subscription prices as the significant factor in the serials crisis. It may be argued that this single contributing factor is over emphasised in discussion of the serials crisis. The problems faced by academic libraries as a result of budget restrictions is significant.

The explosion in scholarly information is not only a key factor but one driven from within HE. However, library budget cuts are one element of a larger problem facing the HE sector which cannot be addressed within the scope of this study. Furthermore, attempts to address the problems associated with the scholarly information explosion tend to focus more on alternative and cheaper formats for publication than on reducing the quantity of published research output. Librarians continue to focus on journal subscription prices and they appear to have legitimate cause for complaint.

There is evidence that the market for commercial journals is anti-competitive and at the very least, does not show much price elasticity. Furthermore, rationalisation, in the form of mergers, has occurred and although users may expect this trend to drive prices down, it has resulted instead in significant price rises.

Publication Costs

The advent of electronic publishing has been hailed by some as an opportunity to overcome these problems. It is argued that electronic publication is much cheaper than publication of hard copy. Proponents of this argument maintain that the cost to print and distribute a journal represents a significant proportion of the total publication cost.

Content is received and refereed free of charge and typically, the author assigns copyright to the publisher who is then free to package the material in any appropriate format and distribute it for a fee.

In an electronic environment, the cost of distributing content is negligible and thus, the total publication cost for an electronic journal should be significantly lower than it is for a print journal. Publishers, among others, argue that fixed costs (or first-copy costs) represent at least 70% of journal production costs and thus that a change in delivery medium could save at most 30% of total costs.

Furthermore, libraries expect publishers to supply electronic journals in multiple formats and end users expect additional functionality from electronic journals, for example multimedia elements, hot links to references, links from abstracting and indexing services or from OPACs to full text.

Clearly, to succeed, any move to replace print journals with electronic journals must be supported by end users and those users will not invest time and effort in learning to use electronic journals unless there appears to be clear advantage in doing so; added functionality, or speed of delivery are examples. However, additional features require time and personnel with expensive skills which adds to production costs.

It is argued that this makes electronic journals at least as expensive to produce as print. A publisher distributing an electronic journal for a fee must also meet the additional cost of controlling access. This is likely to be small if a well-established system such as ATHENS is used (http://www.athens.ac.uk). ATHENS is a JISC-supported service which provides a single password to HE users for accessing new datasets and services within the UK HE community and manages password accounts for the service suppliers. However, although ATHENS is clearly valuable to the HE community, its use may not be consistent with a publisher's commitment to supply statistics on usage to libraries.

Another consideration is that libraries consider it important, having paid for a subscription to a journal, that the volume is still available to their users even if they cancel the subscription at a later date. A publisher can fulfil this requirement by supplying the basic journal content on a portable medium such as a CDROM or by granting permission to the library to create and/or archive a digital copy.

If a publisher itself were to guarantee online access in perpetuity it must migrate such content to new technologies when current technologies become obsolete. These additional costs make it less likely that electronic journals will be cheaper to produce than print journals. To date, publishers have found electronic publishing to be even more expensive than anticipated (Albert Prior, personal communication, 8 February 1999).

The Relationship Between Cost and Price

On balance, it seems that the additional costs associated with publishing a new valueadded product outweigh the costs of reproduction and distribution that are saved. Nevertheless, the argument that journals are overpriced remains valid.

It is important that journals are priced at a level sufficient to recover costs. In a print environment this has never been a problem. On the contrary, commercial journal publishers make large profits, and are sometimes more profitable than companies like Microsoft. Correlation between cost and price is not strong. As an example, Odlyzko cites the 'three most prestigious maths journals' which are published by a commercial publisher, a university and a scholarly society respectively. Prices vary by a factor of seven, suggesting that first-copy costs are not the primary factor determining price.

Journals are priced according to what the market will bear and, until recently, the market has been relatively inelastic; academic journals are considered to be 'must have' items and one cannot easily be substituted for another should the latter become too expensive. Thus, profit margins in print commercial academic journal publishing generally fall within the range 40–60%. When compared with, for example, school text publishing at approximately 12–15%, database publishing at approximately 18–20%, or fiction publishing at approximately 5%, it is clear that commercial publishers of print journals have continued to extract large profits despite the financial pressures facing libraries.

There is a clear need for academic libraries to demonstrate to publishers that the demand for scholarly journals is not inelastic. However, while there are no alternatives to the 'must have' material offered by publishers it is very difficult for libraries to do so.

Non-commercial Electronic Journal Publication in Higher Education

As a solution to the serials crisis various stakeholders within the HE sector have proposed that academics bypass commercial companies and publish electronic journals themselves. There has also been an initiative in the US called the Scholarly Publishing and Academic Resources Coalition (SPARC) which aims to facilitate origination and publication of affordable journals which compete with expensive commercial journals.

SPARC will support sympathetic publishers by guaranteeing a market for their journals. Alternative journal publication models such as these often focus on cost savings gained by:

- Automating the editorial function;
- Dispensing with desk editorial work such as marking up and proof reading; and of course,
- Distributing the material electronically.

Whether costs are reduced or not, a viable economic model must include a costrecovery mechanism. Furthermore, that mechanism should be transparent as users and contributors will consider a publication to be unstable if it has no apparent means of recovering costs.

The additional costs associated with charging subscription fees (e.g. maintaining accounts and restricting access) combined with the 'gift culture' of the Internet that effectively requires most content to be available free of charge, make it difficult to recover costs directly from users.

An alternative to the traditional subscription model recovers costs from authors in the form of page charges and makes journals available to users free of charge. An important element of this model is that page charges should be levied at a rate acceptable to authors as a fee for widespread distribution of their papers; Harnad and Hemus suggest 'dozens rather than hundreds of dollars per page ... $400 for a 20-page article'. Clearly, papers that are refereed and then rejected must also be paid for by the model. Variations on this model would recover costs by charging only for submission and/or acceptance. In common with the models of others who propose to bypass publishers, Harnad's model and variations of it require a reduction in publishing costs when compared with print journals. The Institute of Physics Publishing Publishing (IoPP) and Deutsche Physikalische Gesellschaft (DPG) have recently launched a new pure electronic journal, the *New Journal of Physics*, that is based on this type of model (http://www.njp.org/).

The journal was started after widespread international consultation with librarians and physicists. It is available on the Internet free of charge to users. Authors are required to pay $500 on acceptance of their papers. A discount is available for IoP or DPG members.

Authors are invited to submit only articles of 'outstanding scientific quality; likely to be widely read and highly cited'. Presumably, this criterion is intended to keep the rejection rate low so that the publication fee can cover the costs of papers that are refereed and rejected. The rejection rate of papers in science disciplines tends to be much lower than in social sciences at rates of around 10–30%. This initiative suggests that IoPP and DPG consider it viable that the *New Journal of Physics* be financed by author acceptance fees of only $500. A journal consisting of, say, 120 papers would be produced for only $60 000.

If a journal produced at this cost were to adopt subscription as a price mechanism it could recover costs by selling 1000 subscriptions for only $60 or 500 subscriptions for only $120. Either rate would be very cheap for a physics journal.

This comparison suggests either that:

- Those publishers who claim that 'no-frills' electronic publishing is almost as expensive as print publishing are wrong;
- That the cost of journal production in either format bears no relation to the subscription price and that many commercial publishers are determined to maintain high margins.

Economic Characteristics of the Academic Information Delivery Chain

Authors and Editors

Among these models, there are undoubtedly some that accurately represent the economics of publishing electronic journals at reduced cost. However, the journals produced would almost certainly not incorporate the additional functionality demanded by users as it would be too costly to do so. The incentive for authors to submit their papers to these 'bargain basement' publications and for academics to leave the editorial boards of quality commercial journals to sit on the boards of these journals is unclear.

The importance of academics in their capacity as authors and editors must be recognised if a useful economic model of electronic journals is to be developed. Authors are not simply content originators; they drive the information explosion by seeking the most prestigious outlets for their increasing quantities of journal articles.

Both authors and editors then apply pressure to ensure that their institutional libraries hold the journals to which they are affiliated either as authors or as editors. Thus, academics as authors and editors effectively represent demand in this 'market'.

Libraries

The economic model of electronic journal publication proposed by Andrew Odlyzko identifies library costs as the significant element in the 'serials crisis'. Odlyzko argues that a system-wide perspective reveals that the serials crisis is a library cost crisis.

Libraries have focused on subscription prices as a visible problem which contributes to library budget crises but, in fact, for every $1 spent on journal acquisition, $2 is spent on processing, storing and handling print journals. Furthermore, if publishers were to include many library functions in their delivery systems, libraries subscribing to their electronic journals would save so much in operating costs that they could afford to pay subscription fees at or above their current levels.

Comparative cost–benefit analyses of a hard-copy journal collection and access to an electronic archive, conducted at the University of Michigan supports Odlyzko's arguments that holding a traditional journal collection is an inefficient use of library resources. However, the cost to publishers of compensating for the relative lack of information skills among end users when compared with librarians is not insignificant. 'Ease and relevance of retrieval is directly proportional to the work put into the data beforehand', and that work represents additional cost.

One reason why publishers have found electronic publishing to be more expensive than anticipated is that they have included in their systems some functions that, in a print environment, were undertaken by other information professionals (Albert Prior, personal communication, 8 February 1999).

A controversial element in Odlyzko's model is his explanation of how publishers will make available in digital form archives of previously published volumes. Odlyzko claims that digitisation costs are small (as low as $0.60 per page) and suggests that publishers digitise their back runs and make them available to libraries. This, he says, would be a one-off investment for a publisher migrating to the digital environment. Experience of projects in the UK electronic libraries programme (eLib) indicates that creation of accurate, searchable digital text is much more expensive than Odlyzko suggests.

Furthermore, the cost of this activity would not be recovered quickly. The cost of digitising journal archives is a major market entry problem for existing commercial publishers of academic journals (David Worlock, personal communciation, 9 February 1999). Odlyzko acknowledges that costs vary significantly depending on what level of functionality is required. He claims that the last 20% of functionality accounts for 80% of the costs. Reports suggests that, for users, a primary interest in electronic journals arises from the added functionality of the new medium. Odlyzko's model requires users to differentiate essential functions from those that are nice to have. At present this distinction is likely to be arbitrary. The SuperJournal project found use of electronic journals to be 'an essential pre-condition for answering the question of what readers really want'. Until exploitation of functionality has been developed and explored, it will be difficult for anyone to identify the essential functions of electronic journals in the 21st century.

Users

A system-wide view of the costs and benefits of producing and delivering journal articles must acknowledge the costs and benefits to users. Some of these are referred to above, for example additional functionality is an added benefit as is access to users' desktops; time taken to visit the library is directly related to use of library resources. However, the time that it takes to identify high-quality information and to download it to the desktop is a cost as is time spent learning to use a new interface.

This is demonstrated by the fact that users will not invest time learning to use a new system unless a critical mass of material is available using that system. All of these factors will affect users' uptake of electronic journals but many of them are fluid and are difficult to quantify.

Pricing Mechanisms

The pricing mechanism in traditional journal publishing (annual subscription per title) creates a very low-risk market for journal publishers. The consumer base is widespread and payment is made in advance. In an electronic environment, it is unnecessary to bundle articles into issues before distributing them; it is possible to distribute individual articles on-demand at very low cost to the publisher.

It is possible also to reconfigure bundles to better meet the needs of researchers in specific disciplines and subject areas, e.g. to include in a bundle articles from a variety of journals which may be published by a range of different publishers.

Bundling

For electronic journals, a very low-risk pricing mechanism from the publishers' point of view is a site licence arrangement whereby a publisher's entire list is licensed to one or more institutions as a single product.

This is known as bundling. This not only guarantees payment in advance; it also secures payment for low-use journals which subscribing institutions might otherwise cancel. The UK Pilot Site Licence Initiative (PSLI) is a high-profile example which used bundling as a pricing mechanism. Pricing schemes adopted by publishers participating in the PSLI varied but all represented some form of bundling. Several of the publishers effectively extracted more revenue by offering as a single product all of the titles on their lists. Institutions valued these titles differently; i.e. on a single subscription basis institutions A and B would have subscribed to different titles but during the PSLI both institutions paid for a collection of titles which included their selected journals among others.

The PSLI represented an opportunity to introduce electronic journals to large numbers of users throughout the UK. However, its value as a means of testing the pricing mechanisms and pricing levels was limited. Not only were the costs subsidised by the JISC but publishers were not necessarily testing realistic pricing models.

The Institute of Physics Publishing, for example, made electronic copy of its journals available free of charge to institutions that subscribed to hard copy of those titles. An IoPP representative at that time described this pricing strategy as unrealistic and said that charges would be introduced. The PSLI was criticised for propping up the 'serials crisis'; not only did it mask the effect of rising subscription prices, it also sustained circulation levels of high-cost, low-use journals that many libraries would otherwise have cancelled. For the duration of the initiative, use of PSLI journals was limited; the PSLI resources were used heavily at only six institutions.

It was possible however, to identify 'core' materials that were heavily used and a large number of titles that were used only occasionally. HEFCE suggested that, in future, institutions may use these data to negotiate different rates of discount on titles published by a single publisher. If institutions succeed in these negotiations, one of the benefits of a bundled site licence may be lost to those publishers.

When the PSLI ended, the National Electronic Site Licence Initiative (NESLI) was established. NESLI is a service rather than a project. It was established with JISC funds but the cost of content provided to institutions is not subsidised and NESLI must become self financing.

NESLI will attempt to address the issues raised by the PSLI with a view to meeting the needs of libraries and end users in the UK HE community. A model licence has been developed with a view to agreeing standard terms with publishers.

Not all publishers will agree to all of these terms, but the journals of those that do will be offered through a seamless interface which allows users to access the journals of a range of publishers. The variety of proprietary systems required to access PSLI journals proved to be frustrating for users.

The formal launch of the NESLI service is expected in October 1999. Institutions will also be granted ownership of the electronic copy of journals to which they subscribe; i.e. access will not be withdrawn when subscriptions are cancelled. Other issues being explored include the facility to subscribe to subject-based clusters of journals from a variety of publishers, the facility to link to NESLI journal articles from library OPAC entries, and supply of useful management information in the form of statistics on 'hits' at various levels including table of contents, abstracts and full text.

An important difference between NESLI and the PSLI is that the latter tied the price of electronic copy of journals to the price of hard copy offering subscriptions only to parallel publications. NESLI aims to offer access to the electronic format alone if publishers are willing and institutions wish to subscribe on those terms.

Thus, if Odlyzko is correct and the 'serials crisis' is largely related to the cost of handling and storing print journals, NESLI will enable libraries significantly to reduce the costs associated with journal subscriptions.

Price Differentiation

As well as facilitating sale of products in bundles that vary in size and content from an article to a publishers' entire list, the electronic environment facilitates price differentiation, i.e. varying the price of information with willingness to pay. An example of the potential for price differentiation was identified by researchers working on the ACORN project at Loughborough University. It was suggested that if charges for journal articles from the electronic reserve service were introduced, they may be escalated towards the exam period. This would effectively reduce the load at peak times by charging a higher rate to students who cram for exams.

Price differentiation can be implemented only if differences in user types are easily observable. In a print environment, it is possible to differentiate between different types of journal subscriber, for example professional vs. educational or library vs. individual.

However, it is very difficult to observe user characteristics beyond this, e.g. to observe the quantity of articles read by any researcher or their relative use of tables of contents, abstracts, and full-text articles. In an electronic environment, it is feasible to observe different types of use.

Thus, it should be possible to differentiate between users based on the quality and quantity of the information that they require or for which they are willing to pay. For example, some users may be willing to pay for additional functionality such as hotlinks to all citations in a paper, while others would be willing to forgo this facility to access the text at a cheaper rate. It is increasingly common for authors to publish the text of their research papers on the Internet despite publishers' attempts to protect their exclusive right to publish. It has been predicted that when publishers have to cede exclusivity on individual papers, they will begin to trade in added value, for example retrieval services tailored to individual needs.

PEAK: Exploring bundling and price Differentiation

The PEAK project at the University of Michigan is a collaborative venture with Elsevier Science which aims to test three different pricing models for electronic journals. The models are based on the economic theory on bundling and on price differentiation.. It is argued that:

- 'Non-linear pricing is facilitated by lower transaction costs for fine-grained purchases and feasible direct usage monitoring' by publishers or libraries;
- That bundling can extract revenue from those who value content differently. A key research objective of PEAK is generalisability to other user populations.

The number of possible dimensions which can be manipulated when defining a bundle is very large, for example, the 'article component (abstract, references, text etc.); time limit on usage (unlimited, per use, per year etc.); and usage rights (read only, read and print etc.)'.

To infer anything from data gathered during PEAK, it was necessary that the variables be limited. Only three different pricing mechanisms are being tested. These are described below.

- The electronic journal is supplied on the same terms as a traditional print subscription, i.e. articles are made available on an issue-by-issue basis to all authorised users at a subscribing university.
- The Institution pays in advance for a specific number of articles and may then access articles from any of the 1100 titles available from Elsevier in electronic form. The fee paid is $5.46 per article. If the institution has used these 'vouchers' and wishes to purchase more it must pay for them at the higher rate of $7. Thus, Elsevier and the institution share the risk. Note that both the reduced voucher price of $5.46 and the higher rate of $7 are very low and when converted at the current exchange rate ($1.571/£1 on 19 May 1999) both are cheaper than the price of an interlibrary loan request from the British Library (£4.95).
- Articles are ordered as required and are paid for either by the institution or by individual users within institutions. Articles are more expensive to order in this way than they are in model.

When an individual has ordered an article through PEAK, it is made available to all users at that individual's institution and use of that article is then monitored. On average, each article has been accessed 2.5 times.

The three pricing mechanisms operated by PEAK are effectively two-part tariff schemes as institutions are required to pay $25K to the University of Michigan to join PEAK and then they incur fees for journals and/or articles.

Although there are three discrete pricing schemes, participating institutions need not restrict themselves to one. They may, for example, subscribe to 'core journals' and buy vouchers for additional provision.

Ten institutions are participating in the PEAK project. Very few results have been reported by PEAK researchers but initial results indicate that the traditional subscription is the least popular pricing model. The PEAK project is due to end in August 1999.

Electronic Individual Article Supply

One of the pricing mechanisms being tested by PEAK is electronic individual article supply (eIAS). This mechanism effectively disintegrates the traditional product and increases the publisher's risk. The publisher is no longer paid in advance for a package of around 120 articles to be delivered in 6 or 12 issues throughout the year. The publisher can no longer focus marketing effort on the 120-article bundle and its identifiable market; each article must sell on its own merits and thus is an individual product.

The eIAS model characterises access or 'just-in-time' provision as an alternative to holdings or 'just-in-case' provision. Users can benefit from access to a much wider range of titles than the institution could afford if it maintained journal subscriptions. Furthermore, comparison of the costs of access and holdings models indicate that the former is economically efficient for libraries and is popular with end users. However, to date, the scale of comparative studies conducted has been limited; there may be economies or diseconomies of scale inherent in a large-scale access model which are not yet evident.

IAS in those studies was not a seamless process whereby the end user searched, identified and received articles directly from the supplier and had them delivered electronically to her desktop. Although end users had access to the OPACs of collaborating universities and thus were able to identify the location of requested items, orders were made via librarians at the borrowing and lending libraries and documents were supplied in hard copy by post or courier. To date, access models have tended to rely on library privilege whereby libraries are legally permitted, without paying a copyright fee, to supply an individual with a single copy of a document for the purposes of research or private study.

However, users must sign a print request before they receive their copy of the requested document. Thus, the process whereby the end user searches, identifies and receives the required resource is necessarily interrupted and this interruption represents a significant additional library administration cost.

Furthermore, widespread adoption of an access model which relies on library privilege would undermine the economic incentive to publish as libraries would cancel journal subscriptions thus reducing subscription bases and publishers would receive no alternative revenue from article supply. Publishers are unlikely to comply with library requests for permission to fulfil ILL requests electronically.

Alternative copyright-cleared sources of individual articles in electronic form are available. It is difficult to assess their relative costs and benefits when compared with subscription, however, as services offering copyright-cleared articles tend to operate complex price differentiation policies. These policies can be based on several of the following variables: the country from which a request originates; the type of user; the number of requests; the type of delivery; and the speed of delivery.

Most services offer at least two alternative payment mechanisms, including, most commonly, pay-as-you-go schemes based on credit card payment and payment in advance based on deposit accounts or pre-paid forms. One drawback of pricing electronic articles individually is that the facility to hotlink to citations is less attractive when every link incurs an additional fee. It is worth noting that JISC has agreed in principle to provide sums to help launch an eIAS service in the UK under JISC/PA auspices, but the details of the Tender call have yet to be concluded.

Scholarly Communication and the Market

A recent eLib supporting study compared different models for pricing electronic scholarly journal articles including those based on bundling, price differentiation and IAS. Fishwick *et al.* consider the current academic information delivery chain to be inefficient due to a number of distortions in the supply–demand chain. Among these are that:

- Authors represent a principal source of demand for publication but make no contribution to publication costs;
- Those consuming the information, i.e. the readers, seldom pay for it, preferring instead to obtain it from libraries;
- Much of the journal publication work is undertaken by editors and referees without payment, or with minimal honoraria.

Fishwick *et al.* propose an alternative model which introduces 'normal' market feedback mechanisms into the academic information delivery chain with a view to overcoming the serials crisis and developing an efficient market for scholarly articles.

The most efficient pricing mechanism would be determined by the market; a number of alternatives would be available in the first instance. Publication would be funded by authors and users both of whom contribute to demand. The publisher would receive usage-based payment at a level sufficient to sustain the model.

Editors and referees would be paid to encourage efficiency, and authors would receive royalties to encourage them to submit for publication only material of the highest quality.

Papers would then be available individually or in customised bundles from the publisher database. Included in the system would be a mechanism to support authors who cannot afford to pay a submission fee. Furthermore, payment by authors would facilitate publication of papers that may be important scientifically but are unlikely to be popular among readers at their time of publication. The current system for selecting papers to be published in a journal, peer review, assesses them based primarily on quality rather than wholly on their likely popularity at the time of publication. The contents of a journal issue will contain a selection of papers, some of which will be widely read at the time of publication and some of which will attract very few readers. In economic terms the former subsidise the latter.

When the journal is disaggregated and electronic copy of each article sold ondemand this cross-subsidisation will end and publishers may find it difficult to recover the publication costs of lesser-read papers. The authors of the study acknowledge that publication of such papers may not be guaranteed, and suggest that public support be available to ensure that all important developments are recorded through publication; the merit of all papers would continue to be gauged by peer review. The basic product would be unsophisticated electronic text.

Additional functionality would be available for a higher fee. An important element of this model, it is claimed, would be generation of management data based on usage which would be useful to library managers and publishers. This type of feedback is most useful if users are required to prioritise between materials that are available to them. Thus, it is argued that access should be rationed, even to material obtained by site licence.

Printing and additional functionality are approached in the same way, i.e. it is suggested that if users are required to pay for prints they will filter before, rather than after they print. This argument suggests that end users waste resources by gathering information that they do not really need.

Time, for any student or researcher, is a scarce resource and it takes time to gather information. If end users do need all of the information that they acquire, it may be argued that rationing would prejudice their ability to work effectively. Fishwick *et al.*'s model incorporates elements from many different economic models including Harnad's model. However, in spirit, the model is the antithesis of Harnad's.

Harnad argues convincingly that scholarly communication differs from other types of publication in that it is not a commercial market. Authors of journal articles are not motivated by the promise of royalty payments; they want their papers to be distributed as widely as possible and, in the past, have often paid to acquire offprints so that they could contribute to this dissemination process. This view is reinforced by a recent study of what authors want from publication. Fishwick's argument that structural problems in the current system preclude the introduction of an efficient system that would benefit all stakeholders is compelling but uncomfortable for those who consider scholarly communication necessarily to be qualitatively different from trade commodities.

Whether or not the principle of introducing normal market economics into the scholarly communication chain is valid, certain elements of the model proposed by Fishwick *et al.* are problematic:

- Like many other HE proponents of alternative models for scholarly communication, Fishwick *et al.* claim that print and distribution represent the most significant costs in the journal production process and thus, that distribution in an electronic environment should be significantly cheaper. This would be an important factor in maintaining authors' publication fees at an affordable level. The proportion that print and distribution contribute to publication costs is a contentious issue. However, it may be less important than many authors suggest as publication costs may well be low even though current prices are very high.

- The basic product proposed by Fishwick *et al.* is unsophisticated electronic text. It may be difficult to persuade authors and editors to abandon print journals in favour of such a 'bargain basement' publication. However, if submission fees are introduced, and thus submission in high-quality journals is expensive, those authors not in receipt of large research grants may find that they cannot afford to publish in a high-quality publication.

Thus, the result could be a two-tier system whereby research that is not grant funded is published in the Fishwick *et al.* alternative system and grant-funded research is published in a more sophisticated format.

This problem could be overcome only if all authors, including those in receipt of large grants, are prepared to publish in and thus to support 'alternative' journals that are cost effective for HE such as those proposed by SPARC. This would require a massive attitude shift among important authors. At present authors publish in the most prestigious journals because to do so carries more weight with regard to research assessment and tenure awards. Authors would have to be persuaded of the utilitarian benefits of publishing in 'alternative' cost-effective journals. It is difficult to imagine how such an attitude shift would come about.

International co-operative agreements resulting in HE policy directives may solve the problem but co-operation at a national level let alone at that level is notoriously difficult to achieve. Because this model differs radically from that proposed by Harnad and his ilk, it was also evaluated in the research reported later in this report.

THE MODELS

A variety of different approaches to publishing cost effective electronic journals have been proposed in recent years. Many have common characteristics. Four models will be tested here. The second models non-commercial production of a journal that is available for use free of charge on the Internet as described by Harnad.

The third is a non-commercial journal funded by users by a combination of subscription and eIAS. The fourth is an alternative non-commercial journal model proposed by the authors which differs from the third model only in that costs are recovered through a combination of a modest submission fee and sales of subscriptions and individual articles. None of these models assumes that the production process will be conducted entirely by academics or other stakeholders who have neither experience nor expertise in publishing.

User studies show that professional design is important to user acceptance. Journal production and related tasks such as marketing are undertaken more efficiently by publishing professionals; this is reflected in the models. Tasks that can be automated effectively are automatic in all of the models.

The Conservation Ecology (CE) project has demonstrated that all administrative tasks in the editorial process can be automated and, in an international enterprise, that an automated system can be more effective as it is not constrained by a time zone. Furthermore, the cost of copy editing *Conservation Ecology* is much cheaper than the equivalent cost in a print environment because the bulk of formatting is done automatically1.

Conservation Ecology is published by two permanent employees, a parttime production editor and a part-time systems administrator. All versions of each manuscript are archived by the software. Metadata can be amended at minimal cost as standards change by using a formatting template.

The whole process can be decentralised because all actors in the chain can access files remotely from any networked PC throughout the world. There is no reason why any of the models described here should differ from the others with regard to exploitation of this type of system so editorial costs for each of the models will be based on the CE model.

Variables in the Models

All evidence to date suggests that people prefer not to read at length on screen. They may use the electronic medium to search and identify resources and they will read small portions of text on screen but having established that they wish to read a substantial amount of text such as a journal paper, users obtain a print.

Often electronic journals are not even published in a format suited for reading on screen; electronic versions of journals published in parallel print and electronic form tend to be made available in PDF, a format that is cheap to produce in a parallel production process but is designed to be printed.

The models explored here will be used to examine the economic implications for users and/or their institutions of tending to print or read on screen. One variable with a very significant impact on costs for electronic journal production is the degree of functionality required by users. Most of the models described here require a reduction in production costs.

This implies a lack of additional functionality. It has been suggested that users not only want additional functionality but are unwilling to learn to use new systems unless there are clear functional advantages.

However, despite their expressed interest in additional functionality, in practice end users are most interested in content, browsing (including linking), and printing. Odlyzko asserts that cost-effective journal production requires users to discriminate between those functions that they need and those that they would like.

However, although it is claimed that added functionality will significantly increase journal production costs there are no published data which differentiate the costs of different functional elements. Odlyzko estimates that the last 20% of functionality will incur 80% of the total cost but does not attempt to apply this with reference to different functions.

Variations in electronic journal production costs should be explored but it is beyond the scope of this project to do so. Generally, it is assumed that scholarly journal articles have a limited audience. This characteristic contributes to the expense of publishing such articles.

First copy costs are inevitably spread across a relatively small number of potential users. However, some recent work has suggested that the market for journal articles can be expanded. Odlyzko forecasts increasing use of journal articles by pressure groups. This is plausible given the recent shift in political activity among ordinary citizens towards single-issue politics. Researchers at Project Muse found that institutions that had not subscribed to John Hopkins University Press titles in print did subscribe to journals in electronic form.

MONOGRAPHS AND TEXTS

For the purposes of this report, a monograph is defined as a low-volume work intended for library purchase and use as a resource by researchers. The market for monographs is 'global and export driven'. In contrast, a textbook is defined as being intended to be used as a teaching resource and for student use. If successful, a textbook may be reprinted or new editions may be issued.

Textbooks usually depend on the home market; they are 'developed or adapted in the local market'. However, the distinction between textbooks and monographs is not always clear cut. In any case, it is difficult for publishers accurately to predict the size of the market for a work.

Some works commissioned as textbooks sell so few copies that perhaps they should be categorised as monographs and some commissioned as monographs are far more successful than anticipated and may reasonably be categorised as textbooks. There may be a greater rationale for supplying a textbook in electronic form than for a monograph.

The former is likely to be required by large numbers of students at the same time, while the latter is likely to be consulted by individuals and demand is unlikely to be concentrated to specific time periods. As people do not like to read more than a small amount of text on screen, a monograph in electronic form is unlikely to meet user needs. It would be too expensive, both financially and in time, to print the work. However, if a textbook were required by all students in a large undergraduate class it may be viable as an electronic product as all students in the class could access it at any time, perhaps from their residences, and select those parts that they wished to print. Experience on the ELINOR project suggests that students do not use electronic text in this way; they use it to identify useful materials which they then borrow from the library shelves.

This experience may however, have been due to design, screen resolution and similar factors. As these factors are constantly improving, so a similar experiment run today may generate different results.

Developments towards electronic books for individual use that are portable and facilitate book marking, annotation etc. in the form of Rocket eBook and other similar tools while important, are not library developments and will not be explored in this study.

Monographs

The obvious advantage of digital publishing of monographs is that there is no requirement to invest in inventory (David Worlock, personal communication, 11 February 1999). Nevertheless, digital publication requires investment in first copy costs and, as in most publishing ventures, these represent the most significant proportion of monograph publishing costs. Developments in digital publication of monographs is at a very early stage.

The experience of University presses in the US is that if monographs are made available free of charge over the Internet, sales of hard copy increase 2–3-fold. This is attributed to the reluctance of users to read on screen or to spend time and money downloading and printing substantial quantities of text which are available in a more convenient format from booksellers.

These early projects have explored the market for digital analogues of print monographs. Studies with journal users suggests that it is inadequate simply to deliver in a digital environment material which has been designed for print; to be useful, digital resources should be designed for the medium.

Those publishers attempting to explore the utility of the digital environment for monograph publishing have come to question its suitability and suggest that this environment may change the very nature of the format. For example, use of open review pre-publication may, ultimately, result in a new format: a hybrid between a journal and a monograph.

Publishers are aware that for digital monographs to succeed added value is likely to be important. However, they argue that any additional functionality will increase the cost, and therefore, the price of monographs.

In recent years, 'monograph publishing has almost disappeared in many disciplines because short print runs and library budget problems have made it untenable'. Any increase in cost and price is likely to exacerbate rather than alleviate this problem.

Texts

Publishers have used digital technology to offer university and college teachers the facility to customise texts. For example, Wiley's custom publishing service offers teachers the facility to select chapters from a CD-ROM database of large general texts in a specific subject.

Chapters must be drawn from a minimum of two titles and the teacher must order a minimum of 30 copies. The material is collated, bound and delivered to the campus bookseller for sale to students.

Perhaps custom publishing by the publisher precludes alternative means for students of obtaining the information. Thus, by adapting to the market, Wiley is more likely to maintain its customer share and profitability. Furthermore, when texts represent good value, students may be more prepared to buy them and become less reliant on library provision for core materials. Developments at Wiley use digital technology for production but not for delivery and thus this experiment has limited relevance to the digital library. There is no evidence to date to suggest that texts are being produced for electronic delivery. Development work in this area suggests that, as yet, there is no market for digital texts. The Internet can, however, be used effectively to facilitate sale of peripheral products such as self-marking tests for certification of professional skills such as nursing. Such tests are also delivered free as an value-added supplement to a print publication, i.e. effectively as an incentive to buy/use the associated text.

As with journals, publishers are working with academics to explore ways of utilising the digital medium for teaching. A good example is ChemConnections, a Wiley collaboration with the University of California and Beloit College which is grant-funded by the National Science Foundation.

ChemConnections comprises a number of modules which can be used over a period of weeks for teaching on a variety of different areas of chemistry. Evidence to date suggests that, as yet, publishers are only exploring the utility of the medium for both text and monograph publishing.

Economic modelling is likely to be explored much later in the development cycle, after products have been shown to be sufficiently useful that libraries and/or academic departments would pay for them. At that time, publishers expect developments such as the digital object identifier (DOI) to be important in facilitating commercial transactions. ' As yet use of metadata by monograph publishers is inconsistent and ad-hoc. Given the embryonic state of electronic monograph publishing it is likely that a more consolidated approach to charging models will emerge in the future'. No economic model for producing and delivering electronic texts has been published. Therefore, this area is not the subject of a modelling exercise here.

ELECTRONIC DATASETS

The economic model for electronic reference works is better established than for most other areas of the digital library. A database or dataset consisting of a number of databases is generally supplied on licence either on CD-ROM or online. Where both formats are available the price tends to be similar.

Negotiation of licence terms can be undertaken by institutions individually or by consortia. Economic factors related to licence negotiation are covered below in the section on licensing. In the UK, the Combined Higher Education Software Team (CHEST) negotiates with dataset suppliers on behalf of the JISC to secure favourable access terms for UK Higher Education Institutions (HEIs) and to standardise terms and conditions of use wherever possible.

Standardised terms reduce costs for all parties including individual institutions which must adhere to those terms. Networked access to these commercially supplied datasets from one of JISC's data centres (BIDS, EDINA, and MIDAS) is then offered to the HE community. Each individual institution can choose which of the available datasets it wishes to pay for and, for an annual fee, it obtains a site licence. Institutions then supply end users with access to these datasets free at the point of use.

CHEST licences are usually agreed for five years so institutions subscribing to a dataset commit to take it until the end of the CHEST agreement. The five-year commitment has been cited by several institutions as a reason for not taking JISC datasets. The price of a dataset is obviously important to institutions when deciding whether or not to subscribe but it is not the only factor. Some JISC datasets are made available to the community free of charge but uptake is still not universal. One reason may be that use of datasets by end users can increase demand for journals and ILLs, and thus increase pressure on the workload of library staff.

Another is that even a 'free' dataset involves the HEI in some opportunity costs. An economic advantage to institutions of supplying datasets to end users is a reduction in mediated online searching. Furthermore, as more datasets become available online rather than on CD-ROM, technical support and maintenance costs are reduced. The current annual subscription with a minimum commitment, usually of five years, does not suit many UK HEIs, especially smaller institutions. A recent survey of attitudes to pricing of JISC-funded databases found that institutions would like the option of usage-based payment.

There was also a call to render prices more equitable by allowing a number of small institutions to subscribe as a consortium which would pay at the same rate as a large institution; institution size would be based on student numbers. It is difficult to model provision of datasets to the UK HE community as:

- The term dataset covers a wide range of different types and volumes of content;
- The contribution of the JISC and the terms that it demands from

suppliers are unclear. As this is not a controversial area and economic relationships are established and work effectively it is not modelled and explored here.

COPYRIGHT CLEARANCE FOR DIGITAL LIBRARY

The copyright clearance procedure in the model has been simplified. For example, where an item selected by a lecturer cannot be used because copyright permission cannot be obtained, the reserve service would be required to liaise with the lecturer to select an alternative. This process is not represented. Instead, it is assumed that ultimately, if a list of 14 items is selected by a lecturer, then the ER service will provide the lecturer with 14 items.

Furthermore, although the lead time between receipt of lists of items by the library and the availability of an item in the reserve collection may be longer in an electronic environment due to the time required to clear copyright this would have no financial effect and so is not included in the model. In the Ithink model described here, the number of items for which copyright permission is required is represented by the flow element 'clearance'.

This is defined as the number of items in a class multiplied by the number of classes. The average size of a reading list supplied to the library at Stirling University in 1997 was 15 items. Presumably, there is a degree of overlap between courses especially those in the same department.

This is reflected by a reduction in the average list size of one item thus reducing list size to 14. The number of classes is variable and is manipulated by a slider. The cost of providing a class with materials included in the NERS is determined by the cost of obtaining copyright permissions, the frequency with which a course changes, and the ratio of 'library substitution' to 'text substitution' materials on a reading list.

When seeking copyright permission the Copyright Officer sends details of items required to the relevant Reprographic Rights Organisation (RROs; e.g. CLA in UK or CCC in USA).

She receives permission from the RRO and forwards details to the NERS digitisation staff. The RRO will not have a mandate from all publishers and so the NERS will be required to seek some permissions directly from publishers. When the NERS first approaches a publisher the parties negotiate licence terms. This is a skilled task and costs more than a straightforward request from an RRO.

However, the number of negotiations per list received reduces as the content of the repository increases because the NERS already has agreements with some publishers and can readily identify other publishers which are unwilling to grant permission for digitisation and electronic delivery.

It is assumed that only 10% of requests require negotiation and thus the skills of a more expensive staff member. It is estimated that negotiation takes approximately 3.25 hours work. This includes identification of the rights holder (15 minutes) and negotiation (3 hours). A negotiation such as this will cost £133 or £99 if overhead is applied at a rate of 120% and 60% respectively. This cost is based on a full-time negotiator on a salary of £25K for whom national insurance contributions and employer pension contributions cost an additional 20%, i.e. £5000.

The total cost to the employer is £66 000 if overhead is applied at 120% and £48 000 if overhead is applied at a rate of 60%. If the negotiator is given 8 week's holiday, and works for 37 hours per week, her hourly rate is £41 or £29 if overhead is applied at a rate of 120% or 60% respectively.

Thus, a negotiation lasting a total of 3 hours and 15 minutes costs £133 or £99 if overhead is applied at a rate of 120% or 60% respectively. The cost of processing a request that can be granted by an RRO is estimated as £2 or £1.50 if overhead is applied at a rate of 120% or 60% respectively.

It is estimated that an individual can process 12 requests (including receipt and processing of the permission) in 1 hour. If the individual processing these requests earns £15 000 per annum and the employer pays an additional 20% in national insurance and pension contributions plus overhead at a rate of 120% or 60%, the total cost is £39 600 or £28800 respectively.

If the individual is given 8 week's holiday, and works for 37 hours per week, her hourly rate is £24 or £18 at overhead rates of 120% and 60% respectively. Thus, the cost of processing a single request is £2 or £1.50. The average cost for a permission is calculated based on the premise that 9 out of 10 permissions are secured from the RRO and one out of ten requests requires negotiation. Thus, the total cost of 10 permissions is £151 (2 £2 x 9 + £133) or £113 (£1.50 x 9 + £99) if overhead is applied at a rate of 120% or 60% respectively and, for one permission, it is £15 (£151/10) or £11 (£113/10). This is reduced by 1% for every 1000 items added to the repository to reflect the reduction in the number of negotiations required as the stock of publisher agreements grows.

'Pricing Mechanism: Text Substitution' vs 'Library Substitution' Models

The cost to a library of providing electronic reserve materials for a class will be determined largely by the ratio of 'text substitution' materials to 'library substitution' materials required as the former are much more expensive than the latter. 'Text substitution' is a pricing model for high-use materials and 'library substitution' is intended for materials that would be used for further reading.

Clearly, as a reserve collection is effectively a means of rationing access to high-demand materials, the prevailing model in an electronic reserve collection is likely to be the 'text substitution' model. Any item not required by large numbers of students at the same time is likely to be placed on open shelves. In a print environment, materials in a reserve collection tend to be borrowed, photocopied and returned within a short period as the loan period is often too short to allow a student to read the item. In an electronic environment, high-demand materials made available electronically can be printed by each student.

However, publishers wish fair compensation for this type of use as they consider it a threat to their core business, i.e. text sales. In the 'text substitution' model copyright fees are charged based on numbers of students in a class rather than on use.

This model, referred to as the 'Bookshop Material' model by the Publishers Licensing Society is the default for publishers mandating the PLS to license their copyright material through the Copyright Licensing Agency (CLA). As very few items will be read by all students in a class, this is likely to be a very inefficient way for a library to provide reading materials to users.

The 'library substitution' model proposed by Bide *et al* and described in the CLA Higher Education Digitisation White Paper (CLA 1998) requires the library to pay a one-off fee to the publisher for unlimited use of the material.

The model referred to by the Publishers Licensing Society (PLS 1999) as the 'Library Materials' model is based on the 'library substitution' model but restricts the license to a period of five years rather than granting it in perpetuity. The difficulty of establishing a fair rate for 'library substitution' fees makes this a difficult model to adopt. In the Ithink model described here it is assumed that 'library substitution' prices will be pitched at a level that compensates for loss of library sales.

For the purpose of the model, a mean figure of £29.40 is adopted for all 'library substitution' materials. This figure is based on an estimate of the number of copies of a text that any library would buy to provide for an average class. In 1997, among six universities participating in an eLib supporting study on the impact of electronic reserve services on teaching, students and libraries found that most of the libraries have 'no formal policy dictating that a specific number of copies of a high-demand text should be purchases for every student in a class. One of the libraries holds a copy per 25 students in the reserve collection while one of the larger libraries with a smaller space available for reserve materials, and supplying much larger classes, aims to hold approximately one copy per 100 students.'

For the purposes of this model, it was assumed that the library holds seven copies of each title in its print reserve collection. This figure is the mean of the 6–8 copies held by many libraries and, at the library which provides one copy per 25 students, it would provide for a class of 175 students.

It was assumed that a standard text costs approximately £30. This is lower than the average cost of an academic book; £41 in 1997/98 (LISU 1998). However, since academic books include monographs and texts, the latter is likely to be less expensive than the average of both. If the electronic text were to substitute for the sale of seven copies and thus the licence were to be set at a price that compensates for those lost sales, the price per title would be £210.

However, as a printed text is estimated to cost £30 and the publisher is not required to incur print and distribution fees for ER use of the material, this figure is reduced by 30% to £147.

The electronic reserve collection is likely to require extracts rather than whole books. It is assumed that an extract typically consists of 20 pages, i.e. 10% of a 200-page book. It is reasonable to assume that on a page-for-page basis, an extract would be more expensive than a whole book as the publisher's risk is increased.

For the purposes of the model, it is assumed that an extract is charged at 20% of the £147 referred to above, i.e. an extract of 10% of the whole title, charged at double the price of the whole work. Thus, each extract costs £29.40.

Digitisation

In the model, the NERS digitises every item which is not already held in the digital repository and for which copyright has been cleared. Every item that has been digitised is then stored in the repository. It is assumed that a lecturer selecting materials for her class will be supplied with details of materials held in the repository and will select any available materials that suit her requirements.

The degree to which requested items duplicate those held in the repository is an important variable in the model and may determine its success as the rationale behind a NERS is that economies of scale may be realised in the digitisation and copyright clearance functions.

The total cost of a digitised item includes the cost of acquiring a legitimate, clean original and the cost of capturing the material in digital form. The cost of a clean original scanned and supplied to the NERS by the British Library Document Supply Service and the copyright fee required by BLDSS for each scanned item supplied is £14 plus VAT (£16.45).

The cost of capturing pages in the manner described by the eCLA in their Higher Education Digitisation White Paper (CLA 1998) varies. The HERON project has been quoted a figure of 15 pence per page. It is assumed that a typical extract consists of 20 pages.

Repository

The repository function is related to a single institution. The cost to an institution for this function is related to the number of items that the institution has placed in the repository.

Here refer to the post grant-funded period when the repository will already contain resources gathered over the 3-year grant-funded period. Clearly, overlap between institutions with regard to the material required will reduce costs.

Research on overlap in reading lists in UK HEIs is limited but suggests that overlap is low. Nevertheless, it is assumed that academics will have access to the contents of the repository when compiling reading lists and that they will in a small proportion of cases select items already held in the repository if these suit their teaching purposes. It is reasonable to assume that the resulting duplication of use of a single item (hereinafter simply referred to as "duplication") will increase as the number of items in the repository grows.

In the model, duplication between items requested and items in the repository was varied and the results are documented below. Three different patterns of duplication were tested. The first pattern assumes that duplication between requests and materials held in the repository occurs at a rate of 0.5% in the first project year and increases by 0.5% per annum.

Thus, in the first post-project year, duplication occurs at a rate of 2%. In the second pattern, duplication occurs at a rate of 0.5% in the first project year and this figure increases by 50% beyond each year.

Thus, in the second year there is 0.75% duplication, and in the first post-project year, duplication occurs at a rate of 1.69%. In the third pattern, duplication occurs at a rate of 1% in the first project year and increases arithmetically at a rate of 1% per annum, i.e. duplication is 2% in year 2, 3% in year 3 and so on. The authors of this report consider the first scenario to be the most realistic.

Duplication would be efficient in economic terms, and if suitable materials are available lecturers will select them. Nevertheless, the degree of overlap between courses throughout the country is believed to be very low at present. Furthermore, academic freedom and the individual character of courses offered is an issue.

The authors doubt that lecturers will select more than one or two items from a repository of existing materials and will prefer to select the items they think are best for their students, whether or not already held in a repository. High duplication would obviously produce cost savings.

The more material lecturers use that is already available in machine readable form and copyright cleared, the more efficient the system would be in economic terms. Of course, this requires that suitable materials are available; only then will lecturers select them.

Nevertheless, we believe the degree of duplication between courses throughout the country is very low at present. Furthermore, academic freedom and the individual character of courses offered are relevant issues. We therefore doubt that lecturers will select more than one or two items from a repository of existing machine readable copyright cleared materials, and will in general prefer to select the items they think most suit their students, even if such materials are not in the repository yet.

However, in the absence of clear data regarding the current rate of duplication, our models can only be tentative at this stage. The cost of storing a single item in the repository is estimated at £1.27. This is based on figures supplied for the JSTOR project. JSTOR estimate that $2.5M is required for storage, maintenance and technical migration of a database consisting of backruns of 100 journal titles. Assuming that backruns consist of 100 years and that the average journal volume consists of 120 papers, this is $2.5M for 1 200 000 items, which divides as $2.08 (£1.27) per item. It is assumed here that an average journal paper is approximately equal to an average volume of text held by the NERS.

Role of Booksellers in the Provision of High-Demand Reading Materials

The effect of the introduction of ER on booksellers is not explored in this model. Clearly, the interests of booksellers are closely tied to those of publishers. Students buy their texts through the bookseller and thus, library provision on a 'text substitution' basis is a threat as it bypasses the bookseller. The bookseller is threatened by a 'library substitution' model only if the library acquires print texts from the bookseller.

A comparator print model would reveal the extent to which booksellers would lose as a result of libraries delivering 'text substitution' materials through an ER service. It is beyond the scope of this project to explore such a model.

Comparing cost of content for print and Electronic Reserve Collections

An example of the level of funding made available within the library to provide a print reserve collection at a Scottish University was detailed in a recent eLib supporting study. At Stirling University, 1440 books were purchased every year for the short loan collection at a cost of £28 800. The collection was expected to provide access to high-demand materials for 5544 students. This represents £5.19 per student per annum.

This is a useful comparator for the figures generated during model simulations. In the model, the number of classes affects the total cost of resources by determining the total number of items digitised and stored in the repository, i.e. 14 per class. As student numbers per class decrease, the cost per student of digitising and storing materials for that class increases. If the number of students remains the same, a change in the number of classes affects copyright costs only for 'library substitution' materials.

The NERS incurs a copyright fee per page per student for 'text substitution' materials so the copyright fee per class depends not on the number of titles but on the total number of pages per student. The cost of storage to be shared between institutions participating in the ER scheme will increase every year as more items are added to the repository. In a print reserve collection materials are weeded as well as added to the collection but the NERS is responsible for storing digital copy of items used by HEIs to prevent re-digitisation of materials.

It would be interesting to monitor the percentage of items in the HERON repository that are reused and to determine whether redigitisation might be more efficient than long-term storage of a large collection much of which may never be reused. The effect of varying the ratio of items on reading lists that are categorised as 'text substitution' and those categorised as 'library substitution' is explored. One of the scenarios explored is intended to be compared with the Stirling University print reserve collection referred to above which services 5544 students for a book spend of £28 800 (£5.19 per student). If Stirling University meets the needs of 5544 students, divided into 28 classes of 198, by spending £28 800 on books, the book trade receives £28 800.

An ER system such as the one modelled here and providing material to 5544 students (divided into 28 classes of 198) would generate publisher income of £36 739 if all of the materials in each 14-item list were categorised as 'text substitution'. Thus, without incurring the cost of print and distribution, the publisher would actually increase her income. The figure would fall below the print receipt only at 70% 'text substitution'.

MODEL SIMULATIONS

100% Text Substitution

Overhead on staff costs Applied at 120%

In the model, assuming that the ER collection consists of 14 items per class, there are 100 classes, and duplication occurs at the default rate of 0.5% in year 1 increasing at 0.5% per annum thereafter, spend per student in a class of 50 ranges from £27.38 to £30.17 in (post grant-funded) years 1 to 10 respectively. Spend per student in a class of 200 ranges from £19.18 to £19.88 in years 1 to 10 and spend per student in a class of 400 ranges from £17.82 to £18.16 in years 1 to 10. If there are 400 classes, spend per student in a class of 50 ranges from £27.33 to £30.02 in years 1 to 10. Spend per student in a class of 200 ranges from £19.17 to £19.84 in years 1 to 10. Spend per student in a class of 400 ranges from £17.81 to £18.15 in years 1 to 10.

Overhead on Staff Costs Applied at 60%

In the model, assuming that the ER collection consists of 14 items per class, there are 100 classes, and duplication occurs at the default rate, spend per student in a class of 50 ranges from £26.26 to £29.05 in (post grant-funded) years 1 to 10 respectively. Spend per student in a class of 200 ranges from £18.90 to £19.60 in years 1 to 10 and spend per student in a class of 400 ranges from £17.68 to £18.02 in years 1 to 10. If there are 400 classes, spend per student in a class of 50 ranges from £26.21 to £28.90 in years 1 to 10. Spend per student in a class of 200 ranges from £18.59 to £19.56 in years 1 to 10. Spend per student in a class of 400 ranges from £17.67 to £18.01 in years 1 to 10.

90% Text Substitution to Library Substitution

Overhead on Staff Costs Applied at 120%

If 90% of items in each 14-item list are categorised as 'text substitution' and the other 10% as 'library substitution', if there are 100 classes and duplication occurs at the default rate then in a class of 50 students, the spend per student ranges from £25.98 to £28.76 in years 1 to 10. In a class of 200 students, spend per student ranges from £17.60 to £18.29 in years 1 to 10. In a class of 400 students, spend per student ranges from £16.20 to £16.55 in years 1 to 10. If there are 400 classes, spend per student in a class of 50 would range from £25.93 to £28.62 in years 1 to 10. In a class of 200 students, spend per student would range from £17.59 to £18.26 in years 1 to 10. In a class of 400 students, spend per student would range from £16.20 to £16.55 in years 1 to 10.

Overhead on Staff Costs Applied at 60%

If 90% of items in each 14-item list are categorised as 'text substitution' and the other 10% as 'library substitution', if there are 100 classes and duplication occurs at the default rate, spend per student in a class of 50 would range from £24.86 to £27.64 in years 1 to 10. In a class of 200 students, spend per student would range from £17.32 to £18.01 in years 1 to 10. In a class of 400 students, spend per student would range from £16.06 to £16.41 in years 1 to 10.

If there are 400 classes then in a class of 50 students, the spend per student ranges from £24.81 to £27.50 in years 1 to 10. In a class of 200 students, spend per student ranges from £17.31 to £17.98 in years 1 to 10. In a class of 400 students, spend per student ranges from £16.06 to £16.39 in years 1 to 10.

50% Text Substitution to Library Substitution

Overhead on Staff Costs Applied at 120%

If 50% of the items on each 14-item list are categorised as 'text substitution' and the other 50% as 'library substitution', there are 100 classes and duplication occurs at the default rate, in a class of 50, spend per student would range from £20.36 to £23.15 in years 1 to 10. In a class of 200, spend per student would range from £11.26 to £11.96 in years 1 to 10.

In a class of 400, spend per student would range from £9.74 to £10.09 in years 1 to 10. If there were 400 classes, in a class of 50, spend per student would range from £20.32 to £23.00 in years 1 to 10. In a class of 200 students, spend per student would range from £11.25 to £11.92 in years 1 to 10. In a class of 400 students, spend per student would range from £9.74 to £10.07 in years 1 to 10.

Overhead on Staff Costs Applied at 60%

If 50% of the items on each 14-item list are categorised as 'text substitution' and the other 50% as 'library substitution', there are 100 classes, in a class of 50, spend per student ranges from £19.24 to £22.03 in years 1 to 10. In a class of 200, spend per student ranges from £10.98 to £11.68 in years 1 to 10. In a class of 400, spend per student ranges from £9.60 to £9.95 in years 1 to 10. If there are 400 classes, in a class of 50, spend per student ranges from £19.20 to £21.88 in years 1 to 10. In a class of 200 students, spend per student ranges from £10.97 to £11.64 in years 1 to 10. In a class of 400 students, spend per student ranges from £9.60 to £9.93 in years 1 to 10.

10% Text Substitution to Library Substitution

Overhead on Staff Costs Applied at 120%

If only 10% of items on each 14-item list are categorised as 'text substitution' and 90% as 'library substitution', there are 100 classes and duplication occurs at the default rate, spend per student in a class of 50 ranges from £14.75 to £17.54 in years 1 to 10. In a class of 200, spend per student ranges from £4.92 to £5.62 in years 1 to 10 and in a class of 400, spend per student ranges from £3.28 to £3.63 in years 1 to 10.

If there are 400 classes, in a class of 50 spend per student ranges from £14.70 to £17.39 in years 1 to 10. In a class of 200 spend per student ranges from £4.91 to £5.58 in years 1 to 10. In a class of 400, spend per student ranges from £3.28 to £3.61 in years 1 to 10.

Overhead on Staff Costs Applied at 60%

If only 10% of items on each 14-item list are categorised as 'text substitution' and 90% as 'library substitution', there are 100 classes and duplication occurs at the default rate, spend per student in a class of 50 ranges from £13.63 to £16.42 in years 1 to 10. In a class of 200, spend per student ranges from £4.64 to £5.34 in years 1 to 10 and in a class of 400, spend per student ranges from £3.14 to £3.49 in years 1 to 10.

If there are 400 classes, in a class of 50 spend per student ranges from £13.58 to £16.27 in years 1 to 10. In a class of 200 spend per student ranges from £4.63 to £5.30 in years 1 to 10. In a class of 400, spend per student ranges from £3.14 to £3.47 in years 1 to 10.

0% 'text Substitution' and 100% 'Library Substitution'

Overhead on Staff Costs Applied at 120%

If all items on every 14-item list are categorised as 'library substitution', there are 100 classes and duplication occurs at the default rate, in a class of 50, spend per student ranges from £13.35 to £16.14 in years 1 to 10. In a class of 200, spend per student ranges from £3.34 to £4.03 in years 1 to 10. In a class of 400, spend per student ranges from £1.67 to £2.02 in years 1 to 10.

If there are 400 classes, in a class of 50, spend per student ranges from £13.30 to £15.99 in years 1 to 10. If there are 200 classes, spend per student ranges from £3.33 to £4.00 in years 1 to 10. If there are 400 students, spend per student ranges from £1.66 to £2.00 in years 1 to 10.

Overhead on Staff Costs Applied at 60%

If all items on every 14-item list are categorised as 'library substitution', there are 100 classes and duplication occurs at the default rate, in a class of 50, spend per student ranges from £12.23 to £15.02 in years 1 to 10. In a class of 200, spend per student ranges from £3.06 to £3.75 in years 1 to 10.

In a class of 400, spend per student ranges from £1.53 to £1.88 in years 1 to 10. If there are 400 classes, in a class of 50, spend per student ranges from £12.18 to £14.87 in years 1 to 10. If there are 200 classes, spend per student ranges from £3.05 to £3.72 in years 1 to 10. If there are 400 students, spend per student ranges from £1.52 to £1.86 in years 1 to 10.

Thus, for a class of between 150 and 200 people, the cost to the library of supplying highdemand materials electronically only approaches current cost levels if the ratio of 'text substitution' to 'library substitution' materials on the reading list is as low as 1:9.

Additional simulations on an ER service designed to provide for a specific userbase A variety of simulations were run using figures that correspond with those of a real print reserve service. The example used is the print reserve service at Stirling University as described in a recent eLib supporting study.

This service spends £28 800 per annum to provide a print reserve collection for 5544 students. It is assumed that this total student number is divided into classes of ~200 (198 divides cleanly by 28 classes).

Overhead is Applied to Staff Costs at 120%

If 100% of items on a list are categorised as 'text substitution' the cost to the library ranges from £106 235 to £110185 in Years 1 to 10 respectively. If 90% of items on a list are categorised as 'text substitution' and the remainder are categorised as 'library substitution' the cost to the library ranges from £97 453 to £101 404 in Years 1 to 10 respectively.

If 50% of items on a list are categorised as 'text substitution' and the remainder are categorised as 'library substitution' the cost to the library ranges from £62 328 to £66 279 in Years 1 to 10 respectively.

If 10% of items on a list are categorised as 'text substitution' and the remainder are categorised as 'library substitution' the cost to the library ranges from £27 203 to £31 153 in Years 1 to 10 respectively. If 100% of items on a list are categorised as 'library substitution' the cost to the library ranges from £18 421 to £22 372 in Years 1 to 10 respectively.

Overhead is Applied to Staff Costs at 60%

If 100% of items on a list are categorised as 'text substitution' the cost to the library ranges from £104 667 to £108 617 in Years 1 to 10 respectively. If

90% of items on a list are categorised as 'text substitution' and the remainder are categorised as 'library substitution' the cost to the library ranges from £95 885 to £99 836 in Years 1 to 10 respectively.

If 50% of items on a list are categorised as 'text substitution' and the remainder are categorised as 'library substitution' the cost to the library ranges from £60 760 to £64 711 in Years 1 to 10 respectively. If 10% of items on a list are categorised as 'text substitution' and the remainder are categorised as 'library substitution' the cost to the library ranges from £25 635 to £29 585 in Years 1 to 10 respectively. If 100% of items on a list are categorised as 'library substitution' the cost to the library ranges from £16 853 to £20 804 in Years 1 to 10 respectively.

VARYING THE RATE OF OCCURRENCE OF DUPLICATION

In each of the simulations described there are 28 classes of 198 students and each class is provided in electronic form with materials on a 14-item reading list.

Default Occurrence of Duplication: 0.5% in Year 1, Increasing Annually by 0.5%

If overhead is 120%, and all materials are categorised as 'text substitution', the cost per student ranges from £19.21 to £19. 92 in post-grant funded Years 1 to 10 respectively. If overhead is 60%, and all materials are categorised as 'text substitution', the cost per student ranges from £18.93 to £19. 64 in post-grant funded Years 1 to 10 respectively.

If overhead is 120%, and the ratio of 'text substitution' to 'library substitution' materials on the reading list is 9:1, the cost per student ranges from £17.63 to £18.34 in post-grant funded Years 1 to 10 respectively.

If overhead is 60%, and the ratio of 'text substitution' to 'library substitution' materials on the reading list is 9:1, the cost per student ranges from £17.35 to £18.06 in post-grant funded Years 1 to 10 respectively. If overhead is 120%, and the ratio of 'text substitution' to 'library substitution' materials on the reading list is 5:5, the cost per student ranges from £11.29 to £12.00 in post-grant funded Years 1 to 10 respectively.

If overhead is 60%, and the ratio of 'text substitution' to 'library substitution' materials on the reading list is 5:5, the cost per student ranges from £11.01 to £11.72 in post-grant funded Years 1 to 10 respectively. If overhead is 120%, and the ratio of 'text substitution' to 'library substitution' materials on the reading list is 1:9, the cost per student ranges from £4.96 to £5.67 in post-grant funded Years 1 to 10 respectively. If overhead is 60%, and the ratio of 'text substitution' to 'library substitution' materials on the reading list is 1:9, the cost per student ranges from £4.67 to £5.38 in post-grant funded Years 1 to 10 respectively. If overhead is 120%, and all materials on the reading list are categorised as 'library substitution', the cost per student ranges from

£3.37 to £4.08 in post-grant funded Years 1 to 10 respectively. If overhead is 60%, and all of the materials on the reading list are categorised as 'library substitution', the cost per student ranges from £3.09 to £3.80 in post-grant funded Years 1 to 10 respectively.

Duplication Occurs at a rate of 1% in Year 1 and Increases Annually by 1%

If overhead is 120%, and all materials are categorised as 'text substitution', the cost per student ranges from £19.18 to £19. 80 in post-grant funded Years 1 to 10 respectively. If overhead is 60%, and all materials are categorised as 'text substitution', the cost per student ranges from £18.90 to £19. 51 in post-grant funded Years 1 to 10 respectively. If overhead is 120%, and the ratio of 'text substitution' to 'library substitution' materials on the reading list is 9:1, the cost per student ranges from £17.60 to £18.21 in post-grant funded Years 1 to 10 respectively.

If overhead is 60%, and the ratio of 'text substitution' to 'library substitution' materials on the reading list is 9:1, the cost per student ranges from £17.31 to £17.93 in post-grant funded Years 1 to 10 respectively. If overhead is 120%, and the ratio of 'text substitution' to 'library substitution' materials on the reading list is 5:5, the cost per student ranges from £11.26 to £11.88 in post-grant funded Years 1 to 10 respectively. If overhead is 60%, and the ratio of 'text substitution' to 'library substitution' materials on the reading list is 5:5, the cost per student ranges from £10.98 to £11.59 in post-grant funded Years 1 to 10 respectively.

If overhead is 120%, and the ratio of 'text substitution' to 'library substitution' materials on the reading list is 1:9, the cost per student ranges from £4.93 to £5.54 in post-grant funded Years 1 to 10 respectively. If overhead is 60%, and the ratio of 'text substitution' to 'library substitution' materials on the reading list is 1:9, the cost per student ranges from £4.64 to £5.26 in post-grant funded Years 1 to 10 respectively.

If overhead is 120%, and all materials on the reading list are categorised as 'library substitution', the cost per student ranges from £3.34 to £3.96 in post-grant funded Years 1 to 10 respectively. If overhead is 60%, and all of the materials on the reading list are categorised as 'library substitution', the cost per student ranges from £3.06 to £3.67 in post-grant funded Years 1 to 10 respectively.

Duplication Occurs at a rate of 0.5% in Year 1 and Increases Annually by 50% of its Current rate

The result of this duplication pattern is that in Year 10 post grant-funding, duplication between materials selected by lecturers and material already held in the repository occurs at a rate of 65%.

The authors consider this to be unfeasibly high but have tested this scenario to demonstrate the effect of duplication at an extreme level. If overhead is 120%, and all materials are categorised as 'text substitution', the cost per student ranges from £17.91 to £17.84 in post-grant funded Years 1 to 10 respectively. If overhead is 60%, and all materials are categorised as 'text substitution', the cost per student ranges from £17.63 to £17.55 in post-grant funded Years 1 to 10 respectively. If overhead is 120%, and the ratio of 'text substitution' to 'library substitution' materials on the reading list is 9:1, the cost per student ranges from £16.32 to £16.25 in post-grant funded Years 1 to 10 respectively.

If overhead is 60%, and the ratio of 'text substitution' to 'library substitution' materials on the reading list is 9:1, the cost per student ranges from £16.04 to £15.97 in post-grant funded Years 1 to 10 respectively.

If overhead is 120%, and the ratio of 'text substitution' to 'library substitution' materials on the reading list is 5:5, the cost per student ranges from £9.99 to £9.92 in post-grant funded Years 1 to 10 respectively. If overhead is 60%, and the ratio of 'text substitution' to 'library substitution' materials on the reading list is 5:5, the cost per student ranges from £9.71 to £9.64 in post-grant funded Years 1 to 10 respectively.

If overhead is 120%, and the ratio of 'text substitution' to 'library substitution' materials on the reading list is 1:9, the cost per student ranges from £3.65 to £3.58 in post-grant funded Years 1 to 10 respectively. If overhead is 60%, and the ratio of 'text substitution' to 'library substitution' materials on the reading list is 1:9, the cost per student ranges from £3.37 to £3.30 in post-grant funded Years 1 to 10 respectively.

If overhead is 120%, and all materials on the reading list are categorised as 'library substitution', the cost per student ranges from £2.07 to £2.00 in post-grant funded Years 1 to 10 respectively. If overhead is 60%, and all of the materials on the reading list are categorised as 'library substitution', the cost per student ranges from £1.79 to £1.72 in post-grant funded Years 1 to 10 respectively. The results of simulations designed to test the level of duplication between materials selected by lecturers and materials held in the repository are not encouraging.

They suggest that even when duplication occurs at a high rate, NERS resources are still expensive compared with equivalent print resources. If 50% of materials on a list were categorised as 'text substitution' the cost per student would be double that of the print collection.

Effect on Publisher Income of Varying the Ratio of 'text Substitution' to 'Library Subsstitution Materials in the er collection

These figures are unaffected by the rate at which overhead is applied to staff costs as they represent only publisher income. Clearly, if the cost to the publisher of negotiation were deducted from these figures the net income would be smaller. If all materials on a list are categorised as 'text substitution', the publisher income would be £48 985.

If 90% of materials on the list were 'text substitution' materials and the remainder were 'library substitution' materials, the publisher income would be £44 269. If 'text substitution' materials and 'library substitution' materials each represented 50% of the materials on a list, the publisher income would be £25 402. If only 10% of materials on the list were 'text substitution' and remainder were 'library substitution' the publisher income would be £6535.

If all of the items on the list were categorised as 'library substitution' the publisher income would be £1818. In the equivalent print reserve collection, the book trade would receive £28 000 and the publisher would receive £21 000–£28 000.

To recover the same income from an ER, 'text substitution' would have to represent approximately 57% of materials on a reading list. This would make a list too expensive for the library. It may be argued that as the publisher income is received simply for copyright clearance it is reasonable to expect a reduction in cost when compared to printed books.

However, even if the sum required by the publisher were reduced by 30% to £20 160, 'text substitution' would still have to represent nearly 39% of materials on the list and the cost would still be well beyond the means of the library at £51 640 to £56 496 in Years 1 to 10 respectively. Unfortunately, the library could barely afford to pay for a list whose contents exceed 10% of items categorised as 'text substitution'.

PAYMENT FOR COPYRIGHT FEES

It is clear that, in economic terms, ER does not compare favourably with a print reserve collection even if only 10% of materials included on a class reading list are categorised as 'text substitution'. 'Text substitution' would appear to be inappropriate as a payment mechanism for ER.

It may be argued that this model is designed to be applied to material that, in a print environment, students would buy. It has never been the library mission to supply a copy of a text to every student in a class. On the contrary, 20–30 years ago, some key texts that students were expected to buy would not be stocked by the library. The 'text substitution' model is likely to be perceived as too expensive by libraries unless they pass copyright fees on to students. The effect of passing either print costs and/or copyright costs to students has been explored previously.

Although many in the library community would consider it reasonable that students pay print costs just as, at present, they pay for photocopies, passing the cost of content to students would be contentious. It is argued that students pay for library provision when they pay their fees.

Furthermore, a proposal to pass copyright fees on to students calls into question the role of the library in providing resources for teaching and learning. It could be argued that it would render the library equal to and thus a competitor of other, more competitive, information providers.

Even if libraries were to pass copyright fees on to students, the 'text substitution' model would probably incur costs well beyond what could be recovered from students. This model requires payment from every student in a class but some students will choose not to read some of the selected items. The number of students in a class who actually choose to read every item on a reading list is low.

In the present environment, many students find that time is at a premium as they must take paid employment to supplement other sources of income (CAPP 1998). As a result, they read only the bare minimum necessary to meet course requirements. Evaluation work conducted by the SCOPE project found that fewer than 18% of students who actually purchased a course pack of core readings read more than 50% of the material contained therein (SCOPE 1998).

Furthermore, some students will refuse to print specifically to avoid payment of a copyright fee. Students are reluctant to pay for prints from library resources if the cost exceeds that charged for photocopies.

Thus, if the copyright fee is included in the cost of a print the number of students who choose not to print is likely to be high even among students who wish to read a specific item.

For many students this would appear to be related to student perceptions of the library role rather than willingness to pay for required reading materials as a recent study of student book-purchasing trends suggests that booksellers benefit through increased sales when required reading material is not obtainable from the library. Nevertheless, some students simply cannot afford to pay for learning materials. They depend on the library and thus, the introduction of fees for library resources is, justifiably, resisted by students and librarians alike. It would appear that by taking on production and repository functions, the ER service increases library costs while depriving publishers of sufficient income to sustain a publishing business. The inherent inefficiency in this system is clear: the publisher must incur a significant proportion of production costs to produce hard copy which the ER service then uses to incur further production costs in creating a duplicate.

When publishers are in a position to supply electronic copy directly, this inefficiency may be avoided but it is not clear then what the function of an ER service would be in those circumstances, or indeed whether such a service would be needed at all. When publishers supply their materials directly to the library in electronic form, resources, perhaps with finer granularity than books and journal, could be acquired in electronic form by the libraries acquisitions department and integrated into a digital library.

There may be a role for an intermediary which co-ordinates acquisitions and delivers resources seamlessly through a standard interface just as NESLI does for journals. The repository function would be part of the routine archiving function. It is not clear at present which body will have responsibility for archiving electronic copy but if it resembles the system in print, all material will be archived and a repository of extracts will be redundant. As it stands the NERS does not appear to be economically viable at the levels of duplication we anticipate. To become viable, various actions or assumptions appear to be required. One is that a much higher level of duplication than we expect occurs. Another is that alternative income streams are created. A third is to reduce costs. One possibility is that materials academics have produced for teaching purposes at a single institution is supplied to the NERS for wider distribution. HERON aims to include this type of material in the repository. Such material would be supplied directly by the academic who would also grant copyright permission, presumably at a viable rate. HERON would not be required to acquire and pay a copyright fee for a clean original from the British Library thus eliminating an expensive element of the digitisation cost for published materials.

APPLICATION OF DIGITAL LIBRARY

Internet especially the World Wide Web has given thrust to new ways of communication and knowledge sharing. Digital libraries are considered to be a key application of Internet and web technologies. They enable the creation, organization, maintenance, management, access to, sharing and preserving of digital collections. Digital libraries are created today for different communities and in different fields such as education, health, culture and so on. Digital libraries bring significant benefits to the users. Some of them are - Always Available, Improved Access, Wider Access, Improved Information Sharing and Preservation. In 1986, National Informatics Centre (NIC) and Indian Council of Medical Research (ICMR) jointly set up a centre called ICMR-NIC Centre for Biomedical Information.

This Centre was recognized as the 17th International MEDLARS Centre in 1990 and now is well known as Indian Medlars Centre (IMC). National Informatics Centre (NIC) has been a pioneer in communicating medical research information through the use of Information Technology. This centre is now emerging as a content creator and aggregator. It has developed three major products that are available over Internet:

- UNcat (http://uncat.nic.in) - union catalogue of journal holdings of medical libraries of India;
- IndMED (http://indmed.nic.in) - A bibliographic database of Indian biomedical journals,
- MedIND (http://medind.nic.in) - full texts of Indian biomedical journals being indexed in IndMED and PubMed. NIC has been providing free access to these databases.

DIGITAL LIBRARY OF INDIAN BIOMEDICAL JOURNALS

Digital Library of Indian Biomedical Journals medIND has many functional and process components.

Selection of Journals

The scope of the Collection development policy is well defined to include only those Indian Medical Journals that are either indexed in IndMED or in PubMed database. The selection policy of IndMED is to include peer reviewed journals having at least published on time for the last three years.

At present, IndMED covers 77 Indian biomedical journals. All the articles are assigned metadata using data input worksheet based on Common Communication Format of UNESCO. These articles are indexed using controlled vocabulary 'Medical Subject Heading (MeSH) list of US National Library of Medicine.

It is being updating on an ongoing and timely basis can be accessed at <http://indmed.nic.in> which is searchable through web interface. The securing of intellectual rights has been easier due to rapport existing with the publishers of these journals. To remove any ambiguity and to reach clear understanding with the publishers, a formal Memorandum of Understanding (MOU) was signed with the journals [represented by their editors] to make available their contents for the medIND project.

At present, 37 Indian biomedical journals have signed a formal MOU with NIC. The aim of this understanding is to provide a rights framework under which cooperation is established between NIC and joutnals to provide their full content to the end user free of cost.

The journal publishers provide the content and NIC does all the other activities like conversion, organization, hosting and providing access to the end users. The salient features of MOU are given as below:

- The resulting materials will be stored and hosted on NIC server;
- No fee will be payable to either party for providing content to NIC or converting into digitization;
- On termination of the agreement, NIC shall provide continuing access to the digitized completed up to the date of such termination;
- The copyright of the data would remain with the respected Editors.

Acquisition of Source Materials

The acquisition of material is the important part of project management. The content is of three types - printed version, born digital, and online existing journal archives. This heterogeneous material is converted into homogenous digital content as given below:

Converting Existing Print Media into Digital Format

Bulk of the archival and back volume content received is in form of printed copies of the journals. Each article, editorial and case study is scanned and stored as PDF (multi page) files. The files related to issue of a journal is put in a separate folder. File names are assigned as per a file naming policy that is based on bibliographic properties of content. The journal's content page of each issue is scanned, OCR and converted into HTML file. The content page in HTML format has all the links to the respective PDF files holding the articles.

Converting "Born Digital" Journals

These days, it is common to find journals being composed in DTP packages like PageMaker before they are printed. For such journals, the composed material is acquired with the cooperation of the editors/publishers of the journals. This is directly converted into the PDF files without the need of scanning. The quality of such PDF files is of much better quality. The name of the files is converted in accordance to the file naming convention. The content page of the issues is converted into HTML format and links are provided to the PDF files containing the full text articles.

Archives of On-Line Journals

There are few Indian journals that are already available on-line on the web. However since they are presently hosting on commercial web servers, it may not economical for them for continuing hosting back-volume of the journals. In such cases the archive can be moved to medIND after suitable conversion according to the policy of file names and file organization. This would ensure unique and persistent address for the contents in such archives.

File Naming and File Organization Policy

Unique and persistent URLs for each article are most desirable for such a project. To achieve this there has to be suitable policy for file names and file organization. Such a policy was formulated and adopted. This formed the core on which cross linking between references in IndMED and their corresponding full text file under medIND has been done. Salient features of the policy is as follows:

Directory Structure

The directory structure is as follows: <http://medind.nic.in>/Journal Folder/.../Year-Folder/.../Issue Folder/...Article Files .../Article Folder/

Journal Folder

There is a folder under the site domain for each journal. The name should be unique for each journal folder. A unique three alphabet code has been created for each journal under MedIND called as MJID. This folder contains Year-Issue Sub-Folders and default (index.html) and other html files constituting the home page for the journal.

Year (Sub) Folder

This folder contains the issue subfolders. The Year folder is of three character format 'cyy' whereas c is for century and yy stands for last two digit of the year. For example, Year 2002 would be t02.

Issue (Sub) Folder

This folder is named as "Inn" format having at least two character long. Each Issue folder contains a table of content html file with same name as folder name.

Article File Naming Policy

The file names of articles are given as per the format given below: *<MJID><Century-Year><Issue No.><Pagination> <DOT><File Extension>*

- <MJID>: It is a unique identifier for each journal in IndMED and MedIND. It is of three alphabetical characters.
- <Century-Year>: It represents the year of publication and of three characters. The first character represents the century and is an alphabet. Next two characters are numeric representing the year (first year would be taken if it is a block year).
- <Issue No.>: A variable length of characters, starting with "i" followed by numerical characters represent the issue number.
- <Pagination>: A variable length of characters, starting with "p" followed by numerical characters represents the starting page number of the article. In case more then one articles starts on the same page then a alphabetic character is suffixed to qualify each article sequentially.
- <DOT>: The name portion of the file ends with a dot (.).
- <File Extension>: Three character extensions are suffixed after the dot to represent the common file types.

DIGITIZATION

Thirty-seven journals have signed MOU till now and given the consent for putting their contents under medIND project. The content is being received in hard as well soft copies formats. Each format requires digitization process. These processes are described below:

Conversion from Hard Copies

Steps Involved in OCR to PDF document

- Scanning the document: Resolution has been fixed for text as 300 dpi whereas for table and image, the resolution is 600 dpi;
- Each table is marked as an image as OCR most often distorts table;
- The remaining document is OCRed and saved as Word Document;
- Necessary corrections are performed such as spellings, special characters, colour changing, layout of the text and references;
- Quality checks: Each document is verified and passing quality test, is converted into PDF using Acrobat.

Steps in creating Table of Contents from scanned document

- Scanning the content pages of a journal, OCR and save in Word;
- Necessary corrections are performed such as spellings, special characters in the Word document;
- To design table of content in the same layout as given in the journal, it is designed in HTML format and saved as per naming convention. Hyperlink is given to each article;
- Quality Checks: Each link is being checked for correctness.

Conversion of Born Digital Contents

Steps in converting born digital contents to PDF document

- Content is being received in the form of Page Maker format;
- Converting from Page Maker format to pdf document and save it as pdf file as per the naming convention adopted;
- Checking the completeness of the document;
- In case, image or page(s) are missing, these are scanned locally for completeness.

DESIGN OF DIGITAL LIBRARY MEDIND WEB SITE

The medIND project is having its own domain name at the Internet (http://medind.nic.in). It has pneumonic value and stands for Medical Journals on Internet [from India]. Home page gives details of the project listing of the participating journals.

This listing is hyperlinked to each participating journal home page at the medIND web site. The site provides two approaches to access the journal articles.

Browsing

Journals are hyperlinked and arranged in alphabetical order. Such hyperlinked list leads to pages giving details of selected journals such as editors, instructions to authors, contact address, parent body etc.

Further, this leads to listing of issues of the journal by years/volume wise. The content page provides hyperlinks to the individual article.

Searching

The searching is being provided through the bibliographic database IndMED. Each record of the IndMED has been linked to the individual article in the MedIND site. The searching of the articles can be achieved through from http://indmed.nic.in as well as from http://mednic.nic.in web sites.

The references will display icons indicating the availability of the full text. In developing digital collection, issues of intellectual property rights have been dealt to strengthen the cooperation between editors and content service provider to facilitate access to digital content through Internet to end users in the area of biomedicine on non-commercial basis.

The design of digital collection should be usable, flexible and simple enough to accommodate future changes and also enables other applications to utilize data for development of future applications.

The naming convention of digital collection is acted as bridge between metadata base and full text of content. This project fulfills the demand of providing full text of documents to health professionals free of cost throughout the world. It serves as a model for the development of similar collections in others S&T areas, medIND is a step in the process of making it as an open archive source where Indian journals covered in Medline database as well in IndMED database will be stored and will be provided access free of cost to health professionals throughout the world.

This will give enough visibility and exposure to Indian biomedical journals and demand for Indian literature would be met through the medIND project. In future, more visibility to articles included in medIND journals would be provided by adopting and exposing metadata in OAI-PMH and RSS protocols.

THE DIGITAL LIBRARY MANIFESTO

The term 'Digital Library' is currently used to refer to systems that are very heterogeneous in scope and provide very different functionality. These systems span from digital object and metadata repositories, reference-linking systems, archives, and content administration systems (mainly developed by industry), to complex systems that integrate advanced digital library services (mainly developed in research environments).

This "overloading" of the term 'Digital Library' is a consequence of the fact that there is not yet an agreement on what Digital Libraries are and what functionality is associated with them. This results in lack of interoperability and reuse of both contents and technologies. The current document attempts to put some order in the field for the benefit of its future advancement.

WHAT IS A MANIFESTO

According to the Merriam-Webster Dictionary, a *manifesto* is "a written statement declaring publicly the intentions, motives, or views of its issuer". Similarly, according to Wikipedia, a manifesto is "a public declaration of principles and intentions".

The '*Declaration of the Rights of Man and the Citizen*' in France in 1789 and the '*Declaration of Independence*' in the US in 1776 are two well-known manifestos that have set the stage for the establishment of two major countries and have had major influence on the recent history of the world.

The production of manifestos in subsequent centuries in fact increased; '*The Communist Manifesto*', issued by K. Marx and F. Engels in 1848, and the

'The Russell-Einstein Manifesto', issued B. Russell and A. Einstein in 1955 to confront the development of weapons of mass destruction, are some of the most famous examples. Of smaller scope and within the realm of science, there have been several manifestos as well, which have tried to draw the course for the development of particular research areas. These take more the form of declarations of axioms capturing the strategic ideas of a group of people with respect to a certain topic or field. Examples include the following:

- *'The Third Manifesto'*, from the book 'Databases, Types, and the Relational Model: The Third Manifesto' by H. Darwen and C. J. Date, Addison-Wesley, 2007, which proposes new foundations for future database systems1.
- *'The Object-Oriented Database System Manifesto'*, which describes the main features and characteristics that a system must have to qualify as an object-oriented database system, touching up on mandatory, optional, and even open points where the designer can make several choices.
- *'The Manifesto for Agile Software Development'*, which attempts to uncover better ways of developing software by putting emphasis on different items than traditionally, e.g., individuals and interactions instead of processes and tools, working software instead of comprehensive documentation, and others.
- *'The GNU Manifesto'*, by Richard Stallman, which uses as an axiom the idea that "... the golden rule requires that if I like a programme I must share it with other people who like it" to produce a complete Unix-compatible software system and is given away free to everyone who can use it.

Given the current status of maturity as well as heterogeneity of the relevant research and industrial efforts, the time is right for the Digital Library (DL) field to obtain its own Manifesto. This document is *The Digital Library Manifesto*. It attempts to circumscribe the universe of Digital Libraries and set the foundations that will facilitate integration of relevant research and improvement of system development methodologies.

MOTIVATION

Digital Libraries constitute a relatively young scientific field, whose life spans roughly the last fifteen years. Instrumental in the birth and growth of the field have been the funding opportunities generated by the 'Technology Enhanced Learning; Cultural Heritage' (formerly 'Cultural Heritage Applications') Unit of the Information Society Directorate-General of the European Commission and the 'Digital Library Initiatives' in the United States sponsored by the National Science Foundation and other agencies.

Digital Libraries represent the meeting point of a large number of disciplines and fields, i.e., data management, information retrieval, library sciences, document management, information systems, the web, image processing, artificial intelligence, human-computer interaction, and others.

It was only natural that these first fifteen years were mostly spent on bridging some of the gaps between the disciplines (and the scientists serving each one), improvising on what 'Digital-Library functionality' is supposed to be, and integrating solutions from each separate field into systems to support such functionality, sometimes the solutions being induced by novel requirements of Digital Libraries.

These have been achieved through much exploratory work, primarily in the context of focused efforts devising specialized approaches to address particular aspects of Digital-Library functionality.

For example, the ARTISTE project from Europe's Fifth Framework Programme focused on how to develop an integrated analysis and navigation environment for art images and analogous multimedia content, the COLLATE project from the same Programme focused on how to deal with old film libraries, while the Alexandria Project from NSF's DLI-1 and DLI-2 Programs focused on geospatially-referenced multimedia material. For the most part, every effort so far has been distinct and, in some sense, isolated from the rest. Every project has started from scratch to build a system supporting the particular needs specified in the project's description. Nevertheless, looking back at the individual achievements of all the projects, one may see clearly that there is substantial commonality among many of them; the bottom-up development of the field so far has provided enough 'data points' for patterns to emerge that can encapsulate all efforts.

Despite the young age of the field of Digital Libraries, it has made a long journey from its initial conception to the present state of the art and has reached a level of maturity that did not exist fifteen years ago. There is substantial knowledge and experience that have been accumulated.

This warrants a process of self-declaration that will identify the principle ideas behind the field; it is time for a *Digital Library Manifesto* to set the ground rules for the field and lead to the development of reference documents that will capture the full spectrum of concepts that play a role in Digital Libraries.

As mentioned earlier, the nature of Digital Libraries is highly multidisciplinary. Naturally, this has created several conceptions of what a Digital Library is, each one influenced by the perspective of the primary discipline of the conceiver(s). In fact, Fox et al. observe that the expression "Digital Library" evokes a different impression in each person, ranging from the simple computerisation of traditional libraries to a space in which people communicate, share, and produce new knowledge and knowledge products.

For instance, the 1st Delos Brainstorming Workshop in San Cassiano, Italy, envisions a Digital Library as a system that enables any citizen to access all human knowledge, any time and anywhere, in a friendly, multimodal, efficient, and effective way, by overcoming barriers of distance, language, and culture and by using multiple Internet-connected devices.

An offspring of that activity concludes that Digital Libraries can become the universal knowledge repositories and communication conduits of the future, a common vehicle by which everyone will access, discuss, evaluate, and enhance information of all forms. Likewise, in his framework for Digital Library research, Soergel starts from three very different perspectives that different people in the community have on Digital Libraries, i.e., as tools to serve research, scholarship, and education, as a means for accessing information, and as providing services primarily to individual users.

He then enhances further each one and fuses them all together to obtain the main guiding principles for his vision of the field. On the other hand, Belkin states that a Digital Library is an institution in charge of providing at least the functionality of a traditional library in the context of distributed and networked collections of information objects.

Lesk analyses and discusses the importance of the terms "Digital" and "Library" in the expression "Digital Library", where the former term mainly implies existence of software for searching text, while the latter term refers to existing material that has been scanned for online access, and concludes that the research effort in the field are not usually associated with the users' needs.

Borgman notices that at least two competing visions of the expression "Digital Library" exist: researchers view Digital Libraries as content collected on behalf of user communities, while practising librarians view Digital Libraries as institutions or services. Kuny and Cleveland discuss four myths about Digital Libraries and attempt to bring them down:

- The Internet is 'The' Digital Library;
- At some point there will be a single Digital Library or a single-window view of Digital Library collections;
- Digital Libraries are means to provide more equitable access to content from anywhere at any time;
- Digital Libraries are cheaper instruments than physical libraries. They conclude that Digital Libraries impose reinvention of the role of librarians and library models.

In addition to such a variety of perspectives that may currently exist on what a Digital Library is, the concept has evolved quite substantially since the early idea of a system providing access to digitized books and other text documents. The DELOS Network of Excellence on Digital Libraries now envisions a Digital Library as a tool at the centre of intellectual activity having no logical, conceptual, physical, temporal, or personal borders or barriers on information.

It has moved from a content-centric system that simply organizes and provides access to particular collections of data and information, to a person-centric system that aims to provide interesting, novel, personalized experiences to users. Its main role has moved from static storage and retrieval of information to facilitation of communication, collaboration, and other forms of interaction among scientists, researchers, or the general public on themes that are pertinent to the information stored in the Digital Library.

Finally, it has moved from handling mostly centrally-located text to synthesizing distributed multimedia document collections, sensor data, mobile information, and pervasive computing services. This vision of Digital Libraries seems to resonate well with the concept of "Information Space" that has arisen from the field of Computer Supported Cooperative Work (CSCW).

Snowdon, Churchill, and Frecon have developed future visions about "Connected Communities" and "Inhabited Information Spaces", with the latter being closely related with the vision of Digital Libraries, in that ubiquitous information is a prerequisite for CSCW. In more detail, Inhabited Information Spaces are "spaces and places where people and digital data can meet in fruitful exchange, i.e., they are effective social workspaces where digital information can be created, explored, manipulated and exchanged".

Thus, "in Inhabited Information Spaces, both information and people who are using that information (viewing it, manipulating it) are represented. This supports collaborative action on objects, provides awareness of others' ongoing activities, and offers a view of information in the context of its use". Based on the above and according to the aforementioned DELOS vision of a Digital Library, the latter provides an Information Space that is populated by a user community and becomes an Inhabited Information Space through CSCW technology. The two fields complement each other nicely, in that one focuses on access and provision of relevant information while the other focuses on visualisation and sharing of information.

It becomes obvious that, as envisioned, "Digital Library" is a complex notion with several diverse aspects and cannot be captured by a simple definition. A comprehensive representation encapsulating all potential perspectives is required. This has led to the drafting of '*The Digital Library Manifesto*', whose aim is to set the foundations and identify the cornerstone concepts within the universe of Digital Libraries, facilitating the integration of research and proposing better ways of developing appropriate systems.

Having this broad scope, the Manifesto is followed by a set of separate reference documents, which stand individually but can also be seen as parts of a whole. The '*Digital Library Manifesto*' introduced here exploits the collective understanding that has been acquired on Digital Libraries by several previous efforts by European research groups active in the Digital Library field for many years, both within the DELOS Network of Excellence and outside, as well as by other groups around the world. Its role is one of a springboard for future work. The following sections introduce the entities of discourse of the DL universe. They first introduce the relationships among three types of relevant "systems" in this area: Digital Library, Digital Library System, and Digital

Library Management System. Then, they present the main concepts characterising the above, i.e., content, user, functionality, quality, policy, and architecture, and introduce the main roles that actors may play within a Digital Library, i.e., end-user, designer, administrator, and application developer. Finally, they describe the reference frameworks that are needed to clarify the DL universe at different levels of abstraction, i.e., the DL Reference model and the DL reference and concrete architectures.

THE DIGITAL LIBRARIES UNIVERSE: A THREE-TIER FRAMEWORK

A Digital Library is a live organization that comes to existence through a series of development steps that bring together all necessary constituents.

Unfortunately, these three system notions are often confused and used interchangeably in the literature. Nevertheless, they play a central and distinct role in the Digital Library development process. To clarify their differences and their individual characteristics, they are explicitly defined here as follows:

- *Digital Library (DL): A (potentially virtual) organization that comprehensively collects, manages, and preserves for the long term rich digital content and offers to its user communities specialized functionality on that content, of measurable quality, and according to prescribed policies.*
- *Digital Library System (DLS): A software system that is based on a (potentially distributed) architecture and provides all functionality that is required by a particular Digital Library. Users interact with a Digital Library through the corresponding Digital Library System.*
- *Digital Library Management System (DLMS): A generic software system that provides the appropriate software infrastructure to both:*
  - Produce and administer a Digital Library System that incorporates all functionality that is considered foundational for Digital Libraries and
  - Integrate additional software offering more refined, specialized, or advanced functionality.

A Digital Library Management System is what one may call "system software". As in several other domains (e.g., operating systems, databases, user interfaces), such kernel software may be used as a foundation to produce Digital Library Systems. Depending on the philosophy it follows, a DLMS belongs to one of the following three categories:

- *Extensible Digital Library System:* A complete Digital Library System that is fully operational with respect to basic/foundational functionality required. It is based on an open software architecture, so that further software components can be incorporated on top of the ones already there with ease. DelosDLMS is a prototypical example of a system that is based on this philosophy.
- *Digital Library System Warehouse:* A collection of software components that cover all basic/foundational functionality required

and a set of tools that can be used to combine these components in arbitrary ways (in Lego-like fashion) to create Digital Library Systems offering diverse sets of functionality. New software components can easily be incorporated into the Warehouse for subsequent combination with those already there. BRICKS and DILIGENT are two prototypical examples of systems that are based on this philosophy.

- *Digital Library System Generator:* A highly parameterized software system that encapsulates templates for a broad range of functionality, which includes all basic/foundational as well as any advanced functionality that has been deemed appropriate. Through an initialization session, the appropriate parameters are set and tuned; at the end of that session, software is automatically generated that constitutes essentially a Digital Library System ready to be installed and deployed.

Note that, while the concept of Digital Library is intended to capture an abstract system that consists of both physical and virtual components, the remaining two capture concrete software systems. For every Digital Library, there is a unique Digital Library System in operation (possibly consisting of many interconnected smaller DLSs in the most general case), whereas all Digital Library Systems are based on a handful of Digital Library Management Systems.

It is also important to note that until now, most Digital Libraries have been created by developing DLSs from scratch without any basis on a DLMS. The notion of DLMS has been recently introduced by the DL community in order to overcome the many drawbacks arising from the current DL development process. When the digital library field reaches maturity, one should expect that only a small number of industrial-strength Digital Library Management Systems will be available on the market.

THE DIGITAL LIBRARIES UNIVERSE: MAIN CONCEPTS

Despite the great richness and diversity one finds among existing digital libraries, there are still a rather small number of concepts that are considered fundamental and essentially characterize all relevant systems and, in fact, the entire field.

These concepts are identifiable in every digital library and should be the starting point for any researcher who wants to study and understand the field, for any system designer and developer who is about to embark in an effort to build a Digital Library, and for any content owner who wants to offer it externally. In this section, we identify these concepts and briefly discuss their roles. Given that there are three kinds of "systems" in the digital library world, in principle each one may have, in addition to the common fundamental concepts, a number of other related concepts associated with it.

Nevertheless, from the definitions of these systems in the previous section, one may easily derive that there is a natural inclusion relationship on the concepts that refer to these systems: the set of concepts used to define the Digital Library is completely included in that used for Digital Library System, which is in turn completely included in that characterising the Digital Library Management System.

As a consequence of the above, we introduce below each of these concepts in reference to the highest level of a system (in the three-tier framework) for which it makes sense. All concepts, however, could also be described in reference to lower-level systems, focusing on the characteristics that are of primary concern there. More details can be found elsewhere.

The main concepts that are foundational in the Digital Library world are six. Five of them have been alluded to in the definition of Digital Libraries and are introduced in reference to them: *Content, User, Functionality, Quality,* and *Policy*; one of them has been alluded to in the definition of a Digital Library Systems and is introduced in reference to them: *Architecture*. All six concepts are shown together, influencing the Digital Library framework.

Content

The Content concept represents the data and information that Digital Libraries handle and make available to their users. It is composed of a set of information objects organised in collections. Content is an umbrella concept that is used to aggregate all forms of information that a Digital Library may require to offer its services. For example, metadata play an important role in the information domain because they describe the contents of other information objects and express their structure.

User

The User concept represents the actors (whether human or not) entitled to interact with Digital Libraries. The aim of Digital Libraries is to connect such actors with information and to support them in consuming already available information and produce new information.

As in the case of the previous concept, User is an umbrella concept that covers all notions related to the representation and management of actor entities within a Digital Library, i.e., the digital entities representing the actors, the rights that they have within the system, the profiles of the actors with characteristics that personalize the system's behaviour or represent these actors in collaborations, and others.

Functionality

The Functionality concept represents the services that Digital Libraries offer to their users. In the most general case, the functionality expected from Digital Libraries is extremely rich. One may not expect, however, that all

Digital Libraries must support the complete spectrum. Some core functionality represents the bare minimum that is required by all Digital Libraries, e.g., new information object registration, search, and browse.

Beyond that, depending on the particular needs of its community of users and/or the information it is aimed to manage, each Digital Library may offer diverse additional functionality to serve those needs.

Quality

The Quality concept represents the parameters that can be used to characterize and evaluate the content and behaviour of Digital Libraries. It potentially includes several diverse parameters associated with each class of content or functionality, possibly even with each distinct information object or service. Some of these parameters are objective in nature and can be automatically measured, whereas others are subjective in nature and can only be measured through human experiments.

Policy

The Policy concept represents a set of rules that govern the interaction between users and Digital Libraries. Several mechanisms should be available to enable such interaction and the Digital Library should activate those mechanisms in the form prescribed by its policies. The policy concept includes all aspects of system security, digital rights management, system load control, and other similar issues.

ARCHITECTURE

The Architecture concept (which refers to a Digital Library System) represents a mapping of the functionality and content offered by a DL onto hardware and software components6. Having this as a main concept is important due to the following considerations:

- Digital Libraries are often assumed to be among the most complex and advanced forms of information systems;
- Interoperability of Digital Libraries is one of the greatest challenges of the research community. Having a clear architectural understanding of Digital Library Systems offers ammunition in addressing both the above issues effectively.

In addition to the above primary Digital Library concepts, there is one more that is a derivative of them and is also very useful. That is the concept of Resource, which aggregates the concepts of Content, User, Functionality, and Policy, i.e., all concepts that refer to internal entities of a Digital Library and can be sensed by the external world. There are several aspects of all these concepts that are very similar or identical.

Approached as instances of the more general concept of Resource, the Digital Library should treat them in the same fashion. Having described the main concepts characterising the foundation of the digital library universe, we proceed in introducing four main roles of actors that interact with digital libraries at different levels and for different purposes.

THE DIGITAL LIBRARY UNIVERSE: THE MAIN ROLES OF ACTORS

We envisage four different and complementary roles of actors interacting with digital libraries: *DL End-Users, DL Designers, DL System Administrators,* and *DL Application Developers*.

Each role is primarily associated with one of the three "systems" in the three-tier framework and, therefore, has the view that corresponds to that system. These roles are defined below.

DL End-Users

These exploit the DL functionality for providing, consuming, and managing the DL Content as well as some of its other constituents. They perceive the DL as a stateful entity that serves their functional needs. The behaviour and output of the DL depend on its state at the time a particular part of its functionality is activated.

The state of the DL corresponds to the state of its resources, i.e., it consists of the collections of information objects managed by the DL, its set of authorized users, its functionality, and its set of policies. This state changes during the Digital Library lifetime according to the functionality activated by the users and their inputs. DL end-users may be further partitioned into *Content Creator, Content Consumer,* and *Librarian.*

DL Designers

These exploit their knowledge of the application semantic domain to define, customise, and maintain the Digital Library so that it is aligned with the information and functional needs of its end-users.

To perform this task, they interact with the DLMS providing functional and content configuration parameters. The former capture aspects of the DL functionality perceived by the end-users, e.g., the result set format, the query language, the user profile formats, and the document model.

The latter capture third-party resources that are exploited by the specific DL, e.g., repositories of content, ontologies, classification schemas, authority files, and gazetteers. The values of these parameters, which can be modified during the DL lifetime, configure the specific DL perceived by the end-users because they determine the particular Digital Library System instance serving the Digital Library.

DL SYSTEM ADMINISTRATORS

These select the software components necessary to create the Digital Library System needed to serve the required DL and decide where and how to deploy them. They interact with the DLMS by providing architectural configuration parameters, such as the selected software components, the hosting nodes, and the components allocation.

Their task is to identify the architectural configuration that better fits the DLS in target ensuring the appropriate level of quality. The value of the architectural configuration parameters can be changed over the DL lifetime. Any change of these parameters may result in the provision of different DL functionality and/or different quality.

DL APPLICATION DEVELOPERS

These develop the software components of DLMSs and DLSs, realizing the necessary functionality.

These four roles cover the whole spectrum of actors interacting with digital libraries. Their models of the digital library universe are linked together in a hierarchical fashion. This is a direct consequence of the above definitions since DL end-users act on the Digital Library, whereas the remaining three roles operate on the DLMS and consequently on the DLS and DL as well.

This relationship ensures that roles designed to directly co-operate share a common vocabulary/knowledge. For instance, the DL end-user expresses its requirements in terms of the DL model and, subsequently, the DL designer understands these requirements and defines the DL accordingly.

REFERENCE FRAMEWORKS

The Digital Library Universe is quite complex and comprises multiple elements. The representation of the details of these elements requires the introduction of several frameworks at different levels of abstraction:

Reference Model

it is a set of inter-related concepts that collectively circumscribe and capture the essence of a distinct part of human knowledge, be it a whole scientific field or an individual idea or anything in between. It is a framework that helps in understanding of the basic elements of its concept(s) of concern.

As stated in, "A Reference Model consists of a minimal set of unifying concepts, axioms and relationships within a particular problem domain, and is independent of specific standards, technologies, implementations, or other concrete details".

It can be established at various levels of abstraction, from very high-level and flexible to very concrete and precise. Although independent of them, it often leads to standards that have to be followed by all systems dealing with the particular parts of knowledge corresponding to it. Digital libraries need to obtain a corresponding reference model in order to consolidate the diversity of existing approaches into a cohesive and consistent whole and provide a common basis for further advancement.

Reference Architecture

it is an architectural design pattern indicating an abstract solution in implementing the concepts and relationships identified in the Reference Model. Essentially, the reference architecture acts as a blueprint for the implementation of a DLS. There may be more than one reference architecture that addresses how to design digital libraries systems.

Each of them proposes an optimal architectural pattern for a particular class of DLSs serving the needs of DLs characterised by similar goals, motivations and requirements. For example, we might have a reference architecture for DLSs supporting federated DLs, i.e. DLs built by federating local resources of multiple organizations, and another one for personal DLs, or for specialised applications.

Concrete Architecture

it introduces additional elements making the reference architecture more concrete, e.g. replaces the mechanisms envisaged in the Reference Architecture with concrete standards and specifications. For example, it may specify that the run-time environment deployed on the hosting nodes is CORBA or the Web Services Application Framework, and that the Search functional component is implemented by four specific communicating Web Services.

At the top is the most abstract Reference Model, which guides the more specific Reference Architecture and Concrete Architecture further down. In turn, these should constrain the development of any actual Implementation of a system. The three reference frameworks are the outcome of an abstraction process that has taken into account all the natural Inputs, shown to the left, e.g., the systems already existing on the market, and has taken into consideration all existing Related Work, shown to the right, e.g., best practices and relevant research.

When these frameworks are adopted and followed by the community, the resulting systems will be largely compatible with each other; the interoperability thus afforded will open up significant new horizons for the field. The goal of '*The Digital Library Manifesto*' has been to set the foundations and identify the entities of discourse within the universe of digital libraries. It has introduced the relationships among three kinds of relevant "systems" in this area: Digital Library, Digital Library System, and Digital Library Management System.

It has presented the main concepts characterising the above, i.e., content, user, functionality, quality, policy, and architecture, and has identified the main roles that actors may play within a digital library, i.e., end-user, designer, administrator, and application developer. Finally, it has described the reference frameworks that are needed to clarify the digital library universe at different detailed levels of abstraction, i.e., the Reference Model and the Reference and Concrete Architectures.

'The Digital Library Manifesto' is accompanied currently by two other documents, which correspond precisely to the aforementioned reference frameworks. These documents come as a first attempt to fulfil the needs of the field in these areas.

Clearly, diversity of needs among different digital libraries will continue to introduce new concepts that will require incorporation into the Reference Model and the Reference and Concrete Architectures. Hence, these documents should be considered as first versions of otherwise dynamic documents that will keep evolving, having the Manifesto as a firm foundation.

The *'Digital Library Manifesto'* has been based on the experience and knowledge gained by many previous efforts that have gone on for the past fifteen years around Europe and the rest of the world. We hope it will serve as a basis for new advances in research and system development in the future.

Index